Peace Process in North-East India

ABOUT THE EDITORS

Shukhdeba Sharma Hanjabam is Assistant Professor of Social Work, Indira Gandhi National Tribal University, Regional-Campus, Manipur. He received his doctoral degree from the School of Social Work, Tata Institute of Social Sciences, Mumbai and specializes in human rights and conflict transformation especially in the context of the North-East India.
He can be reached at <hanjabam@gmail.com>.

Aheibam Koireng Singh is Assistant Professor, Centre for Manipur Studies, Manipur University. He received his doctoral degree from Manipur University, Canchipur and specializes on the studies of ethnicity and inter-community conflicts.
He can be reached at <akoireng@gmail.com>.

PEACE PROCESS IN NORTH-EAST INDIA

Editors

Shukhdeba Sharma Hanjabam
Aheibam Koireng Singh

Published for
Department of Social Work
Indira Gandhi National Tribal University, Regional Campus, Manipur
&
Conflict and Human Rights Studies Network, Manipur
by
CONCEPT PUBLISHING COMPANY PVT. LTD.
NEW DELHI-110059

ISBN-13: 978-93-5125-200-9

First Published 2016

Published and Printed by:

Concept
Since 1974

Concept Publishing Company Pvt. Ltd.
A/15-16, Commercial Block, Mohan Garden,
New Delhi-110059 (INDIA)
Phones : 25351460, 25351794, *Fax* : 091-11-25357109
E-mail : publishing@conceptpub.com
Website: www.conceptpub.com

Editorial Office: H-13, Bali Nagar, New Delhi-110 015, India.

Cataloging in Publication Data—DK Courtesy: D.K. Agencies (P) Ltd. <docinfo@dkagencies.com>

Peace process in North-East India / editors,
Shukhdeba Sharma Hanjabam, Aheibam Koireng Singh.
pages cm
Contributed articles.
Includes index.
ISBN 9789351252009

1. Peace-building—India, Northeastern. 2. Ethnic conflict—India, Northeastern. 3. Conflict management—India, Northeastern. 4. India, Northeastern—Politics and government. I. Hanjabam, Shukhdeba Sharma, 1983- editor. II. Singh, Aheibam Koireng, editor. III. Indira Gandhi National Tribal University. Department of Social Work.issuing body. IV. Conflict and Human Rights Studies Network (Manipur, India) issuing body.

DS483.75.P43 2016 DDC 303.6609541 23

Preface and Introduction

Peace remains elusive in the North-East India. The situation of armed conflict has in fact escalated in the region over the years posing a challenge to one's life, livelihood chances and human rights. Increase in the number of armed-opposition groups, who are engaged in turf war, sphere of control/area domination and armed conflict with the Indian State, etc. is a clear indication towards the phenomenon conflict situation in the region. At present, almost every ethnic and sub-ethnic group has an armed opposition group not only for security and protection but also subscribing to the ideology of independence from India and sovereignty. In the case of Manipur alone, the Ministry of Home Affairs states that there are more than 40 "insurgent" outfits operating in the erstwhile sovereign kingdom. In such an alarming situation, the obvious question that strikes one's mind is if any efforts have been initiated from any "concerned" parties, be it the Indian State or any other, to bring about peace in the region. And if such initiatives are present, why is that armed conflict continues unabated? Or does the Indian State solely depend upon militaristic approaches as the only viable alternative to deal with the conflict situation, which it terms as internal security or law and order problem? These questions needs serious deliberations, as today we stand witness to a situation when almost every peace initiatives undertaken by the Indian State has resulted in undesirable fallouts with the exception of the Mizo Accord at least at the macro level.

Broadly, so far India, in the region, has used four models of peace engagement with the armed opposition groups, selectively depending upon the perceived degree of threat to the security of India. However, with the exception of the model of peace building through cease-fire agreement as in the case of the cease-fire agreements entered with the Naga outfits (National Socialist Council of Nagaland (NSCN)-Khaplang, NSCN-Khole-Kitovi and Naga National Council); the remaining three belong to the larger category of peace talk. These include peace talks (with or without ceasefire) at the ministerial level and the level of the Prime Minister, suspension of operation (ceasefire is inherently qualified) and signing of accord after rounds of talks. In each and every case, India has denied involvement of a third party (nation-state or international organization). Peace talk with the United Liberation Front of Asom (Pro-talk or the Rajkhowa faction) and NSCN (Issak-Muivah), respectively, are illustrations of the first model. In the second model referred to as 'Suspension of Operations' (SoO), large numbers of "small" armed groups are currently engaged from across the states in the region and are kept in "designated" camps similar to the case of the NSCN-IM. The last model is characterized by making constitutional mechanisms such as the Bodoland Territorial Council or the *Karbi Anglong Autonomous Council* (KAAC).

Inspite of the presence of such peace mechanisms/initiatives, peace continues to be elusive in each and every state of the North-East. Fratricides have increased in Assam and Nagaland. And in the case of Nagaland and Manipur, numerous Naga outfits have emerged challenging the mandate of the NSCN-IM, thereby undermining the very basis of the secret (*sic.* undisclosed) peace talk between the Government of India and NSCN-IM. Moreover, the peace talk has not arrived to a logical end after years and rounds of talks; bringing about a political solution to the vexed Naga problem remains distant. Similarly, despite efforts from the Government, "genuine" armed outfit has failed to enter into SoO with the Government. Finally, territorial councils, instead of bringing about lasting peace is marked limitations of the constitutional designs, thereby, creating troubles and contention between the inhabitants on the lines of "us" and "them". This has, indeed, posed a challenge to the practice of federalism in India.

The limitations of such peace initiatives on one hand, and on the other, the failure to engage other armed outfits are responsible for the present conflict situation and resultant human rights violations in the region. Over and above, peace initiative of a different kind followed by India, popularly known as Military Civic Action (MCA) Programme, wherein the State forces are used to win the confidence of the civil population through programmes such as hosting of feasts, sports meet, construction of bridges and roads, medical camps, etc. have acted as deterrents against incursion by the armed opposition groups. Beyond the official language of peace, these cannot be construed as peace building as they are largely targeted against the civilian population as deterrent measures and thus, usurpation of the civil space, legitimized by the presence of the Armed Forces Special Powers Act (AFSPA). And such usurpation by the State forces is beyond the norms and practices of democracy. It is our understanding that conflict resolution is the first step towards peace building and it can be possible only when dialogue takes place between the conflicting parties. This is not to deny the role civil society as a stakeholder but the issue of priority. Peace shall remain elusive as long as the terms of engagements remain one dimensional.

With this background, the book chapters in the volume addresses and deals with the themes relating to—Counter insurgency measures: Militaristic approaches, Institution of NIA and Military-Civic Action Programme; Review of Peace Process: MoU, Suspension of Operation and Cease-fire agreements; Peace initiative/building, constitutional measures and others.

The opening chapter is titled, *The Road to Peace in Manipur* by Chitra Ahanthem. She begins by premising that the very idea of 'peace' in Manipur in its current situation is layered. Even as the number of confrontations between the state and non-state security forces has decreased, there has been a rise in the number of cases where the civilian space has been terrorized by bomb blasts, extortions, kidnappings for ransom and kidnapping of minors for induction as child soldiers. On the other hand, the triangular conflict *status quo* arising in the state due to the demands of political identity and territorial status among the Meiteis, Kukis and Nagas has led to a situation where the civil sphere has been infringed. Apart from the major Naga groups and the Kuki armed groups, none of the major Meitei insurgent groups have come forth to the peace table. With various 'civil society groups' and pressure groups already taking their stands on the nature of peace processes operating in the state on ethnic lines and their affiliations, the road ahead for real term peace looks challenging to say the least given the number of armed groups operating in the state and the ethno centric politics driving them. The onus lies with the Government to come clean on the mandates of the peace talks that they are currently engaged in along with a time frame and what concrete steps the talks are aiming to arrive at for without these in place, the event centric approach of SoO and MoU being signed and armed cadres being left to languish in army camps can only backfire, putting the talks and the fragile 'peace' in peril, the chapter concludes.

The second chapter is titled, *The Political Underpinnings of Armed Conflict related Dialogue Processes in Manipur and its Neighbours: Looking for Peace or Containment?* by Laifungbam Debabrata Roy, Immanuel Zarzosang Varte, Namdithiu Pamei explores the principal political foundations and issues of ethnic violence in Manipur and its close neighbours of the North-East region of India that have erupted since the 50s, and the political dialogue processes underway aimed at resolution, focusing on the central function of indigenous peoples, ethnic or national minority rights. It concludes that, the gestures for peace talks by the government indicate a positive step towards reconciliation. However, it is also particularly important to ensure that these gestures are perceived as legitimate and are also genuine desire to engage in solving the vexed issues and bring about peace. Merely, a mechanical process of peace talks will not bring peace but just another temporary solution and therefore containment and management of the problems but never really getting rid of it.

Leaking Pot of Peace Parleys and Accords: Neither Containment Nor Restoration of Peace by Laifungbam Debabrata Roy, Immanuel Zarzosang Varte, Namdithiu Pamei, which constitutes the third chapter of this volume, at the very outset, stated that in the region of North-East India, numerous peace accords have been signed in attempts to bring an end to conflicts. However, many such processes have remained in a state of impasse, unable to overcome the perils of this path to accord. It concludes that, the lack of sincerity on the part of the Union Government, state government and also in many instances, the armed groups themselves have oftentimes made a mockery of parleys and negotiations. Ceasefire agreements and Suspension of Operations have become a platform for capitalization and maximization of benefits and advantages used and manipulated by both parties without restraints. This condition has rendered peace parleys and accords a leaking pot that does not contain nor restore.

The fourth chapter titled, *Restructuring Indian Federalism: The Ideal Way to Peace Process in North-East India* by Rajendra Kshetri and Oinam Momoton Singh articulates that restructuring of Indian federalism and lifting/withdrawal of AFSPA is a long-term initiative of bringing peace in the region of North-East India. Federalism should be cooperative not a competitive, 'persuasive and not coercive', flexible not rigid and above all have positive, not negative character. The people of a federal country should be integrated not only in the geo-political and physical sense of the term but more importantly in the socio-emotional sense. Social and economic development should cover the entire country with a more emphasis on the underdeveloped and peripheral region or territory. There should be no imbalance in this regard as demands for development of underdeveloped and/or neglected areas may give rise to the emergence of more 'Secessionist'/'Separatist' movements as is evident since last four decades in the North-East Region.

Militarism, Human Rights and Democracy in North-East India by Homen Thangjam, which constitutes the fifth chapter of the volume, concluded that the prolonged and continued armed conflict in North-East India sees no immediate end. The Indian State as arbiter of conflict continues to refrain from bringing about a peaceful political solution, other than employing a militaristic approach. Militarism and use of violence has been to neutralize the fighting power of the armed opposition groups as witnessed in its counter insurgency operations. In fact, it has not abandoned its homogenising tendencies both at the ideological level as well as practice. On the part of the non-state actors, too, they are unwilling to come to the table for negotiations. State impunity to violence and seeming acceptance of people to embrace violence has led to the acceptance of aberration of principles and practices of democracy.

The sixth chapter titled, *Inclusion of the Excluded: Towards Uncertainty* by Ch. Rupachandra while premising that most people in the region of North-East India believed democracy as one biggest business concluded that marginalized people took up violence as a means for achieving their share. It concludes that the problem arising out of it need to be redressed by realizing the claims of identity that have moved from exclusive cultural dignity to a new type of economic opportunities by claiming exclusive section of people. This would be very must at the behest of social inclusion which is an integral domain of representative democracy.

The seventh chapter titled *Labyrinth of Neoliberal Crisis: Indian State and its Instrument of Peace* by Malem Ningthouja attempts to go deeper into historicising peace process in and around Manipur with special focus on the objectives and implications at the receiving end, making due emphasise on the role of 'agency' in engineering historical course and question whether or not the discourse of disturbance can be alternatively interpreted. The chapter convincingly argues that there has been disturbances that had not been revealed by the State and its discourses. What are being marked as disturbances can be differently interpreted as syndromes of a disturbing situation for which the Indian

State has been largely responsible. To substantiate, the author used Marxist methodology and argue for disturbance as integral to the structural crisis inherent in Indian capitalist path. The chapter also theorises the driving ideological current embodied in local dynamics of exploitation, misrule, dissent and concludes with alternative perception of peace.

Peace Process of Government of India and NSCN-IM: India's Successful Diplomatic Dancing and Democratic Initiation by L. Muhindro Singh which constitutes the eighth chapter endeavoured to review the *modus operandi* of the ongoing peace process between the Government of India and the NSCN-IM (National Socialist Council of Nagalim-Isak and Muivah). Success of the peace process lies on the part of democratic initiation in the sense that elections in the Hill districts of Manipur are undergoing with the involvement of armed groups who are a party to the ongoing peace process with GoI. Different strategies of politicking that stands against electoral integrity are also appeared freely which seems to be encouraged by Government of India as a part of diplomatic dancing and managing the ongoing conflict. It further maintained that issue of sovereignty was toned down steadily which the success of India's diplomatic is dancing by managing the conflict situation and facilitating assimilation to Indianess by letting space for participating in electoral politics even if the electioneering processes in the hill areas are undemocratic.

The ninth chapter titled, *Regional Security Council for a Viable Peace Process in North-East India by* B. Angousana Sharma strongly pleaded for the formation and commissioning of a Regional Security Council for the North-East States of India. So that "the long been anxiety of the people of the North-East and the dreams of the people to bring a new Sun Rise of peace can be fulfilled".

The tenth chapter titled, *The Fifty Four-Year Indo-Naga Conflict: A Question of Internal Indian Ethnic Conflict or a Conflict between Two Nations* by Kaka D. Iralu while taking a position that Naga can never surrender their lands to India or Myanmar or any other nations on earth, asserted that India on her part must understand that Nagas are not secessionists or terrorists. The Nagas have absolutely no ill intentions of trying to destabilize India or create any problems for India. On their part they want to live in Peace with India as the most friendly neighbour.

Indo-Naga Peace Process: Critical Observation by Yaronsho Ngalung constitutes the eleventh chapter of this book. It started chronologically onwards from the signing of GoI-NSCN (IM) Ceasefire in 1997. It remarked that past interlocutors starting from Swaraj Kaushal and Padmanabhiah to RS Pandey have acknowledged the Naga issue as political, but they all were removed from the interlocutorship. While pointing integration of the Naga areas and sovereignty as the Core issues, he says the integration was met with strong opposition from the neighbours most strongly by the Government of Manipur. He asserted that Government of India had so far not taken any initiative for people to people dialogue to do away with the mutual mistrust. He said past talks had been unsuccessful as it lacks political content. He concluded by stating that Indo-Naga issues is not going to be solved under the Constitution of India. It can only be solved on the basis of the recognition of the unique history and situation of the Nagas which the past NDA regime had done at the time of inking the GoI-NSCN (IM) agreement.

The twelfth chapter titled, *The Conceits of Peace: Civil Societies and Naga's Peace Process* by Soihiamlung Dangmei, at the very outset commenced with a comment that the fragility of the peace process continue to be tested at all levels and demands immense wisdom and integrity from both the parties despite the peace initiative and progress made in the last fifteen years between the Government of India and the Nationalist Socialist Council of Nagalim NSCN (IM). The Naga civil society and traditional organisations supporting the peace process have continued to seek opportunities and initiatives to strengthen political negotiations for a democratic and honourable settlement. Apart from the Naga civil societies, the inclusion of a non-governmental organisation like Kreddha from the Netherlands and with the personality like Yash Ghai, an eminent international constitutional experts, and Anthony Reagan Constitutional lawyer from Australia in the present peace process bring more impetus for peace building and conflict prevention. However, the involvement of civil society remains *ad hoc,* a reflection of the culture of secrecy in an underground organisation and the historical experience of inter-tribal feuds and betrayal. Besides, although the Government of India and the NSCN (IM) rhetorically affirm the value of independent observers to monitor the ceasefire, there has been no progress in integrating civil society into the monitoring mechanism.

The thirteenth chapter titled *International Criminal Court and North-East India* by Sapam Dilipkumar, while contending that the people in the region of North-East India have also been victims of the conflict for the many years without having no way out from the situation. The chapter articulates that bold steps from the part of India to honour the authority of the ICC by signing and ratifying the Rome statute would help in bringing peace in the North-East India.

The fourteenth chapter titled *Polemic on Peace in Manipur: Negative or Positive* by Dhanabir Laishram says Manipur is now on the frying pan and concludes that Conflict transformation can underscore the goal of peace building through empowering a marginalized population exposed to extreme vulnerability in such a way to achieve self-sufficiency and well-being.

The fifteenth chapter titled, *SoO and Resolving Hydra-Headed CHIKIM Insurgencies in Manipur* by Aheibam Koireng Singh gives an exhaustive account of how Ceasefire with CHIKIM armed outfits commenced as a military initiative sidelining the State government following the signing of SoO between the Indian armed forces and eight CHIKIM outfits and later became official with the signing of tripartite agreement between the conglomerate groups of CHIKIM outfit namely, the UPF, and the KNO, State Government and the Centre with definite ground rules that ensures Manipur state territorial integrity, among various others. The chapter concludes by exhorting that SoO being the first ever peace initiative involving the State government, should pave way for substantive dialogue towards durable solution of the hydra-headed CHIKIM insurgencies. Successful resolution of the CHIKIM insurgency through SoO would invite the willingness of other outfits which still eludes the offer for peace talks.

The sixteenth chapter titled, *Suspension of Operation (SoO): Prospects and Challenges* by Sonthang Haokip attempts to highlight the peace and tranquillity which has been brought about with the signing of the Suspension of Operation (SoO), involving both the governments at the Centre and the State with the two Kuki Underground outfits, namely the Kuki National Organisation (KNO) and the United Peoples' Front (UPF). The chapter looks into how with the signing of the SoO Pact, peace and normalcy has finally been restored in the Kuki inhabited areas of Manipur. The chapter attempts to lay more focus on the achievements brought about by it. It also discusses the background history of unification process of the once splinter Kuki UG groups under two conglomeration. The chapter also puts a big question mark (?), about the possibility of looming a destructive future, in the event of the Pact breaking down, before delivering a tangible solution.

The seventeenth chapter titled, *Dimensional Peace in Manipur: Eimi (CHIKIMZ) Expereince* by PM Gangte, started with a premise that peace cannot be achieved by force and that it can only be achieved by understanding. It identified the identity crisis arising out of differences in the adoption of the nomenclature; and the differences in the ideological stance of the two conglomerate groups under suspension of operation in a tripartite agreement, namely the KNO and the UPF as two very crucial issue which comes in the way of fostering unity among the Chin Kuki Mizo Zomi tribes. The chapter winds up with a speculative hope that ZORO (Zomi Reunification Organisation) which is emerging as viable nomenclature could potentially unite the Chin Kuki Mizo Zomi tribes.

Perspectives on Conflict Resolution in Manipur by Shukhdeba Sharma Hanjabam, constitutes the eighteenth chapter of this volume, stated that even after more than 60 years of armed conflict in Manipur, the Government and the armed opposition groups are moving in parallel directions in terms of defining the situation or identifying the root cause(s). The Government has not accepted the position of the armed opposition groups. Similarly, in-spite of engaging with international cooperation (military or otherwise), particularly with Myanmar, Bangladesh and Bhutan, to suppress the armed movement in the State, the Government continues to claim that it is a law and order problem, and most recently, terrorism. There has been no meeting point for the conflict situation of Manipur. Reading from the Governor speeches, it clearly indicates that the Government does not have any policy or political will to address the situation. Any official documents that indicates the existence of Armed Conflict is out rightly rejected or concealed. For instance, the Justice Jeevan Reddy Report on AFSPA was concealed because the report indicates the situation of Manipur as "Internal Disturbance" which can be characterized as non-international armed conflict. The people of the State have already indicated their willingness to resolve the conflict through democratic means. Unfortunately, the Government has not responded to the people as well as non-state actors. Mere appeals for peace talks without any strategy from time-to-time along with military engagements cannot bring about any tangible solution or in addressing the problem. Preaccords talks have not been inclusive; the provisions agreed upon with one group frequently and patently conflict with the interest of others; and the accords either contains provisions to address core conflict issues in a manner that cannot be implemented or they do not deal with core issues at all. Finally, in six decades since Indian Independence, no responsive and accountable political infrastructure has been created either for conflict resolution or for governance itself. The lack or absence of political will is another stumbling block in resolving the conflict in Manipur. The business of conflict seems to be benefitting the political class and other engaging in the conflict. Therefore, they don't want to resolve the conflict else four to five decades is a long time to come up with a policy or a strategy to address the issue, the chapter concludes.

The nineteenth chapter titled, *Constitutional Realism: Peace Process in North-East India* by N. Pramod, at the outset articulates that issue in North-East may be in different forms and nature with different backgrounds and reasons, however, one finds a common feature of such issue occurring in the region, that is why so called "peace process", initiated by the main stakeholders could not either be proceeded or completed with any logical finding, despite having made various attempt in this regard. One of the basic problems for finding such peace building process in the North-East India could be the inactive attitude and conduct of the people, because it is the people who are legally allowed to activate the constitutional machineries. Apparently the Constitution itself does not fail the system but the people, who enforce the Constitution, have miserably failed it. As such, the people of this region have felt alienated from the mainland India in all respects having lost their faith and confident on the working of the constitutional system. Therefore, it is highly essential for both the stakeholders to believe and trust the culture of legalism for building an everlasting peace in the region, the chapter concludes.

The twentieth and concluding chapter is titled *Asoto: Settlement for Peace in the Mao Traditional Culture* by Puni Losii Mao. The chapter gives an exploratory of 'Asoto' is a very old traditional culture of the Mao for coming to terms and extending a network of goodwill and peace within and among the villagers which has been in existence even before Mao people discover the art of writing. The effectiveness of Asoto and the obligations exacted by it from those who participate in it cannot be fathomed from the yardstick of 'Peace Treaty' prevalent in today's parlance'. The chapter concludes that Asoto is still very relevant and important in the present society as some of its terms would still be applicable to better the inter-ethnic and inter-community relationship in a multi-cultural and multi-racial environment.

Acknowledgements

We would like to thank Prof. T.V. Kattimani, Hon'ble Vice Chancellor and Prof. Byomakesh Tripathy, Dean, School of Social Sciences and Professor of History, Indira Gandhi National Tribal University, Amarkantak, Madhya Pradesh for the constant support and encouragement.

We extend our immense gratitude to Prof. Lokendra Arambam, Visiting Fellow, School of Arts and Aesthetics, Jawaharlal Nehru University, New. Delhi and Dr. N. Surjitkumar, Director (i/c), Indira Gandhi National Tribal University, Regional Campus, Manipur for gracing the inaugural session of the roundtable conference as Chief Guest and President respectively.

We also thank the Session Chairs: Irengbam Arun, senior journalist based in Manipur; Kaka De Iralu, renowned social activist based in Nagaland; Dr. Dhanabir Laishram, formerly with Department of Political Science, Manipur University and renowned social activist based in Manipur; and Dr. Aheibam Koireng Singh, Centre for Manipur Studies, Manipur University.

We are grateful to *Kangla Lanpung Journal* (ISSN No: 2321-2357) for the permission to reproduce the following paper published in Volume VIII, Issue II, Summer, 2014

(i) Malem Ningthouja, Labyrinth of Neoliberal Crisis: Indian State and its instrument of Peace

(ii) Homen Thangjam, Militarism, Human Rights and Democracy in North-East India

(iii) Shukhdeba Sharma Hanjabam, Perspectives on Conflict Resolution in Manipur

Our sincere gratitude to Dr. Grace Laltlinzo, Dr. Kamei Beeju, students of Department of Social Work, teaching and non-teaching staff of the Regional Campus, Manipur.

Finally, we thank the Indian Council of Social Science Research, New Delhi for the financial support for the conference.

Contents

Contributors

Prof. Aheibam Koireng Singh, See the editors.

B. Angousana Sharma, had been in SPG (Special Protection Group of the Prime Minister of India) from 1986-1989; deputed in CBI, New Delhi and United Nations Peace Keeping Force and retired as "a Soldier of the Nation" from Sashastra Seema Bal.
Email: <anmolbramhachariya@gmail.com>

Prof. Ch. Rupachandra, is Assistant Professor at the Dept. of Political Science, Kamakhya Pemton College, Manipur.
Email: <rupachandra2010@gmail.com>

Chitra Ahanthem, is Free Lance Researcher. She also writes columns in newspapers and periodicals. Email: <ahanthem.chitra@gmail.com>

Dr. Dhanabir Laishram, has successfully guided many scholars leading to the award of PhD Degree in the discipline of Political Science, Manipur University. He also has been one of the leading opinion makers who speaks in various forums and writes in various newspapers and periodicals.
Email: <dblaishram@yahoo.com>

Dr. Homen Thangjam, is Assistant Professor at the Dept. of Political Science, Maharaja Bodhchandra College, Imphal. Email: <homenth@gmail.com>

Kaka D. Iralu, is well known and widely recognized for articulating the issues relating with the insurgency which is plaguing the region of North-East India. Email: <kakairalu@rediffmail.com>

L. Muhindro Singh, is Senior Fellow, ICSSR, New Delhi and Coordinator, Human Rights Studies Centre, SK Women College, Nambol, Manipur.
Email: <muhinsingh@gmail.com>; <insingh@gmail.com>

Laifungbam Debabrata Roy, Immanuel Zarzosang Varte, Namdithiu Pamei, are associated in different capacities with an organisation, Centre for Education Organisation and Research's (CORE) which enjoys Special Consultative Relations with the Economic and Social Council (ECOSOC) of the United Nations. Email: <roy.laifungbam@coremanipur.in> <varte@coremanipur.org>; <namdithiu@coremanipur.org>

Malem Ningthouja, is Associate Fellow at the Indian Institute of Advanced Studies (IIAS), Shimla. Email: <mningthouja@yahoo.com>

N. Pramod, teaches at Government LMS Law College and has successfully guided many scholars leading to the award of Ph.D. in Law.

Prof. Priyadarshni M. Gangte, is Associate Professor, Dept. of History and Coordinator, Centre for Human Rights, Damdei Christian College. Email: <pm.gangte@gmail.com>

Puni Losii Mao, did his M.Phil. in Political Science from Indira Gandhi National Tribal University, Regional Campus, Manipur (IGNTU, RCM).

Prof. Rajendra Kshetri is Professor at the Dept. of Sociology, Nagaland Univer-sity, Lumani Hills. Email: <aardhikshetri@gmail.com>

Prof. Oinam Momoton Singh is Assistant Professor at the Dept. of Sociology, Dhanamanjuri College of Arts, Imphal.

Sapam Dilipkumar, teaches Law at LMS Government Law College, Government of Manipur. Email: <spmdilip@gmail.com>

Prof. Shukhdeba Sharma Hanjabam, See the editors.

Prof. Soihiamlung Dangmei is Assistant Professor at the Department of Political Science, and Coordinator of the Department of Tribal Studies, Indira Gandhi National Tribal University, Regional Campus, Manipur. E-mail: <soihiam@yahoo.com>

Prof. Sonthang Haokip, is Assistant Professor at Dept. of History, Moirang College. Email: <sonthanghaokip@gmail.com>

Yaronsho Ngalung, is President, The Hao Research Initiative (THRI). Email: <ngalungyaronsho@gmail.com>

Abbreviations

ACMF	:	Adivasi Cobra Militant Force
ADC	:	Autonomous District Council
AGP	:	Assam Gana Parishad
AFSPA	:	Armed Forces Special Powers Act
ANSAM	:	All Naga Students' Association, Manipur
ANVC	:	Achik National Volunteer Council
AOGs	:	Armed Opposition Groups
ASEAN	:	Association of South East Asian Nation
BAC	:	Bodoland Autonomous Council
BLT	:	Bodo Liberation Tigers
BNLF	:	Bru National Liberation Front
CA	:	Chartered Accountant
CFMG	:	Cease Fire Monitoring Group
CHIKIMZ	:	Chin-Kuki-Mizo-Zomi
COFEPOSA	:	The Conservation of Foreign Exchange and Prevention of Smuggling Activities Act, 1974
CRPF	:	Central Reserved Police Force
CCSR		Civil Service Conduct Rules
DGP	:	Director General of Police
DGMO		Director General Military Operations
DHD	:	Dima Halim Daogah
DIG	:	Director-General
DONER	:	Development of North-East Region

FGN	:	Federal Government of Nagaland
FNR	:	Forum for Naga Reconciliation
FPLC	:	Patriotic Force Libration of Congo FPLC
GOC	:	General Office Commanding
GoI	:	Government of India
GPRN	:	Government of People's Republic of Nagaland/Nagalim
GSDRC	:	Governance and Social Development Resource Centre
HNA	:	Hmar National Army
HPC	:	Hmar People's Convention
HPC-D		Hmar People's Convention-Democratic
IAS	:	Indian Administrative Service
ICC	:	International Criminal Court
ICTY	:	International Criminal Tribunal for the Former Yugoslavia
ICTR	:	International Criminal Tribunal for Rwanda
IGAR(S)	:	Inspector-General Assam Rifles (South)
IGP	:	Inspector-General of Police
INC	:	Indian National Congress
IPRA	:	Indigenous People's Revolutionary Alliance
JMG		Joint Monitoring Group
KLA	:	Kuki Liberation Army
KNA	:	Kuki National Army
KNC	:	Kuki National Council
KNF	:	Kuki National Front
KNF-MC	:	Kuki National Front, Military Council
KNF-P	:	Kuki National Front-President
KNF-S	:	Kuki National Front-Samuel
KNF-Z	:	KNF-Zogam
KCP	:	Kangleipak Communist Party

1
The Road to Peace in Manipur

Chitra Ahanthem

Manipur, a sovereign Kingdom came under British rule as a princely state in 1891 after its defeat in the Khongjom war. Following the defeat, the Assam Rifles occupied the Kangla and Manipur became the last independent kingdom to be incorporated into British India. When the British left the Indian sub-continent in 1947, Manipur also regained its independence with the Manipur Constitution Act, 1947, leading to the establishment of a government with an elected legislature and the Maharaja Bodhchandra as the Executive Head. However, in 1949, Maharaja Bodhchandra was summoned to Shillong, the capital of the then Indian province of Assam, and on 21 September, 1949 signed a Treaty of Accession under which Manipur was to be formally merged to India on October 15, 1949. Manipur was a union territory from 1956, becoming a full-fledged State in 1972.

But the signing of the Merger agreement was considered by a majority to be under duress and the first seeds of rebellion were sowed when Hijam Irabot who opposed the merger went underground and raised a band of revolutionaries. Irabot sought the support of Communist Party of Burma, but died before his efforts could bear fruit in 1951. The first Meitei revolutionary movement died with Irabot. It was not until the mid-1960s that Manipur experienced another upsurge in violent, anti-government activities. On 24 November, 1964, the first resistance group was formed with the emergence of the United National Liberation Front (UNLF) which stated as its aim not only an independent, socialist republic in Manipur but also that it had a 'historic mission' to liberate Manipur 'from colonial occupation in the larger context of liberating the entire Indo-Burma region, for a common future" (Bertil Lintner, New Delhi Harper Collins, pp. 146-47). But the UNLF was not be the sole group that would espouse the cause of a 'sovereign Manipur' for over a period of time, there came into being other major groups like the People's Liberation Army (PLA), People's Revolutionary Party of Kangleipak (PREPAK), Kangleipak Communist Party (KCP) and offshoots from these groups due to ideological differences, leadership issues etc.

Apart from the Meitei outfits that are active in the Imphal Valley, the major Naga insurgent group—National Socialist Council of Nagaland—Isak-Muivah (NSCN-IM) has a strong base in four of Manipur's five hill districts, namely, Ukhrul, Senapati, Tamenglong and Chandel. The Nagas who have had a long struggle for their unique place in history and sovereignty with its insurgent movement fragmenting in the journey into the Naga National Council, NSCN (IM) and the NSCN (K) of which, the latter two are more active politically and in terms of their role in the prevailing armed conflict in the state. The ongoing talk between the NSCN (IM) and the Government of India has meanwhile triggered off an active civil response from various groups from among the Meiteis and the Kukis with the main spotlight being territorial integrity.

The demand for Kukiland (land for the Kukis) is a direct challenge to the demand for Greater or southern Nagaland by the National Socialist Council of Nagaland (NSCN-IM). 'Greater Nagaland' as projected by the NSCN (IM) would have to be inclusive of all Naga inhabited areas, thereby forking out major chunks if not the entire districts of Chandel, Senapati, Tamenglong and Ukhrul, to be integrated with the neighbouring Nagaland State.

The intention to drive out Kukis from these four hill districts in fact led to an intense and prolonged "ethnic cleansing" by the NSCN-IM in the 90's. While Meiteis oppose the creation of either a Kuki homeland or a greater Nagaland, the Kukis and Nagas are unable to establish any kind of coordination or cooperation. Thus, the ethnic conflict between the Nagas and Kuki constitutes another problem of the State. Clashes between the two groups are now not heard of. A number of Kuki outfits like Kuki National Army (KNA), Kuki National Front (KNF) and many others had been struggling for a separate State within the Indian Union since the late 80s (SATP backgrounder).

Peace in Manipur?

The very idea of 'peace' in Manipur in its current situation is layered. If at one level, we are to look at the frequency and number of occasions now, in which armed groups or non-state armed actors (various armed groups) have engaged with state armed actors (security personnel) or undertaken attacks and ambushes, there is indeed a decline of such confrontations as compared to the early 80 and 90's. Such confrontations between the state and non state forces lead to a state of fear, harassment and trauma for security personnel would undertake what are called 'combing operations' in the immediate vicinity of sites where attacks took place or where there was suspicion of the movement of the non state actors. It was in the context of such 'combing operations' undertaken by paramilitary forces who were protected under the impunity of the Armed Forces Special Powers Act (AFSPA) that the civilian population of Manipur came to grapple with numerous cases of their civil rights being violated: with numerous cases of forced disappearances, torture in custody, illegal detention, rape and fake encounters even as human rights groups and civil society took to the streets and various other forums to protest against the arbitrary actions. It was the public outrage and agitations but more specifically, the Kangla protest where 12 Meira Paibi women stripped themselves to protest in the wake of the brutal rape and murder of Thangjam Manorama, an alleged former underground care that the situation in the state camc under national and international media and human rights groups. Though 'combing operations' still continue, they are done so under an arrangement called 'joint operations' where paramilitary forces and state police forces work in tandem. Such a move is aimed at deflecting criticism of paramilitary forces and their manner of operations and to co-opt the State police force into the battlefront. This circumstantial marriage has now brought about a situation where the state police force now stands accused of being responsible for a majority of extra judicial killings. Even as the number of confrontations between the state and non-State security forces has decreased, there has been a rise in the number of cases where the civilian space has been terrorized by bomb blasts, extortions, kidnappings for ransom and kidnapping of minors for induction as child soldiers. On the other hand, the triangular conflict *status quo* arising in the state due to the demands of political identity and territorial status among the Meiteis, Kukis and Nagas has led to a situation where the civil sphere has been infringed. The state Highways which are predominantly in areas inhabited by Kukis and Nagas and hence under their control are often used to hold the state to ransom over various 'demands' ranging from Kuki statehood calls to protests over the entry of the NSCN (IM) leadership to Ukhrul and other Naga inhabited areas.

The State of Peace Talks

According to the Governance and Social Development Resource Centre (GSDRC), a partnership of research institutes, think-tanks and consultancy organisations with expertise in governance, social development, humanitarian and conflict issues:

> "Peace agreements are formal agreements aimed at ending violent conflict and creating the conditions for durable peace. They include ceasefire agreements, interim or preliminary agreements, comprehensive and framework agreements, and implementation agreements. The way in which the conflict ends—whether by compromise, or a one-sided victory, for example—typically has implications for the nature of the peace. The signing of a peace agreement is often considered to signal the end of the conflict. Much of the literature argues instead that this signals only the beginning of a process toward ending the conflict given that relapse into violence is common, full implementation of the peace agreement is seen as another key milestone. Key parties to the conflict may agree to peace agreements for tactical reasons, without being genuinely committed to the peace process (Ending violent conflict: peace agreements and conflict transformation)."

In the context mentioned above, the various 'peace process' or 'peace talks' as they are described are at best in a convoluted state in Manipur. Manipur's armed and political conflict is a mix of the fight between armed state actors and non-state actors on one hand and the infighting between the various non-state forces. Broadly put, the non-state forces constitute of two main groups: the valley based ones and the hill based groups. Of these two categories, the hill based ones are again sub divided into the Naga insurgent groups and the Kuki groups while a new entrant that is making its presence felt is a Zeliangrong armed group.

With the Kuki groups, the first Suspension of Operations (SoO) was signed in 2005 with only the Indian army, a fact that speaks volumes of the manner in which the civil administration is kept aside by the armed forces in the region. It was only in 2008, that the existing tripartite agreement came to be signed between the Government of India and the Manipur State Government on one side and various Kuki underground groups on the other side. The Kuki groups that are in a tripartite SoO with the Central and the Manipur state government are again splintered into two umbrella groups: the Kuki National Organisation and the United Peoples Front (UPF). Official sources stated that more than 30 militant groups from both the hills and the valley have entered the peace process since 2008 (Over 150 Manipur rebels surrender, The Telegraph, September 10, 2013). However, there is no real information available on the public domain about the exact number of groups. Interestingly, the term used for peace talks with the valley based groups is 'Memorandum of Understanding' (MoU) though the terms of agreement are on similar lines and just as similarly not disclosed to the public. A few of the hill based groups have a designated camp area where the cadres who have laid down arms are put up but mostly, the cadres who have 'given up arms' are put up in what are called 'designated army camps' in Assam Riffles camps. Out of the scratchy terms of ground rules that are in public knowledge, there is mention that the cadres are not to carry arms and ammunition out of their designated camp area and that they be present in the camp every day. These ground rules are flouted with total nonchalance as evident from the various media reports that have documented all too clearly the manner in which cadres from designated camps have indulged in extortion bids, physical harassment to civilians etc.

The very nature of the peace talks are suspect for a variety of reasons: On February 24 this year, one day after top cadres of the Kanglei Yawol Kanna Lup, MDF were arrested for violating the recently signed peace talks agreement by trying to barge inside the office chamber of the Regional Institute of Medical Sciences Director's office; two persons came forth to claim that they were unwittingly made to join in the surrender and signing of the Memorandum of Understanding programme as cadres of the United Revolutionary Front (URF).

The MoU in question was signed on February 13 at the 1st Manipur Rifles banquet Hall between representatives of the State government, Centre and three militant outfits—Kanglei Yawol Kanna Lup, MDF; United Revolutionary Front, Manipur and the Kangleipak Communist Party, Lamphel. In a press conference, the two said that they had no idea that they will be made to join in the surrender programme and had been hired by one person for masonry work at the Headquarter of 57 Mountain Division, Leimakhong (Two claims they were made part of surrender drama, IFP, 25 February).

The process leading to SoO and MoUs or the requirements specified for armed groups to be a part of the 'peace talks' in Manipur are not made clear while there is no specification on what happens in case ground rules are flouted. In a Kuki designated camp located in Churachandpur district, this author saw the presence of child soldiers thereby throwing up the issue of whether numbers are the sole criteria for armed groups to be recognized as one that can enter into the 'peace process'. In another camp in the interiors of Imphal East district, there were two very cramped rooms meant to house 40 cadres each when it was clear that not more than 10-12 cadres could fit into them. A separate room with double locks was meant to house the arms and ammunition of the armed group, but the few cadres at the designated camp carried the most sophisticated assault rifles. With a paltry sum of Rs. 4000 made out for every cadre made out that armed groups say is supposed to cover the monthly food rations and other essential items, there is a growing incidence of cadres who have taken part on the 'laying down of arms' which incidentally the media has been asked not to term as 'surrender programmes' taking to extortion. If there is any criteria at all for insurgent groups to enter into 'peace talks' with the state and central governments are in place that information is out of public domain. Apart from the Kuki armed groups, the valley based Meitei armed groups have not entered into peace talks with the Government as a unified party but rather as factions with cadres of the same group operating actively.

In another incident that mirrors the lack of transparency and any seriousness on the part of the Government to regulate how former insurgents are being paid their stipends, newspapers in the state reported that Lallumba, the President of the KCP (MC) Lallumba group decamped from the 7th MR Khabeishoi camp on June 9 along with a huge amount of Rs. 1,92,68, 800 meant for a one time rehabilitation package from the government. The amount including monthly allowance of eight months, bank deposits of 114 cadres and 10 politburo members of the outfit which had signed a tripartite peace talk with the Central and the State governments on August 6, 2010 at the 1st Manipur Rifles Banquet Hall (Lallumba of KCP (MC) Lallumba group "decamps" with Rs. 1.92 crores, IFP, July 8, 2013).

Even as the remaining cadres submitted 'complaints' to the state Principal Secretary Home with copies being submitted to the Joint Secretary Home, IGAR (S), GOC 57th Mountain Division, IGP (CRPF) and DIG, there has been no word from the concerned over the fate of the cadres in the camp or in term of the whereabouts of the former leader of the group. There have been numerous incidents when residents in the areas around the AR camps where cadres of various underground groups are kept after entering into SoO and MoU have demanded that the cadres be shifted out of their areas. Such calls have come up on the basis of the cadres 'disturbing the peace' with their involvement in cases of harassment of people in the area, physical intimidation and extortion. To cite an example here: when it came into the public domain that cadres of the KYKL (MDF) who were earlier lodged with the 20th Assam Rifles camp at Chandel Headquarter would be shifted to the Khongjom area of Thoubal district, locals of Khongjom and surrounding villages in Thoubal district including from Sapam, Chingtham, Samram, Langthabal, Langathel, Tekcham took to the streets protesting the move. This came about even as the people of Chandel head quarter district were protesting against the said cadres of the group being stationed at the district (Cadres in 'peace talks' unwanted in both Chandel and Khongjom, IFP). The modalities of the ongoing 'peace' processes in the state clearly shows that what are being undertaken are only superficial events centreed 'signing ceremonies' that are dressed up under the term 'home coming ceremonies' with no real meaning or value in the lives of the common man or any perceptible step towards limiting the level of violence arising out of the conflict situation. Rather, the ambiguity of the terms of the various peace initiatives taken up by the State and Central government with the armed groups on one hand and the fact that major valley based armed groups are yet to bite the peace bait shows that such initiatives do not look to be bringing about any tangible change to the theatre of conflict in the state. The political gains if any of the ongoing 'peace process' in Manipur with various armed groups of the hills and the valley are yet to emerge but already the fissures arising out of the overlapping demands by the Kukis, Nagas in terms of carving out territorial areas with the Meiteis insisting on their territorial integrity has changed the tone of various civil society groups on community lines. On October 10, 2012, when the Union Home Minister Sushil Kumar Shinde, hinted that a 'solution' to the 'Naga issue' was likely before March 2013, when Assembly polls in Nagaland were due, the Kukis opposed the talks, threatening to renew their demand for statehood, even as the Meiteis vehemently rejected the talks, claiming that settlement proposals would disturb the 'unity of Manipur or its territorial integrity'. Further, on November 2, 2012, the Kuki National Organization (KNO), an umbrella organization of 16 Kuki militant groups, threatened to resume armed struggle and to 'secede from Manipur' if the Centre did not begin talks with them.

On the other hand, the United Committee Manipur (UCM), an apex body of the Meiteis, on October 18, 2012, categorically stated that it would demand 'pre-merger status' of Manipur if the ongoing political dialogue between NSCN-IM and GoI disturbed the unity or territorial integrity of Manipur in any way. On October 26, 2012, the United Naga Council (UNC), the main apex body of the Nagas, asserted that a peaceful parting of the Nagas in Manipur and the Meiteis as good neighbours, was the only way to avert a catastrophic situation that would arise out of the prolonged "forced union of the two (Manipur Assessment - Year 2013 by the South Asia Terrorist Portal)".

Overtures and Responses

Apart from the major Naga groups and the Kuki armed groups, none of the major Meitei insurgent groups have come forth to the peace table with ritual appeals being made by the Government on occasions such as Republic Day and Independence Day observations and the groups dismissing the offer. In September 2006, during a session of the Manipur Assembly, Chief Minister Okram Ibobi Singh made a clarification on the floor of the Assembly that in the sixteen years that the State government had introduced a surrender policy for insurgents, only 377 underground activists from nineteen different organizations had actually bitten the bait, an average of twenty persons per organization in the said sixteen years or a little over one person in a year, per organization (Pradip Phanjoubam, Oxford University Press, New Delhi, p. 149). Earlier, while responding to the then Manipur Governor S.S. Sidhu's appeal to militant groups to come to the negotiation table, the United National Liberation Front (UNLF) 'chairman', Sana Yaima (now in NIA custody), in a press statement in Imphal on January 31, 2005, came up with a four-point proposal to "end the conflict satisfactorily once and for all." The proposals mooted were:

1. To hold a plebiscite under the aegis of the United Nations aegis so that the people of Manipur can exercise their democratic right to decide on the core issue of the conflict—the restoration of Manipur's sovereignty and independence.
2. To deploy a UN Peace Keeping Force in Manipur to ensure free and fair conduct of the Plebiscite.
3. UNLF to deposit all its arms to the UN Peace Keeping Force and India to withdraw all its regular and para military forces from Manipur before a deadline prior to the Plebiscite date to be decided by the UN. Also, the UN Peace Keeping Force to call upon all other armed opposition groups in Manipur to follow suit.

4. The UN to hand over political power in accordance with the result of the Plebiscite (UNLF response to Manipur Governor's appeal for dialogue).

The State government rejected the proposals and that was the end of the peace offer. Similarly, when the Manipur Chief Minister, Okram Ibobi Singh reached out to the PLA to shun violence and come forward for peace talks in 2012, the PLA President, Irengbam Chaoren rejected the offer and instead appealed to all armed groups in the North-East to join in a united fight against the Indian state (RPF's chief greets on outfit's 29th B'day *Sangai Express*, 25 February).

According to Ceety Khongsai in the Manipur Chapter of 'Liberation Movements' in the North-East in the *Journal of North-East India* (*Studies*): The Peace initiative of the Government of India in the North-East suffers from ambiguities. The matter becomes more confusing when the GoI-NSCN (IM)'s Ceasefire Agreement intentionally nullifies the repeated "Manipur Territorial Integrity Bills" passed in the Manipur legislative Assembly by appending the words, "without territorial limits. Sensing the impending inter community fracas the GoI was left with no other options, but delete the controversial words from the text of the agreement. However, the public are still in disbelief regarding the sincerity and honesty of the Central government in handling the fluid social atmosphere in Manipur; in the backdrop of the UNC's Alternative Arrangement for the Nagas gaining momentum fresh clouds of apprehensions grips the entire North-East by questioning New Delhi's honesty on the issue. On the other hand, the announcement made by Former Indian Prime Minister Dr. Manmohan Singh that "there's enough room in the constitution to accommodate the demands of the North-East insurgents" categorically invalidate the hypothesis of possible outside-the-constitution solution to the decades old Naga political problem.

Given the context of the ongoing peace initiatives in the State, it is no surprise that there is no real change on the ground. The absence of any of the major armed groups stepping forth to enter into peace talks with the Government casts shadows on the intent of the Government and its various ongoing processes. Writing under the pen name of Yenning (Manipuri word for 'spring'), a leading columnist writing in the *Sangai Express* on the nature of 'Peace talks as counter insurgency measure' has this to say: If at all the government is interested to resolve the conflict in Manipur through peaceful and democratic means, then the first and the foremost step is initiation of a process for identifying the common problems, which are acceptable to both the conflicting groups, through an inclusive mechanism. Mere appeals for peace talks from time to time along with military engagements cannot bring about any tangible solution and least of all, addressing the problem. A charter of demands submitted by United NGOs Mission-Manipur, a conglomerate of over 100 grass NGOs operating in both the hill and valley area pointed out specific pre negotiating measures to be adopted by the government: (i) "Constitute an Independent Commissions for Conflict Resolution in the State; and (ii) develop a framework on pre-negotiation, negotiation and post negotiation with special monitoring mechanisms with due representation from civil society, NGOs and also by engaging International Community as a Third Party to settle the longstanding political conflict in the State". The most important one is to constitute the committee to identify a possible common meeting point within a time frame. However, the process of constituting the committee should be done under the Prime Minister Office or Ministry of External Affairs with the State government particularly the Home Minister and/or elected legislators as facilitators. This will increase the commitment of the government to the AOG (armed opposition group) (Hoi Polloi and Mundanity, Peace talks as counter insurgency measure).

Writing for IDSA, Namrata Goswami asks this rather pertinent question: what could be a feasible formula for peace talks in Manipur? For one, it has to deeply engage with the societal issues that have led to these multiple armed conflicts. Fears of loss of land, demands for political empowerment and economic development, ethnic identity assertion, cultural exclusivity, hill-plain divide, divide between the ethnic communities and the rest of India further fuelled by the absence of an inclusive politics, have created a web of alienation and loss of self-worth. Moreover, the politicization of ethnic differences for electoral gains, rampant corruption in development projects, fears of discrimination, and ethnic distrust creates the structural conditions for armed conflicts aligned along exclusivist ethnic lines. Merely, a mechanical process of peace talks may not salvage years of traumatic experience of conflict, killings, kidnappings and social stress in Manipur since the 1960s (*Peace Gestures in Manipur: Will it Work?* IDSA Publication).

With various 'civil society groups' and pressure groups already taking their stands on the nature of peace processes operating in the state on ethnic lines and their affiliations, the road ahead for real term peace looks challenging to say the least given the number of armed groups operating in the State and the ethno-centric politics driving them. The onus lies with the Government to come clean on the mandates of the peace talks that they are currently engaged in along with a time frame and what concrete steps the talks are aiming to arrive at for without these in place, the event centric approach of SoO and MoU being signed and armed cadres being left to languish in army camps can only backfire, putting the talks and the fragile 'peace' in peril.

References

Goswami, Namrata. 2013. "*Peace Gestures in Manipur: Will it Work*?" Institute for Defence Studies and Analyses, 23 September.

Imphal Free Press 2013. "Lallumba of KCP (MC) Lallumba group "decamps" with Rs. 1.92 crores," 9 July, http://www.ifp.co.in/nws-15474-lallumba-of-kcp-mc- lallumba-group-decamps-with-rs-1-92-crores/

Imphal Free Press, 2013. "Two claim they were made part of surrender drama," 25 February, http://www.ifp.co.in/nws-12668-two-claim-they-were-made-part-of- surrender-drama/

Khongsai, Ceety. 2012. "Liberation movements in the North-East: The Manipur chapter," *Journal of North-East India Studies*, 10 August.

Lintner, Bertil. 2012. *"Great Game East,"* Harper Collins Publishers India, pp. 146-147.

Phanjoubam, Pradip. 2009. (ed.) "North-East problems as a subject and object," *Beyond Counter-insurgency*, Oxford University Press, New Delhi, p. 149.

South Asia Terrorism Portal, 2014, "Manipur Assessment-Year 2014", 8 February, http://www.satp.org/satporgtp/countries/india/states/manipur/index.html

Yenning: 2013, Peace talks as counter insurgency measure, *The Sangai Express* as part of "Hoi Polloi and Mundanity" Column May 26.

2

The Political Underpinnings of Armed Conflict Related Dialogue Processes in Manipur and Its Neighbours

Looking for Peace or Containment?

Laifungbam Debabrata Roy, Immanuel Zarzosang Varte and *Namdithiu Pamei*

Since, the end of the Cold War, most conflicts worldwide have been within states, and in most cases have erupted through ethnic or community mobilisation over enduring grievances. Some of the most terrible recent examples are the long-standing conflicts in Sri Lanka and Sudan, and the genocide in the area of the Great Lakes in Central Africa. The situation in India's Kashmir or its North-East territories is no less tragic. This chapter explores the principal political foundations and issues of ethnic violence in Manipur and its close neighbours of the North-East States of India that have erupted since the 50s, and the political dialogue processes underway aimed at resolution, focusing on the central function of indigenous peoples, ethnic or national minority rights.

Violence involving indigenous, ethnic or national minorities against the State does not operate in a vacuum. To promote peaceful relations in States where the setting is conducive to tension and conflict, it is essential to provide the conditions that encourage all groups, and especially substantial minorities, to feel a shared interest in the society as a whole. They are most likely to do so when they feel that society respects and meets their needs and interests, including those linked to their ethnicity. Such violence may also often lead to or co-exist with conflicts between indigenous peoples or ethnic minorities in an extremely complicated and inter-related or inter-dependent array.

To explain the causes of ethnic conflict and its special brand of violence, many theories have been developed. But, to date, no theory covers all types of ethnic conflict and the circumstances in which they occur. Contrary to what is often believed, many ethnic conflicts do not begin as a quest for territorial sovereignty, but in reaction to grievances which are permitted to fester over long periods of time. And also contrary to assumptions made only a few decades ago by liberal, socialist and Marxist theoreticians, conflicts involving ethnicity have not progressively faded away. It was widely believed in the second half of last century that development, increased urbanization and literacy, the growth of communication networks and globalization would all contribute to the creation of modern societies. All those "quaint" ethnic identities and "tribal" affiliations would eventually be replaced by loyalties to larger communities represented by truly modern political entities like the United States or the European Union. This vision of a Brave New World hasn't quite worked out as many, perhaps most, experts had assumed.

In a multiple conflicts scenario as we have today in Manipur, one factor alone would make us very wary of a simple listing of social, cultural, economic, development, historical and other micro-cosmic scenarios; and that is the lowest common denominator—time frame. The protracted nature of the conflicts means that certain interventions over the decades from civil society, local elected bodies, financial aids and sops, employment generation schemes, faith based organisations, and so forth have all had influence on the outcome, some more than others. Therefore, certain described scenarios, e.g. "underdevelopment", gender roles, emergent non-state opposition armed groups, the notion of "Nagalim", "Kukiland", "Dima Hasao", "Bodoland" or other homelands, alienation from "India", institutional breakdown and so forth are also "products" of the conflicts themselves, and not merely factors from which conflicts have arisen—"conflict drivers". But such overarching conclusions may also be too hasty and incomplete in such chronically complicated and intractable scenarios.

Manipur and its surrounding region is characterised and distinguished by conflicts layered upon conflicts than just a multiple conflicts scenario. Manipur is a layered conflicts 'entity', more like a club sandwich than a fork with multiple prongs. The armed conflicts are only layers among other conflict layers delving into the realm of civil society organisations, communities, even NGOs, district level governance players, academe, etc. The protracted nature of the conflicts in Manipur is also expressed in the seemingly protracted nature of resistance to analysis. Tweeze a tissue out of this sandwich, and you are immediately confronted by another tissue that is linked to another layer. Tweeze more, the whole other layer cascades upon your carefully constructed analytical edifice.

It is precisely in this context that peace building efforts and dialogue processes find themselves immediately trapped in a quagmire. The often teetering and jammed cease-fire, suspension of operations and various 'talks' processes are seen as a "coming home" process. But it is precisely this home that is at the root of the predicament. As soon as the actors "come home", they face the same divisive and discriminatory quandary of rights violations—a situation that has not been effectively addressed by the State. The rights framework provides, presently, the only one that can unravel the issues and point realistically towards a peaceful resolution.

In fact, one is tempted to say that the very term 'peaceful resolution' is a misnomer. The sincerity of the government to peacefully resolve the conflicts in Manipur or other part of North-East has become very questionable. Ceasefire agreement with an insurgent outfit is expected to adopt a progression of steps which would lead to a comprehensive resolution of conflict. Indeed, the path, which a peace process normally takes after a ceasefire is entered into, is expected to be less cumbersome than the one that precedes a ceasefire. Whereas the dynamics that could witness the pre-ceasefire stage could be a long-drawn-out process, with protracted in camera confabulations, engagement of intermediaries etc., a properly managed post-ceasefire situation should ideally result in early resolution. Prolongation of a post-ceasefire period (prior to resolution) should be unnecessary, as much of the groundwork on which a future resolution would be structured on should have already been established preceding a formal cessation of hostility. However, in the context of North-East India, the conflict resolution scenario has become increasingly mired in delays and hindrances, and it appears that adequate attention has not been paid to the pre-ceasefire stage. It is to be noted that the long-drawn protracted negotiations after ceasefires often lack any institution of full-bodied resolutions. This gave rise to questions not only about the efficacy of the strategy that is being adopted for the purpose, but a slew of conflict related apprehensions. Such concerns range from risks of revocation of ceasefires, to factional clashes and violation of ceasefire rules.[1]

However, it will be prudent to note that while military operations against the insurgency movements in the North-East have achieved only limited results, it is the dialogue for peace with them that has brought some order to the region. Dialogue with the Mizo National Front (MNF) culminated in the signing of the Mizo Peace Accord in 1986 ending the 20-year-long insurrection in the entire State of Mizoram in 1986. The December 3, 2003 en masse surrender of the cadres of the Bodo Liberation Tigers (BLT) and subsequent formation of the Bodoland Territorial

Council (BTC) solved a near decade long insurgency in the areas inhabited by the Bodo tribals in Assam. Such experiences, however, have remained rare events. Other peace deals such as the Shillong Accord in 1975 with the Naga National Council (NNC) in Nagaland, the 1988 agreement with the Tripura National Volunteers (TNV) in Tripura, the Bodoland Autonomous Council (BAC) agreement of 1993 with the Bodo hardliners in Assam fell through as new factions, dissatisfied with the terms of the agreement resumed hostilities under new leaderships.

At present, the Union Government has ongoing ceasefire agreements with several insurgent groups in different states. The oldest one with the National Socialist Council of Nagaland-Isak/Muivah (NSCN-IM) dates back to July 25, 1997 and the other one with its bête noire, the National Socialist Council of Nagaland-Khaplang (NSCN-K) has lasted since April 28, 2001. In Assam, the following organizations have ceasefire agreements with the government: Adivasi Cobra Militant Force (ACMF) since September 19, 2001, Dima Halim Daogah (DHD) since January 1, 2003, the United People's Democratic Solidarity (UPDS) since May 23, 2002, Birsa Commando Force (BCF) since August 14, 2004 and the National Democratic Front of Bodoland (NDFB) since May 25, 2005. The Alfa and Charlie companies of the ULFA's 28th Battalion are also on a ceasefire with the government since June 24, 2008. But, the anti-talk factions of the NDFB and DHD are still active. However, after the arrest of their leader, Jewel Garlossa, the anti-talk faction of DHD has also declared a unilateral ceasefire for three months starting June 7, 2009.

Similarly, in the State of Meghalaya, the Achik National Volunteer Council (ANVC) has had a ceasefire agreement with the government since July 23, 2004. In Manipur, the Government has signed Suspension of Operations (SoO) with the Kuki rebel outfits on August 22, 2008. In Tripura, the Nayanbashi Jamatiya faction of the National Liberation Front of Tripura (NLFT) has been observing a ceasefire with the government since March, 2004.[2]

From experiences drawn from the numerous peace parleys and ceasefire agreements in North-East India between the government and the insurgent groups, one is inclined to see it as more of 'managing conflicts' as in business management where the aim is not to resolve the conflicts but to manage and channel the conflicts to suit the needs of the government of India in consolidating its highly debated 'internal colonialisation' of North-East India. There are in fact, several reasons for this policy considered 'valid' by the government. One such reason is that a conflicting, confused, under-developed, corrupted and deprived North-East India is much easier to control and bended rather than a prosperous, well-informed, and developed North-East. The logic for this fallacy is that the more prosperous, well-informed, developed and united a people become, the stronger the capacity to fight back oppression and injustice. Keeping the people confused and informed is the only way India can retain its Queen (as in chess) in the east (as Jammu & Kashmir is in the north) and hence safeguard its commercial centres in Bengal, Bihar, etc against Pakistan and Chinese/South East Asian aggressions. One is reminded of Hitler's 'Mein Kampf'. As long as its interests are served, India can well afford to lose a few hundred or even thousands of its security forces to insurgents; afford to let a few hundred civilians die or afford to spend millions of rupees as the return are much higher than the expenditures. In this regard, the nearest examples will be how the Mizo and Naga uprising in Mizoram and Nagaland were brutally dealt with by the Indian Government. It has no problem in bombing civilian areas in Aizawl or letting its forces commit inhuman atrocities throughout Mizoram and Nagaland.

Another reference is the tripartite Suspension of Operations (SoO) agreements signed between various armed groups, Central and State governments. Except for the lull in violence between the various armed groups after the signing of the Suspension of Operations (SoO) agreement with the Government of India, there is little love lost between them. The term "suspension of operations" is not of military origin. It is rather derived from industries. In the present usage, it merely means a suspension of counter-insurgency operations. The notion of SoO in this context has no relationship to the goal of conflict resolution. It is instead a strategic step taken by the parties involved in the hostilities in order to make room to address other military and political objectives. According to a "best practices" paper released by the Indian Ministry of Home Affairs[3], ceasefire agreements and SoO, provides opportunities such as:

- Firstly, the air of uncertainty as to when and which armed group is going to attack or pose threat to the people is cleared to an extent.
- Peace process is initiated with the insurgent group.
- Increase counter-insurgency measures on the other militant groups operating within the State.
- Maintain vigil over the outfit currently observing ceasefire/ suspension of operations.
- The State can focus attention on the more important and pressing needs for development.

Under the provision of SoO, each cadre is being paid a stipend and other financial assistance. Being paid and provided for by the government, they are, in reality, the unofficial 'militia' of the government[4]. Also, as per the underpinning thrust of the SoO, whenever one group displeases the government or any of its security agency, it will instigate other groups under the SoO to attack former as 'punishment' or bring along cadres from other groups as guides/informers to help catch/punish the erring group.

Lack of success of the peace processes has further created enough misgivings among the active insurgent outfits about the sincerity of the government to drive the negotiations to their logical conclusions. For example in Manipur, the valley based insurgent outfits including the United National Liberation Front (UNLF) have raised frequent questions about the usefulness of a ceasefire with the government and have called for resolution of the conflict only with the intervention of the United Nations (UN). The talks with NSCN (IM) have also not succeeded in setting the stage for a solution to the Naga problem.[5]

"What could be a feasible formula for peace talks in Manipur?" asked Namrata Goswami in her article *Peace Gestures in Manipur: Will it Work?*[6] For one, it has to deeply engage with the societal issues that have led to these multiple armed conflicts. Manipur is a melting pot of diverged aspirations and prejudices within and without the existing ethnicities. It is not only suffering from armed movements of innumerable clandestine organizations, but also from a complex ethnic issues—both internal and external, but where external interferences often provides fuel for internal dissensions. Being inhabited by different groups of people which can be classified broadly into Meetei, Naga, Chin and Kuki, a harmonious existence is being threatened as the interests of one group clash with the other. This has given rise to assertion of group identity; inter group competition for resources, political instability, insecurity and underdevelopment. An understanding of the ongoing issue is therefore, a priority and well known in both government and non-government circles. This very fact often leads one to question the sincerity of both government and non-government peace builders, mediators and facilitators. Maybe, the constraints of armed conflict related dialogue processes in Manipur and its neighbours and the futile search for peace or containment have their sources not only from the government's lackadaisical attitude but maybe even the very reluctance of civil society leaders of North-East India to unite and coordinate their efforts.

There are however several real constraints even for the government to hold peace talks and negotiations in states like Manipur. The prospect of holding a political dialogue between the insurgent groups of Manipur and the Government of India is seriously undermined by the challenges posed by parallel political projects of Nagalim and Zalengam. The existence of the political demands for the integration of the claimed Naga areas of Manipur into the Nagaland state or demand for creation of South Nagalim state in the form of Alternative Arrangement and the demand for the formation of a Kuki state within the territorial space of Manipur are the challenges confronting the Manipuri nation building project. In this context, it is necessary to clarify that the demand for Naga integration or Alternative Arrangement and the demand for an autonomous Kuki state or full-fledged Sadar Hills district are partial manifestations of the movements such as Nagalim and Zalengam respectively.[7]

The accounts of growth of nationalism among the Meiteis, Nagas, Chins and Kukis indicate that the goals of these three major groups of people do not converge. Although these groups of people stayed and lived together side-by-side for centuries, they developed their heritage parallels under the respective ethno-social boundaries. Each group had fought against the British at different points in time. However, there was very little attempt on the part of the various ethnic groups to coordinate these struggles which could have ignited the process of ethnic integration, at least on political lines, during pre-colonial era. The working of the post-colonial government did nothing to improve or bridge the ethnic gap, but rather appear to endorse ethnic demarcation and political fragmentations. The present policy is in fact only an extension of the policy followed by the erstwhile colonial British government. Continuance of such policies encourage ethnic groups in fatally believing that optimization and consolidation of group interests is *sine qua non* for group continuity or as fitting reactions to such thereby often leading a group to choose an option that violates the present territorial, and sometimes, cultural integrity of another ethnic group or groups, e.g., the demands for Nagalim or Kuki State. The diverged ethno-national goals have, thus, created faultlines along ethno-national identity that oftentimes ridiculed the very idea of ethnic integration even before any real attempt at it is made. In fact, any attempts at ethnic integration in Manipur and other parts of North-East India during the last few decades have been the cause of frictions rather than being a panacea. In fact, the belief in zealous optimization and consolidation of group interests has become a trend and considered by many as "necessary evil" and the impact on others candidly accepted as "collaterals"![8]

The other daunting obstacle is the historical interpretation of Manipur's accession to India in 1949. All the armed groups mentioned above propagate the idea that this accession was coerced and not voluntary. An honest and direct engagement with this aspect will help in formulating a constructive and legitimate peace process.[9]

It is also extremely significant to establish a process of peace where the leaders of the armed groups voluntarily come forward for peace talks. Arrested leaders may engage in peace talks, but the credibility, durability and commitment to that process in terms of social healing and conflict prevention in the long run is rather suspect.[10]

The gestures for peace talks by the government indicate a positive step towards reconciliation. However, it is also particularly important to ensure that these gestures are perceived as legitimate and are also genuine desire to engage in solving the vexed issues and bring about peace. Merely, a mechanical process of peace talks will not bring peace, but just another temporary solution and therefore, containment and management of the problems but never really getting rid of it.

Notes and References

1. http://www.vifindia.org/article/2011/august/02/Dialectics-of-Ceasefires-with-Insurgents-in-the-North-East.
2. http://cdpsindia.org/ne_peace.asp
3. http://indiagovernance.gov.in/bestpractices.php?id=14
4. A more or less similar policy was followed by the British in N.C. Hills during the 1850s by forming a 'Kuki militia' to guard the Cachar-Assam frontiers against invading Angamis.
5. Immanuel Z. Varte, "Political Dialogue Among Various Political Armed Groups in North-East India: A Critical Perspective", Paper presented at the Consultative Meet on "The Transitional Justice and Humanitarian Law", 17th January, 2014, Conference Hall of, The Classic Hotel, Imphal organised by United NGOs Mission—Manipur (UNM-M).
6. http://www.idsa.in/idsacomments/PeaceGesturesinManipur_ngoswami_230913
7. *Ibid.*
8. Immanuel Z. Varte, "Ethnic Integration: Issues, Challenges and the Way Forward", Paper presented at a Workshop on "Ethnic Integration in North-East India: Issues and Challenges" Organized by Institute of Social Research and Development, Imphal, Manipur from 20th-21st September, 2013.
9. http://www.idsa.in/idsacomments/PeaceGesturesinManipur_ngoswami_230913
10. *Ibid.*

3

Leaking Pot of Peace Parleys and Accords

Neither Containment Nor Restoration of Peace

Laifungbam Debabrata Roy, Immanuel Zarzosang Varte and *Namdithiu Pamei*

The North-East States of India is most studied as a theatre of insurgency and counter insurgency. Numerous peace accords have been signed in attempts to bring an end to conflicts. As formal agreements, the form of these accords range from the minimalist ceasefire to the scope of mini-constitutions. Often viewed by the parties in conflict as endpoints with the sole purpose of bringing an immediate and permanent end to a conflict; in reality, these expectations have been seldom met. Others view accords as constructs for further negotiations, a change in the course of history, which is essentially a management perspective. The historical narratives of the region have one common character—it is never a level playing field. Hence, such manipulations and 'course correction' do not always lead to peace. The road to an accord—the degree of hostility, the setbacks, the violations of provisional conditions, military strategic calculations, inclusion and exclusion, and so forth—is often more important than the agreement itself. Many such processes have remained in a state of impasse, unable to overcome the perils of this path to accord.

The singular problem in these negotiation processes towards peace is the absence of a principled and rigorous framework adopted and implemented by the Government of India. The Indian Government's surrender policy in North-East India has been flawed from the very beginning employing different yardsticks for different insurgent organizations, given the varying status of peace talks between them. The highest number of surrenders over the years has come from Assam and

Manipur, where surrenders, peace talks and designated camps have mushroomed and occupied much of the government's energies and resources. The government has entered into high-profile new peace talks with the some Naga insurgent groups since 1997, without any breakthrough and at the same without any respite from the violence, due to ceasefire rules violations and 'peacetime' factional fights. The peacetime operational conduct of the security forces has favoured one faction of the Naga insurgency over the other at varying points of time, and the rules in the designated camps have been very liberal. On the other hand the MoUs signed by the Kuki and Meitei groups have been revised lately without appropriate rehabilitation packages that reflect international standards including monitoring by the International Committee of the Red Cross of designated camps and their inmates. There is an overall absence of accountability in parties of the conflicts who have entered into ceasefire arrangements and negotiations, though huge amounts of public money and resources are being used.

John Paul Lederach said, "An agreement represents the process for continuing the conflict with new definition". It's true that accords which have been signed in case of many groups over the years in the region have been at best piecemeal excluding the important stakeholders out of the realm of these accords. These arrangements have proved to be impermanent and undercut each other. These accords also have demonstrative affects as they have prompted numerous other ethnic groups to demand the same privileges as are available to others by way of accords. Johann Galtung has promulgated the idea that peace building involves radical change to overcome contradictions that lie at the root of conflict. Peace building has been characterised as "a comprehensive concept that encompasses, generates, and sustains the full array of processes, approaches, and stages needed to transform conflict toward more sustainable, peaceful relationships." There is a consensus amongst most academics and policy-makers that peace building entails a multi-layered approach involving many sectors and including local, national, regional, and international actors. This paper reviews how peace processes in the North-East India have failed on every count to reflect this consensus.

The premise underlying our enquiry is that mere deployment of the word 'peace' should not be insulated from critical scrutiny peace processes that are of questionable durability and produce a poor quality of peace. Where peace processes and peace accords minister to conflict manifestations than causes; reinforce rather than challenge inter group divisions; attend to the interest of armed groups but neglect less vocal and more vulnerable constituencies and fail to deliver quality of life changes to many inhabitants—there is need for a critical peace impact assessment (Roger MacGinty 2006: 106).

All across Manipur and its neighbouring states is the evidence of flawed, stalled and faltering peace processes. In Region of North-East India, in which the role and status of nations and communities within the state-nation is still being battled and negotiated, the Naga conflict is India's oldest separatist insurgency on which the Indian state honed its militarist counter insurgency strategies. Analogously, the Indian state developed a genealogy of 'unfinished' peace accords that divided the struggle, co-opting the moderates and radicalising the 'rebels'. The latest demarche is the 1997 Ceasefire Agreement has stopped vertical violence between the State and the Naga nationalists, but reinforced inter factional violence and rampant extortion. The stuttering peace process has produced a no war no peace stalemate that has undermined the moral high ground of the Naga nationalists. State and market penetration has created a new socio-economic context with consequences for national movements anchored in traditional tribal structures. Demographic shifts, especially the youth bulge have produced new challenges and new opportunities. The protracted ceasefire has created an expanding middle space for 'civil society' activities. It needs reiteration that while a society coming out of conflict carries over the structural grievances of the past, it also is marked by the transformed context of the present which produces new challenges and opportunities.

In Assam, successive Bodo Accords (1993 & 2003) have attempted to contain the minoritization anxieties of the Bodo plain tribes. However, by conceding to the Bodo movement's demand of territorial autonomy, it has left even more vulnerable the less vocal minorities in the 'Bodo' homeland. The territory of the 'homeland' is no longer mono-ethnic, but multi-ethnic, multi-lingual and multi-cultural and in many areas the ethnic Bodos have become a minority. Consequently, the promise of self-rule of the Bodo majority is compromised by demographic anxieties. With ethnicity determining territorial inclusion and claims to entitlements, identity politics has unleashed ethnic cleansing in these multi-ethnic spaces. Histories of population flows have established settler populations, and the borders of post-colonial state making have made for continuing flows of 'illegal' migrants. Communal politics gives an edge to the targeting of Bengali speaking population. Such peacemaking has prompted the mass displacement of successive communities—Santhals, Bengali Muslims—the casualties of an ethnic homeland politics.

In neighbouring Mizoram there is the much lauded success story of the Mizo accord (1986) which swapped independence for statehood and delivered a sort of 'sustainable' peace. However, the sustainable peace which was to usher in development is now constrained by the tiny state's over dependence on the Central Government. While its minimal level corruption is significant, the benefits of state patronage and resources have not included Mizoram's small minorities, whose politics are becoming increasingly contentious. Mizoram's cohesive society keeps at bay the sectarian politics that have vitiated peace in neighbouring states, but post conflict ethnic Mizos have internalised the values and practices of long years of militarism. When coupled with the xenophobia fostered by identity politics, it has produced an anti democratic culture of intolerance and vigilantism against 'outsiders', vulnerable groups and women. Mass displacement of the Hmars is witness to Mizoram's exclusionary politics. Evidently the Mizo Exception has failed to deliver quality of life changes to many of its inhabitants.[1]

In bold, crude words, ceasefire agreements in North-East India appears to be just another excuse to prolong the conflict that supplies India's military and police forces with a perennial source for counter-insurgency and consolidatory strategies. Counter-insurgency training camps such as Counter-insurgency and Jungle Warfare School (CIJWS) and also soldiers in the front have greatly benefitted from the experiences afforded by the insurgents. There has also been rumours that many Indian Army officers choose to be posted in insurgency affected North-East India as it afford them the chances of getting medals and quick promotions depending on how much arms seized, insurgents 'killed' in encounters, 'insurgents' convinced or coerced to surrender during their tenure in the region. North-East India has, in fact, become the hunting ground for military honours and glory for young, ambitious military officers. Given such, it is not surprising to see the military reluctant to repeal militarily empowering legislations like AFSPA and also reluctance to constructively assist in resolving conflicts. The military is often found to favour ceasefire agreements that are more temporary in nature but nonetheless affording them maximum opportunity to exploit it for their own gains.

Another very pertinent point that is to be taken into account when analysing the peace parleys and accords in North-East India is the nexus between insurgency, corruption and failure in delivery of services-especially at the civil and political administration. Take for instance Manipur, where insurgency and insurgents have become an indispensable part of the daily excuses for unaccounted public money and failure in delivery of services. If power corrupts and absolute power corrupts absolutely, then terror enervates and constant terror creates anomie. This is as true for societies as for individuals. In the region of North-East India, the world is divided not merely by ethnicities or religions or gender or class but into those who hold absolute power with impunity, and those who are subject to it without recourse. Insurgency and insurgents have become a major source of earning for politicians and bureaucrats alike with millions of rupees meant for public purposes siphoned away and blamed on the insurgents for plethora of reasons such as causing delays in execution, extortion, protection money etc while at the same time millions being 'spent' by the government on security and counter-insurgency. Given the hype on insurgency and frequent fatal encounters and bombings, there is little the central government or its vigilance agencies can do nor are many that very enthusiastic to delve too deep in the mud for several equally obscure 'reasons' that apparently appears to restrain them. In sort, the insurgents are the perfect excuse and escape pod for many, who otherwise, would have been in the dock for corruption and financial misappropriation and it will be no surprise if the insurgents themselves get a 'cut' from these transactions.

Furthermore, analysis of the process of negotiations across multiple accords revealed that there was little intention or capacity on the part of the parties to address the grievances which drove the conflict. The core issue at 'the peace table' seemed to be to enable the contending group leaders to come to power in an autonomous unit as reflected in the Assam accord process (1985). Texts of accords are marked by an asymmetry of power where the government always somehow maintains the upper hand. In such unequal peace processes between a constituted state and movements for self-determination, it is the state that chooses when and with whom to talk. Routinely, the state when challenged by competing national movements, questions their legitimacy and whether there is a sole spokesperson who can deliver on an agreement. Empirical evidence shows that state designed peace processes seem either to deliberately exclude, or are unable to include all stakeholders reinforcing a crisis of unity and legitimacy and fomenting more violent discord. This pattern can be picked up in the Naga, Kuki, Zomi, Bodo and several accords signed between armed groups, Union Government and the State governments in North-East India.

Persistence of armed conflict in North-East India and the rising instances of collateral damage have assumed significant dimension mainly in view of different interested quarters expressing their concern to resolve the outstanding conflict through political dialogue. Here, the basic question that needs to be addressed is whether or not the present situation is appropriate for holding political dialogue.[2]

Such a concern has arisen mainly because of the prevailing understanding that holds any kind of political dialogue between the insurgents and the Government at the present situation as a path towards capitulation. In this context, it is reiterated that the auguries and caveats regarding cessation of hostilities must encompass unorthodox methodologies that can constitute newer ideation. Long-term policies should govern negotiations, ceasefires and resolutions with wayward groups in the region, shedding the imperative of short-term expedience.[3]

The crisis of cultures and societies in Manipur societies partakes of the larger crisis of our contemporary civilization. Sadly, the abundance of thoughts is unfortunately matched by the unavailability of actions. While the abundance of thoughts should also be followed by the abundance of actions, this sadly is absent.[4] Whereas ceasefire agreements have led to a reduction in the insurgency-related fatalities in the respective states, the Union government has not been able to carve out a road map toward a situation of permanent agreement. In many cases, the process of dialogue is yet to formally start with the outfits even after a decade(s) of signing the agreements.[5] The lack of sincerity on the part of the Central government, State government and also in many instances, the armed groups themselves[6] have oftentimes made a mockery of parleys and negotiations. Ceasefire agreements and Suspension of Operations have become a platform for capitalization and maximization of benefits and advantages used and manipulated by both parties without restraints. This condition has rendered peace parleys and accords a leaking pot that does not contain nor restore.

References

1. South Asian Conference concept paper on "Why Peace Accords and Peace Processes Falter? Resolving Ethno- Nationalist Conflicts and the Challenge for Democracy and Equality", 26-27 March, 2013.
2. http://e-pao.net/Indo_Manipur_political_dialogue_How_feasible_is_it_Part_1
3. http://www.vifindia.org/article/2011/august/02/Dialectics-of-Ceasefires-with-Insurgents-in-the-North-East
4. Immanuel Z. Varte, "Ethnic Integration: Issues, Challenges and the Way Forward", Workshop on "Ethnic Integration in North-East India: Issues

and Challenges" Organized by Institute of Social Research and Development, Imphal, Manipur from 20th-21st September, 2013.

5. http://cdpsindia.org/ne_peace.asp
6. In Nagaland, fratricidal clashes between the NSCN-IM and the NSCN-K have remained a major issue of concern. In Assam, even after its moves for peace, ULFA continues to indulge in sporadic acts of violence.

4

Restructuring Indian Federalism

The Ideal Way to Peace Process in North-East India

Rajendrakshetri and *Oinam Momoton Singh*

Introduction

The constitution of a state/country is a body of rules and regulations, written or unwritten, whereby the government is organized and functions. It is a collection of principles according to which the powers of the government, the rights of the governed and the relations between the two are adjusted. A constitution may be either unitary or federal on the ground of concentration and distribution of powers. A unitary constitution is one which vests all power in a Central Government while a federal constitution distributes powers between the Central and regional/State governments in such a way that there is no chance of conflict between the two as far as possible. An independent and impartial judiciary is also there to act as an umpire between two governments and to interpret the provisions of the constitution as and when required.

The Constitution of India does not fit into any rigid definition of federal or unitary. The members of the Constituent Assembly, by drawing on the experience of the great federations like the United States, Canada, Switzerland and Australia, pursued the policy of pick and choose to see what would suit them best. The Constituent Assembly took the decision to have a federal constitution with a strong centre because of the circumstances of the time at which the decision was taken. The need for a strong Central Government was felt for handling the situation arising out of communal riots that preceded and accompanied the partition of the country, for meeting the food crisis, for settling the refugees, for maintaining national unity and for promoting social and economic development. India was made a Union of States rather than federation of states. Thus, the federal character of India was not the result of an agreement by the states to join in a federation and no state has the right to secede from it. However, in a true federation the constituting units/states have the freedom to come out of the union. The Central/Union Government has been given more power and it is stronger than the State Governments. The State governments have to respect the laws made by the Central Government and cannot make any law on matters on which there is already a Central law. The centre can give directions to the states which they must carry out. Both the houses of the Parliament—Lok Sabha and Rajya Sabha—do not represent the states equally. The populous states have more representatives in the house than the less populous states. When emergency is declared, the Union/Central Government becomes all powerful and the State Governments come under its total control, losing their autonomy. The Union Parliament does not need the approval of the state legislatures to amend the Constitution and this act is contrary to the federal provision that the Union and the State legislatures take part in the amendment of the Constitution with respect to all matters. The overwhelming financial power of the Union and the dependence of the States upon the Centre for grants-in-aid for discharging their functions places limits on federalism. The role of Planning Commission has been contributing to the strength of the Central Government in financial matters. It exercises control over the working of the State governments and consequently reduce the position of the States to the units of local administration in a unitary system of government. But, trying to hammer the multiple identities of the citizens into a singular identity would fracture the political community rather than solidifying it.

Brief Political History of North-East India

The North-East India comprising seven states—Assam, Arunachal Pradesh, Nagaland, Manipur, Mizoram, Meghalaya and Tripura—has the distinction of experiencing persistent underdevelopment and insurgency. Most of these states were parts of colonial Assam except the former princely States of Manipur and Tripura. The region of North-East India got its strategic importance as it is surrounded by China, Myanmar, Bangladesh and Bhutan. It is covered by both the hills (70%) and the plains (30%) and majority of the population inhabiting the region belongs to mongoloid race. The region is at a location far away from the consciousness of Indian leaders. It is linked to the Indian mainland by a slender 20 km corridor, known as 'Chicken Neck,' through North Bengal. Outdated legislations such as the 'Inner Line Permit', 'Protected Area Permit', 'Restricted Area Permit' and Armed Forces Special Powers Act are being imposed in the region. This makes the region a strictly landlocked hinterland region of India, isolating it from the international community. The people of this region feel that they are neglected, exploited and discriminated. The Indian state treats the entire region primarily as the supplier of raw materials and a market for goods produced in the rest of the country what British Imperialism did in and to India in its two hundred years of colonialism, Independent India is doing in and to the North-East India.

Politically, Assam has been invaded but has never served as a vassal or a colony to an extreme power till the advent of the Burmese in 1821 and subsequently the British in 1826. The colonial period began with the establishment of the British control after the Yandaboo Treaty in 1826 and the post-colonial period began in 1947 after the Independence of India. The State of Assam was formed on 26 January, 1950. It has a unicameral legislature with 126 seats. The State is represented in the Lok Sabha by 14 MPs and 7 MPs in the Rajya Sabha. Mizoram, a small state covering an area of 21,081 sq.km., was formed on 20 February, 1987 as the 23rd State of India. It has a unicameral legislature with 40 seats and the state is represented in the Parliament by 2 MPs, one each in Lok Sabha and Rajya Sabha respectively. Another small state, Nagaland, was formed on 1 December, 1963 and is represented by one MP each in Lok Sabha and Rajya Sabha. It too has a unicameral legislature with 60 seats. Manipur is another small state in North-East India with its own long history since 33 A.D. The introduction of democratic institutions and principles in the state was coincided with the emergence of educated elite groups in the 1930s when the state was under the British rule. The enactment of Manipur State Constitution Act, 1947 was the solid foundation for the establishment of a government based on democracy. After the lapse of the British paramouncy in August, 1947, assembly elections were held in 1948, under the Manipur State Constitution Act, 1947, on the basis of adult franchise and a representative government was formed under the Chief Ministership of Maharajkumar Priyobrata Singh. However, the newly Independent India and it government in New Delhi pressured the king to sign a merger agreement with India. Maharaja Bodhchandra signed the Merger Agreement under duress on 21 September, 1949 A.D. at Shillong. Following the Merger Agreement, Manipur was made a Part-C state. Manipur, from a Part-C state, become a Union territory in 1956 and was finally granted statehood in 1972. The state has a unicameral legislature of 60 seats and is represented by 2 MPs in the Lok Sabha and one MP in the Rajya Sabha. The state's electoral politics is marked by politics of defection, re-defection, coalition and counter-coalition causing great political instability. From 1972 to 2001, there had not been any government which completed the tenure of five years.

The States of the North-East India remained virtually isolated from social and political development taking place elsewhere in the country. In the process of nation building since 1947, sub-national challenges to Pan-Indianism have come from several quarters of the region. The sub-nationalism in the region implies an aspiration for an independent country or the pursuit of greater autonomy within the existing politico-legal framework of the country. The multi-ethnic, multi-linguistic region has been witnessing some of the worst crises-insurgency, secessionism and linguistic turmoil. The piecemeal approach of New Delhi to the problems in the North-East India also has given rise to a built-in cause of separatism in the region. It is argued that the government's response is a total failure in resolving the recurring sub-nationalist challenge to Pan-Indian constructs. The alleged neglect and economic exploitation by the Indian state are the contributory reasons behind the growth of the secessionist movement in the region. The insurgency or separatist movement in Assam started in the 1970s. It stems from the alleged neglect and internal colonization by the Indian government with its federal centre in Delhi. Several insurgent organizations like the United Liberation Front of Asom (ULFA), Adivasi National Liberation Army, Karbi Longni N.C. Hills Liberation Front (KLNLF) and National Democratic Front of Bodoland are active in the state. ULFA is perhaps the largest and oldest group, being founded in 1979 and it seeks to establish a sovereign Assam via armed struggle. The Indian government had banned the organization in 1990 and classifies it as a terrorist group. Military operations against the insurgent groups by the Indian Army that began in 1990 continue till the present day. In the past two decades, more than 30,000 people have died in the clash between the rebels and the government.

It was Mizoram in the 1960s. The Mizo National Front (MNF), formed on 22 October, 1961, had the specified goal of sovereign independent Mizoram by resorting to armed insurrection. The Government of India bombed the city of Aizawl with Toofani and Hunter jet fighters on 5 and 6 March, 1966 to suppress the secessionist movement. This was the first time that India used its Air Force to quell a movement among its citizens. The MNF was outlawed in 1967. The Mizoram Peace Accord (the official document entitled Mizoram Accord, 1986, Memorandum of Settlement) was signed between the MNF and the Union government on 30 June, 1986. Statehood was a pre-requisite of the accord so that Mizoram became a federal state of India on 20 February, 1987. In Nagaland, it was such that the Naga National Council (NNC) was a political organization of Naga people and it was active from the late 1940s to the early 1950s. Under the leadership of Angami Zapu Phizo in the 1940s, it successfully campaigned for the secession of Naga territory from India and creation of sovereign Naga state. The NNC leaders had an understanding that the Nagas were never Indians and that the Naga territories were never a part of India at any time before the advent of British. A seven member's delegation of the NNC consisting of Phizo, Khrisanisa, Kughato, Kezehol, John Angami, T. Sakhrie and Lhousihtuo were sent to New Delhi in 1947 to propose their view that the Nagas be left outside the Indian union when the British withdrew from British India. This idea was rejected by the Indian government. However, Nagaland declared its independence on 14 August, 1947. This event led to serious conflict between NNC and government of India. In 1956 the Federal government of Nagaland was formed by NNC and it maintained an army called Naga army. With the declaration of the Naga Hills as disturbed area on 29 January, 1956, the army started moving in and Nagaland passed through a period of undeclared war waged between the Indian army and the Naga army with the result that innocent villagers suffered the most in different forms. On 6 September, 1964, the Indian government and the Federal government of Nagaland declared bilateral ceasefire. The abortive attempt to kill Hokishe Sema, the Chief Minister of Nagaland, by the Naga underground on 8 August, 1972 provoked the government to formally withdraw the ceasefire and consequently enforced the Unlawful Activities Act, 1967 and banned the activities of the Federal government of Nagaland, the Naga army and the NNC on 1 September, 1972. The Shillong Accord was signed on 10-11 November, 1975 at Raj Bhavan, Shillong between the Naga underground consisting of six members delegation led by Kevi Yallay, brother of Phizo, and the government of India represented by L.P. Singh, then Governor of Nagaland. However, on 21 November, 1975, Th. Muivah, the General Secretary of the NNC and six members of his delegation including Isak Chishi Swu, issued a statement that the people of Nagaland have nothing to choose in place of their national freedom and that they will by no means be a party to any settlement that may entail the loss of their right to sovereign existence. The statement called the negotiators of the agreement traitors and disclaimed their authority to settle the Indo-Naga issue within the Indian union. The present National Socialist Council of Nagaland (NSCN) was formed on 31 January, 1980 and it was split into two groups as NSCN (IM) under the leadership of Isak Chishi Swu and Th. Muivah and NSCN-K under S.S. Khaplang on 30 April, 1988. As of now, both the groups are in ceasefire with the Indian government.

Insurgency problem in Manipur stated slowly in the late 1960s and 1970s. Between 1992 and 2010, at least 5665 people were killed in insurgency related incidents in the state and Manipur remains the most volatile state in the region of North-East India. The genesis of insurgency in the valley areas of Manipur can be traced to the emergence of the United Liberation Front (UNLF) on 24 November, 1964. Since then, several other outfits like the People's Liberation Army (PLA) founded on 25 September, 1978; People's Revolutionary Party of Kangleipak set up on 9 October, 1977; the Kangleipak Communist Party (KCP) that came into being in April, 1980 etc. have emerged in the state and they have been demanding a separate independent Manipur. The hill areas of the state have been affected by different brands of insurgency. The alleged forced merger of Manipur and the delay in the conferring of full-fledged statehood to it was greatly resented by the people of Manipur. There was the failure of the elected representatives of the Manipur state Assembly formed under the Manipur State Constitution Act, 1947 to explain the merits and demerits of Manipur's merger to India to the king who signed the merger agreement with India. Added to these is the long neglect or step motherly treatment of the region (state) by the Central Government which promote feeling of alienation among the People of North-East India. The Government of India has been trying to suppress the secessionist movements in the region by force. The armed forces are given sweeping powers by the Armed Forces (Special Powers) Act-1958 and there has been the process of militarization of the region. The display of sophisticated weapons, armored vehicles and thousands of army and paramilitary forces create fear psychosis among the general public. The security forces take every opportunity to terrorize the general masses by way of combing operation, illegal detention, custodial killing, indiscriminate firing, fake encounters, torture, rape, molestation and killing of women etc.

Indian Federalism and American Federalism

Both the United States (US) and India have federal political structure.

The US became a federal republic state by promulgating its constitution in the year 1789 while India became a socialist, sovereign, secular, democratic republic in the year 1950. The strong Central Government in the US is called Federal Government and Central government in India. Both the countries have written constitution on the basis of which the Federal political structure has been set up and function. Both of them are also characterized by supremacy of the Federal or Central Government. There are provisions of amending the constitution to meet the growing socio-political and economic needs and demands. There are also basic divisions with regard to division of labour in their federal set-up—executive, legislature and judiciary—with clear cut separation of powers.

Differences also exist between Indian federalism and US federalism. The constitution of US is very rigid than the Constitution of India. The Constitution of India is very voluminous containing as many as XXII parts, 395 articles and ten schedules whereas the US constitution is very brief and rigid running into only a few pages. The provisions meant for amending the US constitution are very rigid and more formal. Between the period 1789 and 1992, the US constitution has been amended only 27 times whereas the Indian Constitution which came into force in the year 1950 was so far amended 98 times. In the US all the states affiliated with the Federal government in addition to their allegiance to the Federal constitution have their own constitutions to regulate their own governance. In India, on the other hand, all the States affiliated with the India Union owe their allegiance only to the Constitution of India and do not have their own constitution. The US has the Presidential form of government and therefore, the President is the head of the state. India has Parliamentary form of Government where the President is only a nominal head and the Prime Minister and his cabinet is the popular sovereign to whom the real power is vested. The process of nominating a candidate for contesting the Presidential election by a political party in the US is comparatively simpler than the Indian system of electing the Prime Minister from a party which enjoys a majority in the Lok Sabha. The US follows the bi-party system while India has a multi-party system and a complicated process of election. The Indian Prime Minister holds power for five years as long as his political party enjoys majority in the house. But the US President holds power for a period of four years irrespective of his affiliation with a political party, republican or democrat and irrespective of his party's success or failure in the elections for the House of Representatives or House of Senate. In the US, a person can hold the post of President for two terms only, but in India there is no such restriction to hold the post of Prime Minister or President. The Indian Prime Minister and his cabinet are collectively and directly responsible to the Parliament and indirectly to the people whereas the US President has constitutional obligation and duties and is answerable to the people.

The lower house or Lok Sabha in India is more powerful and its members are directly elected by the people. The members of the Lok Sabha represent their constituencies on the basis of their popular strength. In the US, the members of House of Representative are elected on the basis of the popular strength of the State. But irrespective of the size of the State or its population, each State in the US has only two Senate members totaling 100 members in all in the US. Moreover, the House of Senate or the upper house is more powerful and its members are directly elected. In India, the upper house or Rajya Sabha members are indirectly elected by a system of proportional and transferable voting system. Differences also exist in the judicial system of the US and India. An accused or a witness in the US can dispose from the place where he is imprisoned using advanced technology. Such facilities are yet to develop in India. A judge in the US can hold his office for life as long as he enjoys his good health. But in India, a district judge unless elevated retires at the age of 58 years, a High Court and Supreme Court judge retires at the age of 65 years. Each State, whether inhabited by people of India origin/ Chinese origin/African origin or otherwise or small or big in size or populous or not has equal representation to the upper house and the representatives have equal right/privilege and power in formulating policies for the welfare of the State in particular and for the whole US in general. Such a unique feature of federalism is not found in Indian federalism where the voices of small and less populous states highlighted by their representatives are generally ignored and neglected. This fact in one way gives birth to the feeling of alienation among various groups in India and this is perhaps the main reason why separatist movements exist in India in one form or another but not in the US.

Indian Federalism: Root Cause of Alienation/Insurgency in the North-East India

The real working of Constitution of India shows that the Central Government has grown stronger and that the states (particularly small states) have become just like administrative units of the Centre. India's Constitution is being described as federal in form, but unitary in spirit. It is also described as quasi-federal. It is a fact that federalism in India has a strong bias towards the Central Government. Representation in the Parliament varies widely from one state to another depending on a number of factors including demography and total land area. The State-wise representation to the Union Parliament as well as the state having either bicameral or unicameral legislature can be highlighted in the tabular form as under

Table 4.1: The State-wise representation to the Union Parliament as well as the State having either bicameral or unicameral legislature

State	*No. of MPs in Lok Sabha*	*No. of MPs in Rajya Sabha*	*Total*	*Bicameral legislature*	*Unicameral legislature*
Andhra Pradesh	42	18	60	Yes	—
Arunachal Pradesh	02	01	03	—	Yes
Assam	14	07	21	—	Yes
Bihar	40	16	56	Yes	—
Chhattisgrah	11	05	16	—	Yes
Goa	02	01	03	—	Yes
Gujarat	26	11	37	—	Yes
Haryana	10	05	15	—	Yes
Himachal Pradesh	04	03	07	—	Yes
Jammu & Kashmir	06	04	10	Yes	—
Jharkhand	14	06	20	—	Yes
Karnataka	28	12	40	Yes	—
Kerala	20	09	29	—	Yes
Madhya Pradesh	29	11	40	—	Yes
Maharashtra	48	19	67	Yes	—
Manipur	02	01	03	—	Yes
Meghalaya	02	01	03	—	Yes
Mizoram	01	01	02	—	Yes
Nagaland	01	01	02	—	Yes
Odisha	21	10	31	—	Yes
Punjab	13	07	20	—	Yes
Rajasthan	25	10	35	—	Yes
Sikkim	01	01	02	—	Yes
Tamil Nadu	39	18	57	—	Yes
Tripura	02	01	03	—	Yes
Uttarakhand	05	03	08	—	Yes
Utter Pradesh	80	31	111	Yes	—
West Bengal	42	16	58	—	Yes
Telangana	17	Not decided	17	Not decided	Not decided

The above Table 4.1 clearly shows that Uttar Pradesh has the largest number of MPs (111), 80 MPs in Lok Sabha and 31 MPs in Rajya Sabha followed by Maharashtra (67) with 48 MPs in Lok Sabha and 19 MPs in Rajya Sabha. The state having the 3rd largest number of MPs in the Parliament is Andhra Pradesh with 60 MPs (42 MPs in Lok Sabha and

18 in Rajya Sabha). Among the States in North-East India, Assam send largest number of MPs in the Parliament and the region of North-East India as a whole is represented by only 24 MPs in the Lok Sabha and 13 MPs in the Rajya Sabha. Many states like Uttar Pradesh, West Bengal, Tamil Nadu, Rajasthan, Maharashtra, Madhya Pradesh, Karnataka, Gujarat, Bihar and Andhra Pradesh are sending more MPs to the Parliament than the whole North-East India put together and thus more advantageous while playing crucial role in law making and policy formulation procedure of the country. It is a common practice in Indian democracy that decisions with regard to diverse fields are taken by the group with majority support of the members in the two houses of parliament. As the North-East India is represented merely by 37 MPs only, that too belonging to different political parties with different ideologies, the region is not given the due importance while taking any major policy decision. This phenomenon is so much pervasive today that no political leaders/parties in the region have been able to chart out their own course of action with wisdom san Delhi or central leaders. This is not to mean together that the Delhi centric approach is unhealthy for the region, but it also cannot be said that the trend is healthy either. The lack of adequate physical connectivity between North-East India and South-East Asia, for example, is an outcome of skeptic mindset of Indian policy makers and this constitute one important factor that hindered the possibilities of economic development in the region. Thus, Indian federalism promotes alienation of the People of North-East India from the mainland India. The table further shows that only 6 states in India—Andhra Pradesh, Bihar, Jammu & Kashmir, Karnataka, Maharashtra and Uttar Pradesh—have bicameral legislature and the rest have unicameral legislature. It means that the people of the states with bicameral legislature have more representatives of the people to safeguard their interests than other states with unicameral legislature. It will be a better option for the states of North-East India to adopt/introduce bicameral chamber in their respective state so that people have more representatives who can promote their welfare.

India stands on the principle of unity in diversity. It aims at forging a union. There are prevailing diversities that are sought to be preserved. There must be an overriding sense of unity to bind diverse people together. It is not possible that all the unit states of Indian federalism are of equal size or they have equal density of population. However, it should be essentially such that there should be no inequality in matters relating to the distribution of powers in the highest possible way. The number of

MPs sent by the State governments to the Rajya Sabha varies from 1 to 34 and 1 to 80 in the Lok Sabha. This factor of inequality creates dissatisfaction that has harmful effects on the political behaviour of the State governments. It is and will be a positive alternative to have equal representation of all states in the parliament irrespective of size and population. Extreme care should also be taken to remove regional economic imbalance. Introducing legislative council in all states is also a better option in India. This will give a sense of equality and parity among the people and most importantly, the sense of belongingness to one country.

North-East India and Armed Forces (Special Powers) Act, 1959

The Armed Forces (Special Powers) Act, 1958 (AFSPA) is one of the most draconian legislations that Indian Parliament has ever passed in its parliamentary history. This act was implemented in the states of North-East India at Assam and Manipur and was afterwards amended in 1972 to extend to all seven states in the region of North-East India. It has been justified on the plea that it is required to stop the North-East states from seceding from the Indian Union. The provisions of the Act provide special powers to State Governors, whereby they can on their own discretion and without informing the elected representatives, by notification in the official gazette, declare the whole or part of the State or Union territory to be disturbed area. Bypassing duly elected representative political authority is tantamount to *de facto* imposition of emergency. The AFSPA automatically comes into force when the government of India designated a territory as a disturbed and empowers the armed forces to arrest without warrant, to conduct search and seizure without warrant and to shoot even to the causing of death on mere suspicion. It also provides virtual immunity from prosecution by requiring prior permission from the Central government and this permission is almost never given. The Act has led to grave human rights violations including extrajudicial execution, enforced disappearance, rape, torture and other ill treatment. It effectively undermines civil authority. For instance, the civil law ceased to operate in Senapati district of Manipur after the Oinam incident (1987) due to excess committed by the Assam Rifles, the Deputy Commissioner and the Superintendent of Police were wrongly confined, humiliated and prevented from discharging their official duties by the security forces. In Nagaland, consequent to the Kohima incident of 1995, even the Superintendent of Police, Kohima was stopped at gun point by army personnel. Here, it may be mentioned that the Supreme Court of India appointed Justice Hegde Commission in January, 2013, in response to a public interest litigation seeking investigation into 1528 cases of alleged extrajudicial executions committed in the State of Manipur in North-East India between 1978 and 2010. The Commission was established to determine whether six cases identified by the Court were extrajudicial executions or encounter deaths as claimed by security forces. In its report submitted to the court in April, 2013, the Commission found that all seven deaths in the six cases it investigated were extrajudicial executions and the AFSPA was widely abused by security forces in Manipur. It also said that the continued operation of the Act in Manipur has made 'a mockery of the law' and that security forces have been "transgressing the legal bounds for their counter-insurgency operations in the State of Manipur". The commission also made a statement made by the Jeevan Reddy Committee, a committee formed to review the AFSPA in 2005, which said that the law had become "a symbol of oppression, an object of hate and an instrument of discrimination and high handedness".

The frustration and anger of the people produced by the Act are so high that spontaneous agitations against the Act and security personnel involved in the act of human rights violation have been made throughout the region of North-East India. For instance, 12 elderly women in Manipur stripped themselves naked and demonstrated in front of the Assam Rifles headquarters at Kangla carrying placards bearing the words 'Indian Army Rape Us', a lone lady, Irom Sharmila Chanu, has been on fast up to death for more than a decade and another Manipuri, Pebam Chitaranjan, had gone to the extent of torching himself to death on 15 August, 2004 (he received about 85% burn of his body and succumbed to the injuries on 16 August, 2004) demanding the repeal of the Act. AFSPA does not give peace a chance. It divides rather than unites people and dehumanizes human being. It sends a wrong/dangerous signal to the people living in the peripheral areas. Restructuring of Indian federalism must be followed by lifting/withdrawal of AFSPA from the region.

Suggestive Note

India urgently needs to initiate peace process with a vision—a long-term vision where peripheral Indians feel at home, equal and at par with their counterparts elsewhere in the country. Building peace process is a serious business and should not be treated as something/some kind of a play thing to be used and thrown away at the behest of some vested leaders/

groups/community. It is necessary for the state to resort to new strategies and plans to hook and book the vested groups/community and instill the confidence of being Indian among the people of peripheral areas in the country. The perceived discrimination or neglect and underdevelopment posed a threat to the peace and integrity of the nation. It is time to have a holistic approach to the challenges of peace in the country, particularly in peripheral areas. National leadership must also be in the hands of those who have national image and who can infuse the sentiments of national integration in the mind of their people. That is why India needs, more than ever before, political leaders with visions, not political dealers. Political statesmen, not political pygmies.

Restructuring of Indian federalism and lifting/withdrawal of AFSPA is a long-term initiative of bringing peace in the region of North-East India. Federalism should be cooperative not a competitive, 'persuasive and not coercive', flexible not rigid and above all have positive, not negative character. The people of a federal country should be integrated not only in the geo-political and physical sense of the term, but more importantly in the socio-emotional sense. Social and economic development should cover the entire country with a more emphasis on the underdeveloped and peripheral region or territory. There should be no imbalance in this regard as demands for development of underdeveloped and/or neglected areas may give rise to the emergence of more 'Secessionist'/'Separatist' movements as is evident since last four decades in the region of North-East India.

References

Banerjee, D. (2012), Repeal the Draconian AFSPA, *North-East Sun*, Vol. XVII, No. 15, New Delhi.

Chandra, Bipan; Mukherjee, Mridula; Mukherjee, Aditya. (2008), *India since Independence*, Penguin Books, New Delhi.

Chaudhury, Soma (2009), *Life in a Shadow Land*, *Tehelka*, Vol. 6, No. 32, New Delhi.

Government of India, Ministry of Home Affairs. (2006), *Report of the Committee to Review the Armed Forces (Special Powers) Act-1958*, New Delhi.

Independent Citizen's Fact Finding Mission. (2009), *Democracy Encountered: Rights Violations in Manipur*, New Delhi.

Johari, J.C. (1993), *Comparative Politics*, Sterling Publishers Pvt. Ltd., New Delhi.

_______(2011), *New Comparative Government*, Lotus Press, New Delhi.

Kashyap, Subash C. (2010), *Our Constitution,* National Book Trust, New Delhi.

Kshetri, Rajendra. (2006), *The Emergence of Meetei Nationalism,* Mittal Publications, New Delhi.

Kshetri, Rajendra (2010): "Peripheral India" *Sangai Express*, Imphal, 12th November, 2010, Imphal, p. 2.

Phukan, Girin. (Ed). (2004), *Inter-Ethnic Conflict North-East India*, South Asia Publishers Pvt. Ltd., New Delhi.

Phanjoubam, Tarapot. (2003), *Bleeding Manipur*, Har Anand Publications, New Delhi.

Singh, Oinam Momoton. (2013), *The Issue of Armed Forces (Special Powers) Act, 1958 in Manipur*, International Research & Review, Vol. 2, No. 4, Varanasi.

Retrieved Materials from Websites:

History of Assam, available at [http://en.wikipedia.org/wiki/History_of_Assam], retrieved on 29.4.2014.

Assam Separatist Movement, available at [http://en.wikipedia.org/wiki/Assam_separatist_movements], retrieved on 29.4.2014.

Insurgency in North-East India available at [http://en.wikipedia.org/wiki/Insurgency_in_North-East_India] retrieved on 30.4.2014.

History of Mizoram, available at [http://en.wikipedia.org/wiki/History_of_Mizoram], retrieved on 30.4.2014.

Naga National Council, available at [http://en.wikipedia.org/wiki/Naga_National_Council] retrieved on 1.5.2014.

Nagas Struggle for Sovereignty (Naga Political History), available at [http://nagalimonline.tangkhul.com/modules.php?name=Forums&file=viewtopic&t=64], retrieved on 1.5.2014.

Armed Forces Special Power Act and Violation of Human Rights in North-East India, available at [http://samaj-thesociety.blogspot.in/2010/08/armed-forces-special-power-act-and.html, retrieved on 5.5.2014.

The Armed Forces Special Powers Act: Time for a renewed debate in India on human rights and national security, available at [http://www.amnesty.org/en/library/asset/ASA20/042/2013/en/d47290df-5a65-42ec-ac49-de305f299229/asa200422013en.html] retrieved on 5.5.2014.

The Similarities and Differences Between American Federalism and Indian Federalism, available at [http://general-law.knoji.com/the-similarities-and-differences-between-american-federalism-and-indian-federalism/], retrieved on 5.5.2014.

5
Militarism, Human Rights and Democracy in North-East India

Homen Thangjam

Introduction

In a memorial lecture delivered on June 30, 2013 at Imphal, scholar and creator of alternative theatre, "theatre of the earth", Padma Shri, Shri Heisnam Kanhailal observed:

> Simmering discontent that started from around 1960 finally erupted into a war of independence against India in the 70s. Manipur became a contested land for both the Indian army and the liberation army. Even today, the Manipuri society exists amidst confusion and mayhem. Government's imposition of various types of laws to subjugate the people has become the burning issues and resulted into existential crisis. It has been nearly 50 years since people have been living in this manner. Brutal oppression continues (Kanhailal, 2013: 2).

Further he remarked:

> On a daily basis there are *bandhs* and ceaseless economic blockades for more than 100 days. All this happens in the midst of armed-conflict between the State armed-forces and armed opposition groups. All of us are living, leading the lives of victims. Violence has become a characteristic feature, embraced and practiced, for any activity. Whenever there is a *bandh* or a strike, instead of seeking solidarity from the public, *bandh*

> supporters warn the people to follow their *diktat,* if not, they have to face the consequences on their own. Are these verdicts non-violence or violence? There is no respect for human life any more. There are no qualms in taking away a life. Where can one find a more decadent society than ours? (Kanhailal, 2013:5 and 12).

Heisnam Kanhailal clearly captures the popular angst as well as the existential reality of the region of North-East India (hereafter NER) in general and the State of Manipur in particular. It would not be an exaggeration to add that in contemporary Manipur, violence influences not only the high politics but also the everyday life of the common people. In fact, the prolonged and continued armed conflict in North-East India has impacted onto the social, economic, political and everyday life shaping into a practice. This is reflected in three visible trends. On one hand, State enjoys impunity to violence under the cloak of the Armed Forces Special (Powers) Act, 1958 (hereafter AFSPA). The Act, which was imposed initially in the hill areas of Manipur in 1958 and all over the state in 1980, provides immunity to the state actors and they cannot be tried in civilian court of justice.[1] And on the other hand, armed opposition groups continue to rely on violence either to achieve the goal of independence or to enforce their mandate upon the people. Moreover, we witness seeming acceptance of violence by the people both as a means of resistance against the excesses of the armed groups (state and non-state actors) as well as a method of settling disputes amongst themselves, and thus caught in the grips of the cycle of violence.

My argument is that these trends have led to the acceptance of aberration of principles and practices of democracy. And human rights violations are considered to be collateral damages. In order to put the issues into perspective and understand the prevailing malaise of militarism as well as the democratic condition in the state, the chapter focuses on the genesis of the armed conflict in Manipur. Further, the chapter proposes that the juxtaposition of the Indian State (with a civilizational narrative) with other erstwhile independent nations such as Manipur, which was once a sovereign kingdom in the South-East Asia, finds mismatches. In this midst, what has become an alarming trend is the practice of violence, which has captured popular imagination and used in dealing with any issue.

Contesting Narratives and the Armed Conflict

The genesis of armed conflict in Manipur may be traced back to the last days of British imperialism. The Asiatic kingdom became a colony of the British after its defeat in the Anglo-Manipur War of 1891. End of British colonialism in the Indian Sub-continent in 1947 they provided the historical context for the emergence of conflict situation in the State. In fact, the conflict in Manipur is rooted in the contested merger of Manipur with Indian Union in 1949. A pertinent demand of the armed opposition groups in Manipur has been the restoration of the pre-1949 sovereign status of Manipur. Since then, the narrative of "nation" and "sub-nation" becomes a major point of contention among different political and cultural positionalities, which has rendered the erstwhile kingdom in a cauldron of violence.

The Nation Narrative, Nation Building and the Enemy Within

The modern idea of nation-state was introduced in India through colonial intervention. The post-Enlightenment ideals of value-neutrality, objectivity, impersonal and bureaucratic structures of governance and representative rule, developed in Western countries as a part of reform movements and protests, had a basis in popular thought. In India, such ideals, which became the basis of nationalism, were a gift from the modernity package brought by colonialism.

In rejecting the colonial rule, Indian nationalism had to assert its distinctive identity by differentiating itself from the identity of the colonial masters, while simultaneously internalizing the Enlightenment rationality of Western thought for its own formation. But as Bikhu Parekh (1997) notes, the cultural limitation of liberal democracy imposes certain constraints upon those imitating the same both in terms of skills as well as the craft. Out of such emplacement emerged the Indian dilemma: a contradictory and conflicting nation-self in which the nation-state had to be at once itself and the other than itself. This dilemma leads the Indian State appropriating the colonial character, questioned and rejected during the freedom struggle, thus resulting into a situation of state-linked "internal colonialism" (Nandy, 1983:12). The state uses legitimizing core concepts like national security, development, modern science and technology as justificatory ideologies for domination. Violence is used to sustain these ideologies. Legitimacy to this violence is drawn from the accepted dominant theory of state so as to monopolise absolute violence.

At the policy level, what was followed by the political elites, following the withdrawal of the colonial state, was the tendency to take an excessively constitutional or constructivist view of the political dynamics.

It was widely believed, in the Indian nationalist circles as elsewhere, that the making of a successful nation-state was basically a matter of legal and political construction. In spite of differences on principles for the creation of a new society, the constructivist premise went unquestioned among the political elites. Legacies of administration, political order, rule and defiance surviving from earlier political formations—empires, royalties, rituals of exaltation and subordination, etc.—thus, have not completely vanished, but remain in something like a substructure of the political world (Doornbos and Kaviraj, 1997:12). Administrative convenience once decried against the British colonial rule was continued and legal homogenization of the political world entirely structured by the institutions and initiatives of the ruling elites, who went all out to serve their own interests. The materiality of having a physical nation (territoriality) whose resources could be exploited for the elites' benefits, under the garb of social equity and redistributive justice could only be envisioned by the educated elites at the expense of illiterate masses.

Over the years, what has occurred in India is the resurgence of historical legacies often as memories, which do not have any definable locus in institutions but pervade the political world, subtly altering the meanings and results of political actions (Doornbos and Kaviraj, 1997:12). For example, the recent period in India has witnessed an increasingly lucid appreciation of the subtle ways in which historical past remain active through their effects. The patterns of traditional politics operate as deeper, subterranean influences on the formal architectures of modern parliamentary politics. Caste and religious politics have in recent times developed forms which are impossible to describe in terms of the dichotomy between the "traditional" and the "modern". In the case of the North-East India, ethnicity have emerged as historical units vying for space both in the mainstream politics as well as serve as canons for self-determination. Whether ethnic groups in the North-East India are historical entities or these are modern political constructs shall be deliberated in the subsequent sections. It is worth noting that the politics of identity revolves around these structures, which are responsible for most of the violence in the region.

The story of the political integration of India as a nation-state was through the logic of citizenship and economics. The ideas were mainly borrowed from the (western) modern paradigm of nation-state theory. In this enterprise, what was inculcated is the principle of individuating the individuals whose locomotion in life is propelled by self-interest and profit. While this is true for most part of India, the North-East India and some parts of India had a different story to tell. The logic of "strategic importance" was given paramount significance over those two processes. For example, Manipur was "taken over" through a militaristic maneuver. The enforcement of Merger Agreement on October 15, 1949 led to the dissolution of a democratically constituted Legislative Assembly. In Manipur, after the departure of the British in 1947, elections based on universal adult franchise was held in June 1948 and the Maharaja inaugurated the first Assembly Session on October 18, 1948.

The State, as a social and political practice and as a system of inclusion and exclusion *par excellence*, has tried to solve the problem of conflicting identity claims by producing precise distinctions and differences between citizens and aliens, by domesticating particular identities and by creating a coherent sovereign identity. As Bauman describes the modern state:

> National states promote "nativism" and construe its subjects as "natives". They laud and enforce the ethnic, religious, linguistic, cultural *homogeneity*. They are engaged in incessant propaganda of *shared* attitudes. They construct *joint* historical memories and do their best to discredit or suppress such stubborn memories that cannot be squeezed into a shared tradition—now redefined in the state-appropriate quasi-legal terms, as "our common heritage". They preach the sense of *common* mission, *common* fate, *common* destiny. They breed, or at least legitimize and give tacit support to, animosity towards everyone standing outside the holy union (Bauman, 1991:64; emphasis by Bauman).

This state has become more and more a contested space. As Appadurai notes, the "nation-state" is a battle of imagination with "state and nation seeking to cannibalise each other" (Appadurai, 1990:304). Groups with ideas about nationhood seek to capture or co-opt state power, and states simultaneously seek to capture and monopolise ideas about nationhood. Thus, a platform is set for separatism and micro-identities to become political projects within the nation-states. Ideas of nationhood appear to be steadily increasing in scale and regularly crossing existing state boundaries.

At the same time, logic of citizenship, although the Constitution provides the parameters, remains questionable when seen in the context of the state's relation with its minorities. The application of a Western worldview of state formation in the developing countries with ideals of singularity—single identity, single source of sovereignty, single legal system, a single system of rights and obligations, a unitary conception of citizenship, and a single mode of relating to the state—presupposes that members of the state are all agreed in defining themselves primarily as individual citizens rather than as members of specific ethnic, religious or other communities. The presupposition is that members of the state form a single and homogenous people, and qua people they are sovereign. Since, they form a homogenous unit, the majority is entitled to speak and act in the name of them all (Parekh, 1997:192). Any attempt to develop or sustain loyalties to their pre-modern identities, other than given by the state, or go against the majority principle, are viewed with suspicion and hostility. For the state, these minorities are the "Others"—the enemies within or the "objective enemies". Take for instance, when movements are initiated demanding autonomy in the form of recognition of language, culture, or in more radical terms, self-determination, they are viewed as anti-national. Catalytic explosions of such demands are not viewed as failure of the state to provide a framework for order and justice. Thus, the very idea of turning the North-East India into an "alien space" where martial law like AFSPA operates suggests that people of the region is closer to Hannah Arendt's "objective enemies"[2] whose definition is created by virtue of their existence in a particular position at a historical moment in time, and that they do not fall within the self-definition of a state. The idea of "national security" which the Indian State emphatically nurtures may in the long-run create incurable conflicts where the state starts subscribing to totalitarian ideology of creating "Others" within the country. From the perspective of the "nation-state", an ethnic group claiming a right to produce difference and make distinctions which transcend the official state ideology is treated as an "enemy within". The state enacts several suppressive methods to deal with these "enemy within". In India, AFSPA seems to be a pointer towards this method. The hardening character of the state emerges in reinforcing greater violence at the moment of slightest opposition. Ethnic communities in India's North-East India have been targets of such violence, not only officially at the hands of powerful state machinery, but also at the hands of all those who take their legitimation from state ideology.

Economic logic of integration is also used as another tool for nation building. This was successfully achieved through the development of capitalism across nations. In the developing countries, too, economic integration formed a compulsory component of the nation building process. In India, the idea of economic integration was associated with the concept of "planning". However, official justification of "planning" was projected as a means to achieve social justice. There seems to be inconsistency in what the Indian State intends and what it projects. While the intention of the Indian State is to achieve economic integration, it projects a different picture of targeting social justice as its goal. The result is quite imminent. Each stage of planned economy produced elites which sought to benefit the most from the state. They developed the idea of India as a nation-state based on "materiality". Instances are that of the neo-rich peasants in the Green Revolution belt, and emerging new elites in other regions of the country at recent times.

What is being achieved in this entire process of legal, political and economic integration is a strong Indian State, whose military play a substantive role in safeguarding the "national interest", which only endorses the unitary spirit of a nation-state.

Counter Narrative: The Manipuri Discourse

Assertions and demands for self-determination mainly by the Manipuris harp back to the historical legacies—of an autonomous kingdom with a civilizational foundation or having been the constant defenders of the territory against the marauding Burmese, or most recently of the story of defiance against the British colonial rule—which they believe was undone through merger with the Indian Union (Oinam and Thangjam, 2006:123). Although ascribing to different political ideologies and method of armed struggle, a common narrative shared by the valley based armed opposition groups[3] is that Manipur was a sovereign kingdom where different ethnic communities existed harmoniously and was never a part of the British India that ruled over India for more than 400 years. Such an articulation has produced a nationalist discourse that fits into an imagination of nation and territoriality. First claim is that Manipur has a 2000 years old political history and one of the most ancient kingdoms in the South-east Asia (Akoijam, 2002). When British Paramountcy lapsed, the first political act committed by the people of Manipur was the promulgation of the Manipur State Constitution Act, 1947 and adoption of a partially democratic government by holding an election based on universal adult franchise in 1948. Thus, Manipur had the distinction of possessing a constitution based on free will with the king as its constitutional head. However, the democratic sovereign status ended with five initiatives taken up by the Indian Dominion.

First step pertains to a secret agreement between the Dominion of

India and the Manipur State Durbar wherein the Durbar was persuaded to send a representative to the Constituent Assembly of India on July 1, 1947 (Singh, 2009:61-62). Second step pertains to signing of the Standstill Agreement and the Instrument of Accession on July 11, 1947 (Singh, 1988:70). Third step relates to stationing of a *Dewan*[4] in Manipur by the Government of the Dominion of India on April 10, 1949 (Singh, 1988:95). The signing of the Manipur Merger Agreement, 1949 on September 21, 1949 and forceful integration of Manipur into the Indian Union on October 15, 1949 can be regarded as the fourth step (Singh, 1988:93). Finally, through the promulgation of two orders, namely, the Manipur (Administration) Order 1949 and the State's Merger (Chief Commissioner's Provinces) Order, 1950, the Manipur State Constitution Act, 1947 and the Manipur State Assembly were dissolved (Singh, 1988:125 and 127).

The dissolution of the Manipur State Constitution and its democratic Government eventually has led to one of the most protracted armed conflict in Manipur. As a matter of fact, the armed opposition groups or insurgent groups of Manipur have been resisting the presence of Indian State in Manipur. They are fighting against the Indian military forces to restore the pre-1949 political status of Manipur with the ultimate aim to reconsolidate the democracy that had existed then. The armed opposition groups pick up October 15, 1949 as a specific historical moment when the independent political existence of Manipur came to an end. As such, the day is observed every year as "National Black Day". They are demanding the revocation of the Merger Agreement. It may be recalled that the Manipur Merger Agreement which was signed on September 21, 1949 became operative on October 15, 1949.

Resistance to the Indian State is articulated as a national liberation struggle by claiming that it is not even a demand for independence. It is instead, as the Chairman of the United National Liberation Front (UNLF), RK Sanayaima, who is currently in prison, asserts, "A question of regaining the lost sovereign independence of Manipur by driving out the Indian Occupation Forces from the soil of Manipur" (Annual Statement of the Central Committee, United National Liberation Front on its 41st Foundation Day, 2005 in *The Sangai Express*, Imphal, November 24, 2005).[5] Similarly, Revolutionary People's Front (RPF) and its military wing People's Liberation Army (PLA) also claims that the existing issue is not an internal matter of India as the Government of India (hereafter GoI) understands, but purely a conflict between two nations. The conflict, according to RPF, is between Manipur and India and this is due to the annexation of Manipur by India in 1949. It, therefore, considered it irrational to hold unemployment and underdevelopment as factors responsible for launching the liberation movement. RPF also holds the view that their struggle is not a separatist or secessionist movement on account of the fact that they are not asking or demanding even an inch of the Indian Territory that existed as in 1947. Claiming that Manipur was never a part of India, the armed opposition group insists that their resistance is a movement for national liberation which is aimed at restoring the independence of Manipur.

Counter Narrative: Multiple Ethno-discourses

Manipur is a multi-ethnic state. Major ethnic groups are the Meeteis, Nagas and the Kukis and officially thirty-three tribes are recognised as the scheduled tribes. The Manipuri discourse is regarded to be nationalist and representing only the Meetei ethnic group by other ethnic groups such as the Nagas and the Kukis. At the same time, they also reject the idea of India. What we witness in Manipur, at the micro-level, is an ongoing process of identity constructions and reconstructions resulting into clashes, both physical and otherwise. It is in a way, the invigoration of Appadurai's (1990) nation-state as the battle of imagination or platform for separatism and micro-identities to become political projects within the nation-states. In other words, undercurrent of ethno-nationalism marks demands for separatism and such political projects operate within the discourse of the nation-state.

Though ethnic consolidation began during the colonial period, emergence of ethno-nationalism is a post-colonial development. The democratic and representational form of government that was adopted in the newly independent countries has substantially influenced the process. In the case of Manipur, it was only in the 1990s that ethnic and religious strife of various shades became prominent with the heightening of ethno-nationalist assertions. Unification and formation of ethnic identities, today, have balanced the control of political space, which Meeteis as an ethnic community has been enjoying for long. In spite of the recent consolidations, population are known by their tribe identity. In fact, the number of scheduled tribes in the state has increased to thirty-three not out of migration but out of division into sub-tribes. This is not to suggest that there is no migration at recent times. While tribes split into sub-tribes largely for administrative benefits, they also consolidate into larger ethnic identity in the political domain. These ethnic conglomerations, which are very recent, have not only brought new equation of power, but also added newer dimension to the concept of the "other".

Both the terms Naga and Kuki as functional categories came into use with records of the British military officers and administrators (Mackenzie, 1884, reprint 2001). Though the names may be in use earlier, self-appropriation of identities with these names came much later. Take for instance, the name Naga, which is more of a British creation in the 1880s, though the term existed before the British came to the North-East India (Thangjam, 2008). The name was identified with a large number of tribes for better administrative purposes—to club different tribes under one administrative umbrella. It was much later that the first self-appropriation came into being with the creation of the Naga Club. This name as a political identity became clearer in 1947 when the British left its South-east Asian colonies. Phizo, as the champion of Naga self-determination, called for a separate Naga state outside the Indian Dominion. Thus, the term got projected by the Naga national workers that Nagas achieved independence one day before India did. Creation of Naga political identity is still in process, latest being the inclusion of tribes like Anal, Moyon, Monsang, Maring, etc. in 1990s into a common Naga identity. This is a major achievement of the NSCN (IM). In spite of inter tribal rivalry (Singh and Singh, 1989) the appropriation of Naga as a political identity shaping on a common political platform has enabled to seek for "equal" participation of the constituting tribes.

Identities are continuously negotiated in encounters, which are political and involve power.[6] Arendt (1970:52) also notes that power "springs up whenever people get together and act in concert". Furthermore, ethnicity is employed in order to draw boundaries as to who belongs to the group and who does not. An ethnic group is about boundary maintenance; ethnicity is a way to structure interaction, which allows the persistence of differences. Ethnic communality is, therefore, always an artifact of boundary-drawing activity: always contentious and contested, glossing over some differentiations and representing some other differences as powerful and separating factors (Barth, F. (ed.), 1969; Bauman, 1992).

The problems with the Kukis are, however, different. Though the term Kuki is also a creation of the British, the tribes constituting this category has close cultural affinity linguistically as well as by custom. Of course, it would be an exaggeration if one projects these tribes under one cultural head. Unlike the Nagas, Kuki as a political identity has not yet been fully appropriated. It remained more as a convenient name coined by the British administrators. Though attempts were made for unification of all the tribes under Kuki, it was short-lived. Controversies over the nomenclature to identify the various tribes under a single name have been the major problem inhibiting the consolidation of these tribes. Failure to integrate the Kuki tribes, either through equal participation or dominance of one over others, also shows the thin fabric, which fails to tie them as a cultural unit or block. It further shows the difficulty of seeing Kuki as a cultural identity before being a political one. Recent attempt by some scholars to float the concept of "Zale'n-gam" (Haokip, 1998) by including all these tribes into Kuki is yet another attempt to create Kuki both as a political and a cultural identity. Success or failure is yet to be seen.

These new identities-in-formation uses the discourse of Western liberal democracy and its ideological constructs though it is hard to presume if those values have really been internalised. Political consciousness in its collective form becomes not only exclusive in approach, but also takes violent turns—ethnic conflicts being its outcome. "A factor which, perhaps, contributes towards a violent expression of aspirations for political independence is the absence of a language native to a community in terms of which to generate a complex, nuanced, authentic and imaginative articulation of the idea of freedom. In the absence of such a language, the articulation takes place in the language of ideologies fashioned elsewhere and not internalised to any appreciable degrees" (Miri, 1999:14). Rise of violence in its varied forms emerges mainly because of non-internalization of the borrowed discourse. This doubt on internalization remains even after conceding the arguments by many in the "South" that borrowed categories from the West no more remains the same while in operation in the developing countries. That concept like "secularism" in the Indian context has to be understood differently for the discourse has totally changed from the place of its origin. This line of argument has already been conceded while studying the idea of nation as used in the political discourses in the region. However, the success or failure of these identity formations in terms of achieving the spirit of democratic values is yet to be accounted.

The ideas of nation, self-determination and human rights that all the major tribes and communities in the state use in their respective discourses are within the firmament of strong tribal kinship and bond. The idea of a Naga nation or a Kuki (and for that matter, pan-Manipuri) draws legitimacy from the same discourse, that of the Western liberal democracy. Interestingly, each of these identities emerges with consciousness, which is opposed to the idea of India as a nation-state, though both the Indian

State as well as these ethnic nations borrows their legitimacy, again, from the same discursive context (Akoijam, 2002). The very complexity of these identities lies where Naga "nation" and Kuki "nation" operating within the territory of Manipur are, in addition to their opposition to the Indian nation-state and the Manipuri "nation", mutually opposed and antagonistic. This is indeed alarming that instead of being accommodative these identities have turned exclusive and hostile. At present, the wider "world view" remains more in symbolism than in content (Bhagat and Thangjam, 2006: 66). Yet, this should be seen, particularly of the Nagas and the Kukis, as a struggle to come out of tribal moorings, failure being only a pathway.

Militarism and Counter Insurgency Operations

Violence has become the *ultima ratio* of (late) modern politics, because "subjectivation" has liberated political understanding and framed the world in a "technological" and instrumental manner. The basic political subject is violent by virtue of its very composition (Campbell and Dillon, 1993). According to them, security is the foundational value around which the political subject revolves. Security is not merely the main goal of the political subject of violence; it is, rather, the very principle of formation of that political subject. The political subject of violence, invoking constantly security, comes in a variety of forms: God, rational subject, nation, state, people, class, race, etc. (Campbell and Dillon, 1993). The Indian State justifies use of violence to maintain security of the "Indian nation-state" and adopt militarism as a means. Militarism here is understood as a behaviour or condition in which states resort quickly to the use of their armed forces in response to international or domestic threats or go to great lengths to mobilize people and resources for war. Militarism is also the belief that military responses are usually the best ones, and that the military is the most important institution in the state (Vagts, 1959).[7] Or in other words, "It is the extension of military thinking over civilian institutions and civilian planning and over civilian authority" (Regehr, 1980:129-30).

The fragility of the foundation on which the Indian State rests necessitates the invocation of a sense of "supreme national interests" in its citizen *vis-à-vis* other interests and its corollary obsession with security. This is the outcome of a "deeply wounded" memory of partition and subsequently, wars with its neighbours after Independence.[8] One of the unfortunate fallout of these events is the collective psyche that treats the minorities with eyes of suspicion. What follows is the denial of alternate voices and interests. The homogenising trend (dealt above), in interest and value, of the Indian nation-state, has increased all the more ignoring competing and contradictory interests that exist in societies. Such homogenizing tendencies justify the adoption of militarism and use of violence while dealing with ideologies or movements interpreted to be inimical to national sovereignty. That in recent times there is a constitutive relationship between politics and violence has become more glaring if one takes into account the unfolding events in North-East India.

Pervasiveness of militarism with regard to North-East India can elucidated from the very framing of the region itself. In the 1950s, GoI evolved and adopted an approach towards North-East India, which was founded on two edifices. First is the Nehruvian model of non-interference into the traditional socio-economic structure of the region and second is the national security perspective. Given the low level of understanding and appreciation of the region among the policy makers in Delhi, the surest shortcut to policy was one based on security by virtue of the region sharing international boundary with Myanmar, China, Bangladesh and Nepal. So, security emerged as the guiding principle for all policy interventions, development or otherwise, in the region. But the question is—security for whom?

The security principle, or rather the insecurity of GoI, drove it to adopt AFSPA (Assam and Manipur) way back in 1958 when there was hardly any insurgency in the region. According to Amar Yumnam, "The Government of India could never get rid of its insecurity and abandon the security principle even when it belatedly realized that the North-East India. Region needed a development agency for transformation" (Yumnam, 2005: 201). As a result, when the North Eastern Council (which should have been there in 1958 instead of AFSPA) was established in the early 1970s, it was placed under the Home Ministry. But the Home Ministry, Yumnam adds, could never evolve a development strategy for the region as it is neither competent nor oriented for such a task. This "politicization of economic issues" has reached its height recently with the requirement of certificates from the Home Ministry for the provincial government to get funds sanctioned from the Ministry of Finance (Yumnam, 2005:201).

The battle of imagination envisioned by Appadurai (1990) where groups with ideas about nationhood seek to capture or co-opt state power, and states simultaneously seek to capture and monopolise ideas about nationhood is clearly manifested in the form of armed conflict. Precisely on this account, armed liberation movements in India by different insurgent groups and ethno-nationalism that has emerged and shaped the course of these movements found a strong response from the Indian nation-state. The Indian State comes ever more strongly with its military might. Equally, the logic of military employment rests on the notion of security. As far as Manipur is concerned, the government had granted full-fledged statehood to Manipur in 1972 as a response to subversive activities undertaken by the Revolutionary Government of Manipur in the late 1960s and early part of the 1970s. It was also a pre-emptive strategy of the Government to prevent further escalation of subversive activities in the state. But from the 1980s when armed opposition escalated, militarism marks the government's efforts to contain the liberation movement. Since then the Indian State has been routinely propagating national/internal "insecurities" to allow the Indian State to exercise its monopoly over violence. Imposition of AFSPA in the region is to ensure India's sovereignty and territorial integrity.

Counter Insurgency Operations

As against the intermittent commitment in conventional wars, the Indian Army has been fighting insurgency almost continuously since Independence. As early as 1955, Jawaharlal Nehru ordered "the Indian Army to conduct a counter insurgency campaign against the rebel Naga tribesmen in North-East India, a campaign that has since haunted the region" (Cohen and Dasgupta, 2010:4). And since then it has been involved in counter-insurgency operations in almost all of North-East India in an ever escalating area of operations. In fact, counter-insurgency operations have provided the staple operational fare for the Indian Army more than any other, except, perhaps, the Israeli Army (Sinha, 2006).

Different types of counter insurgency operations undertaken in North-East Region are discussed briefly in the following sections:

(a) *Isolating the Populace from Armed opposition groups (Grouping of Villages)*: Drawing on the British experience in Malaya in the 60s, Indian Army tried the concept of grouping of villages as a means to isolate the rebels from the populace. It was tried out both in Nagaland and Mizoram. In Nagaland it was given up in the face of fierce opposition from the moderate Nagas. In Mizoram the experiment produced mixed results. S.P. Sinha opines, "A study of the existing literature on the Indian experience leads one to conclude that such measures may have been acceptable means by colonial powers to quell insurgencies, but the fallout of adoption of such measures against own people is extremely contentious and repugnant" (Sinha 2006:3).

(b) *Employment of Air Power*: Air strafing was resorted to in Nagaland at Purr and in Mizoram at Aizwal and Lungleigh Districts to save the Assam Rifles posts from being run over by armed opposition groups. Since the 60s, helicopters have been used extensively for movement of troops, casualty evacuation and reconnaissance as integral part of counter-insurgency operations. In Operation Stinger conducted in October, 2005 and Summer Storm in April, 2009, drones were used to locate hideouts of rebels in Loktak Lake in Manipur.

(c) *Political and Diplomatic Initiatives*: Counter-insurgency operations are politico-military in nature. In the context of North-East India insurgencies, political initiatives have been taken at two levels, internal and external. At the internal level, peace talks are underway with National Socialist Council of Nagalim-Isaac and Muivah and United Liberation Front of Asom (ULFA). In the case of Manipur, there has not been peace talk or political initiative to end the armed conflict. However, Suspension of Operation (SoO) prevails. Under this model, peace talks do not occur but surrendered militants are given shelter by the government. At the external level, political and diplomatic steps have been taken to deny safe sanctuaries to the armed opposition groups in neighbouring countries such as with Myanmar, Bhutan and Bangladesh.

(d) *Re-organising of Infantry Battalions for Counter-Insurgency Operations*: One of the earliest attempts to reorganise the infantry battalions for counter-insurgency tasks was the creation of I-Battalions in the 1960s by converting some of the existing battalions drawn from some selected regiments. These units were to be permanently deployed in the Naga Hills and Tuensang Area with their personnel being periodically turned over from within their respective regiments. In the early 90s when the requirement of forces for internal security duties increased, it was envisaged to raise "a paramilitary force with Army's ethos" under the Ministry of Defence, designated as Rashtriya Rifles (Roychowdhury, 2002:219). It has been deployed exclusively in Jamu & Kashmir (J&K), except for a very brief period in the

North-East India. Today, there are Indian Reserve Battalion and Village Defence Force, exclusively created to combat insurgency in the North-East India.

(e) *Composition of the Assam Rifles*: Assam Rifles was raised primarily for deployment in North-East India and comprised men from these areas. In 2004, Gen. V.P. Malik, former Chief of the Army, recommended that the force should comprise 60-70 per cent of its personnel from the North-East India.

(f) *Military Civic Action Programme*: In the expanding American empire after 1898, civic action went hand in hand with military measures in the Philippines, which included a variety of public works projects to improve communication and health (Beckett, 2001:36-37). It was practised in Malaya in counter-insurgency operations against the communist guerrillas in the sixties by the British forces. Over the years the Indian Army has expanded the scope of civic action. In official parlance it is known as "Winning the Hearts and Minds" of the local population. It has moved beyond initiatives by local commanders to deploy resources for creating the basic infrastructure like provision of potable water, primary health centres, primary schools and improving village roads. Operation Good Samaritan in Manipur and Sadbhavna in the Kargil sector of J&K are examples. This method is perceived by the people as an attempt on the part of the Indian Army and para-military forces to prevent the armed opposition groups from penetrating the local population and procure intelligence.

(g) *Unified Command*: One of the cardinal principles of counter insurgency operations is the unity of command. At the operational level it means integrated civil-military operations under one military commander appointed by the civil government. The concept of unified command in counter insurgency-operations was first experimented in Kashmir. In Assam a three-tier system was evolved. At the top was the Strategic Planning Group (under the Chief Secretary) to lay down the policy. The second tier, the operation group, was headed by General Officer Commanding (GOC) 4 Corps, the senior military commander in Assam. The third tier was headed by the District Collector, supported by the battalion commander and the superintendent of police of the area. The strategic group at the top had GOC 4 Corps, State Director General of Police (DGP) and Inspector General of

> Police of Border Security Force and Central Reserved Police Force as members. GOC 4 Corps attended the meeting whenever the chief minister chaired it (Roychowdhury, 2002:121). In Manipur, the Chief Minister insisted that the DGP of the state head the unified headquarters, which resulted in the Army keeping out of it. In Tripura the situation was different; there were no army formations in Tripura. The Deputy Inspector General of Assam Rifles, who, if he was a serving brigadier, had army battalions serving under him. Tripura, too, adopted a unified headquarters model headed by the Chief Secretary.

What has emerged in the militaristic approach is that the agents of the State (the army, para-military forces and police), rather than approaching the affected people as citizens, treats them as "subjects". Thus, military and paramilitary forces are "deployed" for the maintenance of "law and order" in the region. An unofficial report puts that there are more than 60,000 security personnel deployed in Manipur (Rupachandra, 2012). According to Namrata Goswami, a defense analyst, "The overt presence of the armed wing of a democratic state like India, i.e. its army, has fostered the idea of a militarised India amongst the population" (Goswami, 2010:11).

Deployment of the state security personnel such as the army, para-military forces and state police, as a part counter insurgency operation can be read as "interventionist policy" in an alien space. While not questioning the merit of such approaches, rather the very premise of treating the people of the region as aliens is itself questionable. Incursion of the military into the civil spheres and violence meted out through counter insurgency strategies, despite the motto of use of minimal force, tells a lot about the nature of the Indian State. The terms of engagement formulated in the past, that is use of minimal force, is deemed to be no longer valid and needs to be redefined. General Shankar Roychowdhury, a former Army Chief, defines it as "adequate minimum force, the adequacy of weapons and firepower for each situation to be determined by the field commander. This included heavier weapons like mortars or artillery whenever required" (Roychowdhury, 2002: 98).

Practice of Violence

As much as the State discourse is built on violence, its counterpart, the non-state armed groups are also built on the same logic. The "non-state" if understood as "State in becoming" highlights interesting trend that is near equivalent to the State discourse—of monopolising violence. But more alarming trend is the "non-state" discourse that no more seems to confine to its "classic" opposition to the State, but more so towards the contending groups and the people. Propaganda warfare, intimidation, extortion, etc. have become the hallmark of their operation over the latter. Militarism is largely reflected through these operations. In the militarized situation, ordinary people are caught in the crossfire, lives remain dear, and human rights continue to be violated. Table 5.1 shows the number of people killed in Manipur from 2001 to 2011.

Table 5.1: Insurgency related Fatalities in Manipur: 2001-2011

Years	*Civilians*	*Security Forces*	*Militants*	*Total*
2001	70	25	161	256
2002	36	53	101	190
2003	27	23	148	198
2004	40	41	127	208
2005	138	50	143	331
2006	107	37	141	285
2007	150	40	218	408
2008	131	13	341	485
2009	77	18	321	416
2010	26	8	104	138
2011 (till December 4)	22	10	27	59

Source: South Asia Terrorist Portal, 2011. http://www.satp.org (accessed on Saturday, August 3, 2012, 2:30:16 PM).

From Table 5.1, we can see that a total of 2,974 persons were killed in the stated period of time. More than 60 per cent were militants and civilian casualties constituted nearly 30 per cent. We witness escalation of fatalities from 2007 to 2009. A disturbing feature of the armed conflict is the kind of impact it has on the demographic profile of the indigenous population. More than 90 per cent of the victims were from the indigenous stock.

One of the major problems associated with tabulation of casualties related with insurgency is that very often, civilians killed in fake encounters or extrajudicial encounters are grouped in the category of militants. Such instances are high in compilations (insurgency related statistics) done by Government officials or organizations sponsored by the Government. Take for instance, The *Sangai Express* reported that altogether 1,528 people including 31 women and 98 children were killed in fake encounters by the security forces in Manipur between 1979 and May 2012. Of these, 419 were killed by the Assam Rifles, while 481 were killed by the combined teams of Manipur Police and Central Security Forces (*The Sangai Express*, Imphal, June 19, 2012). In October 2012, a Public Interest Litigation was filed by NGOs—Extra-judicial Execution Victims' Families Association of Manipur and Human Rights Alert—to the Supreme Court of India against extra judicial executions carried out by the police and the security forces in Manipur. The petition gave details of each of the 1,528 people killed in fake encounter since 1979. The Court randomly selected six cases out of the 1,528, and found the security forces to be guilty. In order to address such issues, as recommended by the international community, India needs to ratify the Convention against Torture and Other Cruel, Inhuman or Degrading Treatment or Punishment as well as the International Convention for the Protection of All Persons from Enforced Disappearance.

At another level, the apprehension expressed by Campbell and Dillon (1993) that the political subject of violence constantly invokes security, amongst others, holds true in the case of Manipur. What has aggravated the situation in the region (largely in the state of Manipur) is the prolonged and continued armed conflict. Violence has impacted onto the social, political and everyday life shaping into a practice. Take for instance, civil society bodies very often resort to non-violent methods such as *bandhs* and economic blockades to voice their grievances or resist against excesses committed by the State actors or non-state armed opposition groups, but ultimately take recourse to violence. Heisnam Kanhailal (2013) correctly captures the popular angst and predicament. "Groups of *bandh* supporters move around in vehicles and raze down commuters' vehicles, innocent people are beaten up with sticks for defying their verdict" (Kanhailal, 2013:12). This elucidates the fact that impact of militarism in the functioning of civil societies has become highly pronounced.

At the societal level, too, violence is constantly used to settle dispute or any issue. Take for instance, houses of suspects in any crime is dismantled and razed to the ground. The family members of the suspects or accused are expelled from the locality by Kangaroo Courts. There are incidences in which self-styled moral cops raid restaurants and parade young girls and boys before the public for allegedly indulging in "immoral activities". In the more extreme cases, suspects behind the killing of any person are publicly lynched. These are the classic cases of mobocracy hijacking the rule of law and the role of police, judge and executioner, etc. Editorial of the *Huyen Lanpao* (April 03, 2011) affirms that the conflict situation which has besieged our society has given rise to the concept of street justice. It states that this is no longer a law and order problem. It is a problem of a society where ethical and social values are being spurned and mocked at. In the year 2012, when unabated crimes continued in Manipur, editorial of the *Sangai Express*, Imphal (August 21, 2012) expressed that the definition of an "anarchic state fits Manipur to the T". The editorial was written on the occasion of lynching of a suspect in the murder of girl child.

Conclusion: Issues of Human Rights and Democracy

The foundations of democracy in the North-East India are based not so much on values and principles, but on political expediency (Goswami 2010:12). When violence has been embraced and accepted as a practice in contemporary Manipur, the notion of rule of law, ethos of tolerance, dignity of life and human security have become utopian ideals. Although a civilian government is in place, elected through periodic elections, militarism continues to be the guiding principle. As a result, human rights continue to be violated and lives extinguished. Such loses are regarded to be collateral damages by the state actors. At the same time, these are considered to be "objective" casualties to achieve the political goal of self-determination on the part of the armed opposition groups. Finally, to the common people who have embraced violence as a practice, even if dreadful, and become vigilantes, such dealings are about "justice" as law keepers are unreliable, corrupted and too engaged in fighting the armed opposition groups. The prolonged and continued armed conflict in North-East India sees no immediate end. The Indian State as arbiter of conflict continues to refrain from bringing about a peaceful political solution, other than employing a militaristic approach. Militarism and use of violence has been to neutralize the fighting power of the armed opposition groups as witnessed in its counter insurgency operations. In fact, it has not abandoned its homogenising tendencies both at the ideological level as well as practice. On the part of the non-state actors, too, they are unwilling to come to the table for negotiations. State impunity to violence and seeming acceptance of people to embrace violence has led to the acceptance of aberration of principles and practices of democracy.

Notes

1. In 2004, after a statewide protest against the rape and murder of Th.

Manorama Devi by the Assam Rifles, AFSPA was partially lifted from the seven assembly segments of Imphal Municipality areas.

2. "Objective enemies" or "enemies of the people" refer to classes of people who are liquidated simply because of their group membership.
3. By valley based armed oppositions groups I am referring to those which are largely derived from the Meetei ethnic stock. However, this is not to deny the presence of membership from other communities. Major valley based armed opposition groups include the United National Liberation Front, Revolutionary Peoples Front, People's Revolutionary Army of Kangleipak-Pro, Kangleipak Communist Party, Kanglei Yawol Kanna Lup, etc. which at present forms the CORCOM (Coordination Committee) to wage a unified war against India.
4. This is a title which had undergone shifting meaning in India. During the Mughal era, the *Dewan* served as the chief revenue officer of a province. Later, when most vassal states gained various degrees of self-determination, the finance—and/or chief minister and leader of many princely states were known as a *Dewan*. Exceptionally, a ruler was himself titled Dewan or Nawab notably in Junagadh, where Shah Nawaz Bhutto was the prime-minister of the former princley state. In the case of Manipur, *Dewan* became the highest ranking officer to look after the affairs of the princely state, which was the violation of the existing Constitution of Manipur with the King as the Constitutional head.
5. UNLF made its visible presence as an armed opposition group only in 1991 after nearly three decades of establishment.
6. On the political nature of human encounters, see Hannah Arendt, 1958.
7. In feminist analyses, intellectual and cultural histories, or "bottom-up" historical accounts, militarism is a factor of inequality or an aspect of cultural hegemony (See, for example, Enloe, 1983).
8. In 1905 partition of Bengal took place. Again in 1947 British India was further fragmented into India and Pakistan, and part of Bengal went to present day Bangladesh.

References

Akoijam, A. Bimol, 2002. Cry for Homeland: A Political Psychology of Identity Politics. *MRFD Bulletin*, 2 (3), pp. 12-23.

Appadurai, Arjun, 1990. Disjuncture and Difference in the Global Cultural Economy. *Theory, Culture and Society*, 7 (2-3), July, pp. 295-310.

Arendt, Hannah, 1958. *The Human Condition*. New York: A Doubleday Anchor Books.

_______, 1970. *On Violence*. New York: Harcourt, Brace & World.

_______, 1968. *The Origins of Totalitarianism*. Revised edition 1973. New York: Harcourt, Brace Jovanovich.

Barth, F. (ed.), 1969. *Ethnic Groups and Boundaries: The Social Organization of Culture Difference*. Boston: Little, Brown and Company.

Bauman, Z., 1991. *Modernity and Ambivalence*. New York: Cornell University Press.

_______, 1992. Soil, Blood and Identity. *The Sociological Review*, 40 (4), pp. 675-701.

Beckett, Ian F.W., 2001. *Modern Insurgencies and Counter-insurgencies*. London: Routelage.

Campbell, D. and Dillon, M., 1993. The End of Philosophy and the End of International Relations. In: Campbell, D and Dillon, M. (eds.). *The Political Subject of Violence*. Manchester and New York: Manchester University Press, pp. 1-47.

Cohen, Stepen P. and Dasgupta, Sunil, 2004. *Arming Without Aiming: India's Military Modernization*. New Delhi: Penguin/Viking.

Doornbos, Martin and Kaviraj, Sudipta (eds.), 1997. *Dynamics of state formation: India and Europe compared*. (Indo-Dutch Studies on Development Alternatives–19). New Delhi and London: Sage.

Enloe, Cynthia, 1983. *Does Khaki Become You?: The Militarisation of Women's Lives*. Boston: South End.

Goswami, Namrata, 2010. India's North-East India 2020: Four Alternative Futures. *IDSA Occasional Paper 13*, July, pp. 1-26.

Haokip, P.S., 1998. *Zale'n-gam: The Kuki Nation.* Delhi: KNO Publication.

Kanhailal, Heisnam, 2013. Manipuri Society and Its Art and Culture: Contemplation of a Victim Artist. Translated from Manipuri by Thangjam, Homen and Khuraijam, Senate for DTKF. Fourth Dr. Thingnam Kishan Memorial Lecture, 2013. Imphal: DTKF.

Mackenzie, Alexander, 1884. *The North-East Frontier of India.* Reprint 2001. New Delhi: Mittal Publications.

Malik, V.P., 2004. Security on the Borderline. *The Indian Express*, 18th September. Retrieved from http.//www.theindianexpress.com (accessed on Monday, September 10, 2012, 4:42:55 PM).

Miri, Mrinal, 1999. Welcome Speech: India's North-East and North-East's India. In: Aggarwal, Kailash S., (ed.). *Dynamics of identity and intergroup relations in North-East India*. Shimla: Indian Institute of Advanced Studies, pp. 13-16.

Nandy, Ashis, 1983. *The Intimate Enemy: Loss and Recovery of Self Under Colonialism*. Delhi: Oxford University Press.

Oinaṃ, Bhagat, 2005. Receiving Communities: The Encounter with Modernity. *Eastern Quarterly,* 3 (II), July-September, pp. 86-96.

Oinam, Bhagat and Thangjam, Homen, 2006. Indian 'Nation-state' and Crisis of the 'Periphery'. In: Biswas, Presenjit and Thomas, C.J. (eds.). *The Meaning, Metaphor and Method of Peace in India's North-East: Essays of Concern and Commitment.* New Delhi: Regency, pp. 49-78

Parekh, Bikhu, 1997. Cultural Diversity and the Modern State. In: Doornbos, Martin and Kaviraj, Sudipta (eds.). *Dynamics of State Formation: India and Europe Compared.* (Indo-Dutch Studies on Development Alternatives–19). New Delhi & London: Sage, pp. 177-203.

Regehr, Ernie, 1980. What is Militarism? In: Eide, Asbjorn and Thee, Marek (eds.). *Problems of Contemporary Militarism.* London: Croom Helm, pp. 127-139.

Roychowdhury, Shankar, 2002. *Officially at Peace*. New Delhi: Viking.

Rupachandra, Yumnam, 2012. UNLF Owns up Manipur Blast. *Seven Sisters Post*, September 6. Retrieved from http://www.sevensisterspost.com (accessed on Sunday, September 9, 2012, 3:40:25 PM).

Singh, H. Bhubon, 1988. *The Merger of Manipur.* Imphal: Pritam Haobam.

Singh, L. Ibungohal and Singh, N. Khelchandra, 1989. *Cheitharol Kumbaba* (Manipuri text), Imphal: Manipur Sahitya Parishad.

Singh, Y. Mohendra, 2009. *The Status of Manipur (1823-1947)*. Imphal: Yumnam Indira Devi.

Sinha, S.P., 2006. C.I. Operations in the North-East. *India Defence Review*, 21 (2), April-June, pp. 1-6.

Thangjam, Homen, 2008. Colonial Administration, Knowledge and Intervention: Colonial Project of Ethnicization in Manipur. *Alternative Perspectives,* III (IV), July-September, pp. 18-31.

Vagts, Alfred, 1959. *A History of Militarism: Civilian and Military.* Revised edition 1967. New York: Meridian.

Yumnam, Amar, 2005. Development Intervention in the North-East: A Critique. *Eastern Quarterly*, 3 (III), October-December, pp. 196-205.

6
Inclusion of the Excluded
Towards Uncertainty

Ch. Rupachandra

The geographic location of the region of North-East India makes more vulnerable and became to be the core of hostility with massive negative outcomes from the onlookers. Since, we are talking about lack of infrastructural development, the problem of connectivity, absence of passionate response from stakeholders in the political process and frequent instability, there seems poor governance in the state of affairs as it generate more helplessness to the policy makers, planners, academicians and young researchers to arrive at a commonly acceptable platform to bring an amicable solution. Academically, social movement has been defined as collective effort to resists a change. In a certain set-up of political system, it sometimes refers as political violence where violent action of a group of people against the government to highlight's its discontents. This term refer to a situation where in a large scale institutional malfunctioning, politics acquires an appetite for all spaces-both public and private. Thus, all violence becomes political. Insurgency, terrorism, revolutionary movements etc. are some forms of political violence though their practices may be different. The region of North-East India represents a unique feature of social movements, different from the rest of the country. Autonomy movement based on ethnic identity, secession movements etc. are some of the underlying dynamics in this region.

After partition, the scenario of the region had changed as international borders surrounded it. It lost it access to the sea through the entry point at Chittagong where Brahmaputra and its tributaries was a water ways of commerce, where it now becomes landlocked. The traditional land routes through East Pakistan (now Bangladesh) had been cut off. And it accordingly multiplied longevity, transportation cost along with new and circuitous road. Before partition the distance through Calcutta from Agartala was only 400 km., but in post partition, it had multiplied four times to 1600 km.

From the early political history of the region, it comes to know that the region provide a complexities of issues and challenges. This is often critique with the century of misrule, rampant human right violations, insensitivity and ignorance of the issues. Even these lead to the security concern for the territorial integrity of the Nation. From the very beginning, the redrawing of Map cutting across the natural habitation, customs, food habits etc. have severe implications in the working of political system in the region. Regarding Manipur situation, the state has witnessed structural flaws and institutional malfunctioning in the working of the democratic institution. The arguments like controversial merger, subsequent downgrading of this princely state to part 'C' status, Union Territory and finally statehood in its transformation of political domains also need to analyze. Moreover, in the name of maintaining law and order, imposition of anti-people legislation, draconian laws which lead to rampant human rights violations, extra judicial killings, and extortion, a new dimension of political violence emerges and creating beneficiaries of conflict become an everyday parlance. The recent proposition and opposition to bifurcate the boundary of the state along ethnic lines is also a contentious issue. It goes thoroughly into poor governance as it led to instability for over the decades.

Unabated Violence

There has been much engagement in both the policy makers, planners, academic communities and young researchers about the present unrest in North-East India. The government even put forwarded the six inter-dependent components to meet the challenges *viz.*,

(i) Empowerment of the people by maximizing self-governance and participatory development through grass-roots planning. Such planning will help to evolve development strategy based on the resources, needs and aspirations of the people.

(ii) Rural development with a focus on improving agricultural productivity and the creation of non-farm avocations and employment.

(iii) Development of sectors with comparative advantage agro-processing industries, modernization and development of sericulture, investment in manufacturing units based on the resources available in the region, harnessing the large hydroelectric power generation potential and focus on developing services such as tourism that will help to accelerate development and create productive employment opportunities.

(iv) Maximising self-governance, introduction of participatory planning, rural development and development of sectors with comparative advantage call for significant augmentation of capacity of the people and institutions both in the government and private sectors. Capacity development will have to address the issue of imparting skills among the people to enhance their productivity, generating a class of entrepreneurs within the region willing to take risks. They will also have to be provided with the necessary support through the creation and development of institutions at all levels to undertake planning.

(v) Augmenting infrastructure, including rail, road, inland water and air transportation to facilitate a two-way movement of people and goods within the region and outside, communication networks including broadband and wireless connectivity, and harnessing of the vast power generation potential, all of which will open up markets for produce from the region, attract private investment, create greater employment opportunities and expand choices for people of the region. Making the Look East Policy meaningful for the region by connecting it with Southeast Asian markets. Connectivity of North-East India with ASEAN would require opening up the sea route through the Chittagong port and the land routes through Myanmar and China. In addition, opening up the land route through Bangladesh could enormously benefit both countries and diplomatic efforts should focus on improving relations with the neighbours.

(vi) Ensuring adequate flow of resources for public investments in infrastructure, implementing a framework for private participation in augmenting infrastructure and creating an enabling environment for the flow of investments to harness the physical resources of the region for the welfare of the people.[1]

But such strategy for an inclusive development had witnessed numerous shortcomings. It is evident that peace has eluded much of the region at serious costs to the political process. Prolonged violence in the region has also impacted on the character of the state and on its democratic credentials. Rule of law, limited government, checks and balances, freedom of press and regular elections which rulers can lose are some of the effective countermeasures against this type of violence. But, such political processes of the largest representative democracy on Earth become helpless to the major stakeholders.

Historically, most lethal type of violence, i.e., violence by rulers against subjects, is theoretically the most tractable case. In principle, the deprivation theory seems fit to explain the present unrest in the North-East India region, i.e., violence by the deprived section of people. In the international scenario, political violence appears to be growing in both scale and intensity throughout the Globe. Often, the state allows atrocities to take place, and may even promote them. But most of the third world countries are now facing these similar problems. Even developed countries like Great Britain and Canada faced the problem of secession in Northern Ireland and Quebec respectively. Political violence kills human beings, destroys natural resources and wildlife, and wipes out productive physical capital. Although such violence is itself endogenous to a range of complex factors, once ignited, it can become the direct cause of untold human suffering, loss of life as well as massive economic decline and political instability.

The evidence on the direct destructive impact of political violence on human, natural and physical capital is abundant. However, the overall general equilibrium, development costs of political violence are, in fact, much larger. This is particularly true for long-drawn out violence, such as civil wars; or short-duration but highly intense violence, such as riots or uprisings. In addition to its direct destructive effect, political violence undermines the micro-security of the individual as well as the macro-security of communities, nations and countries. Therefore, it can change behaviour, preferences as well as institutions and public policy.

Government concern to the present unrest basically in Manipur and the region as a whole is centreed round the strategic importance of the region. The eruption of violence and development of anti-centric feelings among the people can't be subsided. There is no reason why mostly educated youths will become all the more indignant as the infamous draconian law, the AFSPA has been pressed in the service that no longer serve the purpose, but only evokes worldwide condemnation on the counter productivity. What is most unfortunate and appalling is that a nation claiming to be the largest democracy on Earth instead of nurturing a law-based State, has been active in an exercise to keep law and justice, more so the humane consideration. This reminds the people again and again of the fallacy of the Merger Agreement that is now considered to be the turning point in the history of Manipur and will always prompt the younger generation to look back with resentment and spew venom on the Government and the erstwhile State Authority. People have experienced the repeated subversion of humane values in contrast to aspiration of our founding fathers of democratic India who even contribute more funds than the rich nations to develop democracy in the global arena. Conflict between the people of Manipur and the government is now more clearly visible in the form of armed insurgency in the State while the small border State having its written history of an Asiatic domain for more than 2000 years has been involving itself in the nation building process ever since, it was brought into the fold of Indian Union in 1949. Moreover, it seems that the government has adopted, broadly three approaches to dealing with violence in North-East India:

(i) Use of force against the warring groups,
(ii) Accommodation of ethnic aspirations based on ethnic identity,
(iii) Enhanced transfers to the region for its socio-economic development.

The first has been the state's 'counter insurgency' approach and remaining two are of adjustment policy. Though, we have experienced various shortcomings in the implementation of these approaches thereby creating more beneficiaries' of conflict. Outbreak of violence in Nagaland soon after Independence led by the Naga National Council and in Mizoram in 1966 which even used first air power by Independent India against the Mizo National Front (MNF), and by groups in other parts of the region in successive years, all led to strong military responses declaring rebel groups as unlawful, deploying central security forces, including the army thereby creating an venerable situation in the region.

Plight of Stakeholders

Discrimination and exclusion of marginalized groups are concern for the working of representative democracy. The very much inspiration of our founding fathers for the liberty, equality, justice and fraternity to all the people irrespective of caste, creed, gender etc. had totally sidelined over the decades. People's of the region were seen as racially distinct from other groups that make up India's 'unity in diversity' and their physical appearance denoting Tai, Tibeto-Burman, and Mon-Khmer lineages is central in interactions with fellow brethrens and it generates the feelings as separate entity. Moreover, some analysis refers the present racial prejudice against people of North-East India by the fellow brethrens of mainland, may be due to their Mongoloid feature and discrimination is often regarded as institutional racism. Here, trying to bring different ethnic communities of the region of North-East India within the ambit of the nation-state was a great experiment. Indeed, it become the greatest challenges in the process of nation building because, most of these communities had not been a part of social and political developments which took place in the rest of the country, and they have become a part of independent India without self-consciously involving themselves in the struggle for independence.[2] People of the region were apprehensive about the on-going attempts of national integration without any degree of psychological integration. Vivid example for such attitudes has been seen from the attitudes, behaviours of the people of mainland through their brethrens over the decades and even it is going till date.

This is now widely accepted that developments in state and society in post-independent India have not conformed to the expectations as discrimination and exclusion still persists in our society. With the retreat of the state from major economic activities since the 1990s,[3] the socio-economic gap between social groups has in fact increased. Disparities among social groups have also been the result of particular forms of discrimination and exclusion prevalent in society. Discrimination and exclusion marginalizes certain groups from full participation in the social, economic, political and cultural life of the country.[4]

History reveals that government had sideline the people aspiration over the decades besides it become an important yardstick on the part of governance. The abundant natural and human resources were kept more or less from the people's sight. Bishnuram Medhi former Chief Minister of Assam reacts when Nehru denied for a refinery in terms of national security that "if defence cannot undertake to protect the refinery located in Assam how will protect the oil fields and transport system in the eastern region… in that case we do not understand, how the defense will be able to protect the pipeline to Barauni, 140 miles of which will necessarily have to pass along the Pakistan border. We also do not understand how the pipeline would be more defendable than the railway system as a good bit of it will have to pass at a distance of only 20 miles from the border."[5] Further, regarding the connectivity which becomes a main dilemma of the people had not much in the reliable conditions. After partition, whole the atmosphere had changed. From Agartala to Calcutta is 2,200 km by road or train. That is nearest Indian port. It will cost at least a few hundred rupees for a second class fare by train *via* the Siliguri neck. But it is hardly six kilometers to the nearest rail and road head in Bangladesh, Akhaura where it is only 150 km to the main port of Chittagong as it is considered as the one of the finest natural harbours in Asia.[6] If we analyze how far the government initiative to solve the main constraint, it would be in misnomer. The projects like setting up of Trans Asian Highway, Rail connectivity to each and every state capital etc. were in namesake only giving one reason or another. It is said that broad gauge reaches Guwahati only in the 1980s that much of the small gauge railways elsewhere in India had converted to broad gauge. In this period, a region that remains battered by insurgency, potential international threats and supplies most of the country's tea export and a large chunk of its oil.

Notwithstanding several promises put forth by the Constitution, various forms of discrimination continue to persist in our society because the Constitutional remedy is often inaccessible to the main stakeholders and even minorities ethnic communities, literally taking away the equally quotient of their rights in terms of implementation. The Indian experience of a secular Indian nationalism which was developed during the independence struggle came to be opposed by the centrifugal tendencies based on regional, ethnic, linguistic and communal identities.[7] In a representative democracy like ours economic development and social development are mutually reinforcing. Disparities in economic development and social development are also mutually reinforcing. Socially excluded are economically marginalized. Economically, marginalized remain socially excluded. Therefore, it becomes two sides of a same Coin and it happens to be an important yardstick for national integration in the processes of nation building.

Apart from the region known for its resources in natural, agricultural and horticultural products, many people argued that the development initiatives were mainly focuses on big dams which are not without their share of environmental hazards. Some people even argued that big dams have never solved any problems but only have created ones. They point to the high seismicity of the Himalayan ranges and to the swiftness and big silt loads that rivers like the tributaries of the Brahmaputra carry in Arunachal Pradesh. These, experts say, will halve the life span of a dam in these areas from the normal areas from the normal life of about 100 years.[8] But the same thing is going on as the proposed mega dams in different part of the region besides not getting environmental clearance from the concerned Ministry, the processes to construct such venture is carried on. Even the vigilant right's groups, NGOs etc. have highlighted the possibility of the loss of large scale flora and fauna, mass migration, environmental degradation, but the government did not hear the people's aspiration. Since development becomes main agenda for government, may be the centre or state, it is true that we need to exploit the resources, but we need to think about the future generation. But it had not gone to the way of meaningful development, though may be in the certain infrastructural development particularly in the urban areas, served the interest of bureaucrat's, politicians and other some vested interest although it does not goes to the needful who were the major stakeholders of the issue.

Recurring Ethnic Aspiration

Development of all ethnic groups and minority is possible if larger interest of the state is served. We have experience such phenomenon where various ethnic armies who were formed on the ethnic lines demanding homeland (autonomy) due to the lack of development and many other issues and their demand seems to be lasted in the autonomous district council. After getting the demand they are in the same way as earlier stated. We need to re-analyze the present instability in Assam where most of the present states of North-East India were a part of it. But the demand for more autonomy or separate state is still boiling. Those needy and major stakeholders doesn't get the real benefit of (basically in the remote areas) the basic amenities, infrastructure, improvement of livelihood, connectivity etc. and they were living as a 'second class citizens.' Therefore, it lacks democratic politics in governance as it generates more demand of autonomy.

Regarding Manipur situation in this connection, there is a long history of demanding autonomy. Different analysts have given their opinion as it was a carbon copy Jharkhand from Bihar, Gorkhaland from West Bengal, Telangana from Andhra Pradesh. They have the overview that it is possible to get their demand within the state (a state within the state). That is what the different minorities groups in the region had in their perception. The epicenter of such autonomy demand, i.e. Nagaland had nowadays faced the same issue. Dimasa had claimed Dimapur as their main demand, Eastern Naga groups had demanded for a separate state out of Nagaland etc. Since the main insurgents' outfit of the region, NSCN-IM and other Nagas outfits' were in the peace process with the government of India over the decades for a greater Nagalim, it had caused tremendous hardship to people and government. But despite many rounds of peace negotiations, including at the highest political level, signs of a settlement are not hopeful. The people of Manipur had analyzed the repeated assertion of "no solution is possible without Naga integration" which need to revaluate the stand of the government of India. Demanding of Naga inhabited areas of the State of North-East India had openly advocating an ethno-nationalist strategy. In the last two decades, expansion movements of ethnic identity have witnessed the ethnic cleansing not only in the state but also to other part of the region. Even some the elite who used to play community card along ethnic lines become a concern on the part of the governance.

Pointed out four major rules which have regulated the Central government's attitude towards regional demands for greater autonomy and statehood, Paul brass says that centre has always tried to accommodate the following demands:

1. Demands for regional autonomy, short of secession;
2. Demands based on language and culture and not on religion;
3. Demands for autonomy backed by popular support of the particular region; and
4. Demands for split up of multilingual states with support from different linguistic groups.[9]

As a result, this strategy of accommodation has resulted in the creation of separate political units and the regionalization of politics, thereby increasing anti-centric feeling. But this has not been generally true as it is a fact that creation of different territorial units for hill peoples of the region of North-East India has met the ethnic aspiration to a large extent and has drawn these people into country's democratic process, yet grave regional imbalances and continuance of internal colonial pockets' have tended to stock fires of secessionists insurgency in the area. Under development and relative deprivation syndrome have been major factors contributing to growing sense of alienation from rest of the country among a sizeable section of youth of the region of North-East India.[10]

The newly crafted area under certain provision of autonomy has pumped in disproportionate sums of money by the government without trying to build up an infrastructure for proper dispersal and utilization of such funds. Here, "Secessionism has been attempted to be countered by many countries through liberal concessions to separatists. Federalism or regionalism will be most attractive if it is coupled with policies whose effect is to raise the cost of successful secession."[11] But it becomes rather paradoxical that the sense of deprivation grew even as the process of development, however such initiative was in slow pace. The emerging middle class elite of these region soon realised that struggle for jobs, privileges of as well as political space would not be easy in a system where uneven economic development was the rule and strong regional disparities prevailed. Thus, ethnic or sub-nationalist mobilisation initially on economic grounds would be resorted to by the emerging middle class who would also be the spokesmen of the masses.[12] The elite emerges along with a middle class in urban and rural areas, a class of growing tastes and ambitions, the larger community—excluded from this small minority of the privileged—will become disillusioned with the failure of the system to provide them with jobs, money, hope. As this happens swiftly—for the same experience is repeated across India wherever elites among the underprivileged have emerged—there will be violence and greater violence, and insurgency will be seen as the only way of redressing the problem.[13]

Another major ethnic community of Manipur, i.e. Kukis had also on the same line. Regarding their aspiration, Kuki State Demand Committee had strongly come out against the claim of the NSCN-IM and its frontal organization. Even it called an indefinite blockade for a Kuki state prior to the Naga solution. Kuki Inpi, Manipur had asserted that the any settlement reached with the NSCN-IM may affect the interest of other tribal communities, whom are 'equally or more deserving' of such an 'alternative arrangement' and added that accommodation of a particular section could result in denial of justice to the larger society. They even argued that Kuki uprising of 1917-1919 is one of the historical legacies where Kuki people show their resentment against the colonial rule. This anti-colonial struggle had cemented the relationship of the Kukis across the villages and brought the Chiefs closer to each other. The Kuki identity was also widened. With the British Raj coming to an end, the Kukis formed the Kuki National Assembly (KNA), in October 1946, to press forward the cause of the Kukis and demand for a homeland for themselves. However, with the merger of Manipur into the Indian Union in 1949, this demand was subsided. The territorial claims of the Kukis include the districts of Churachandpur, Chandel and some portions of Tamenglong, Senapati and Ukhrul, whereas the Nagas claim the districts of Tamenglong, Senapati, Ukhrul and Chandel. Thus, the Kukis and Nagas have overlapping and conflicting territorial interests over all the hill districts of Manipur, except Churachandpur. This conflicting territorial claim has turned into inter-tribal warfare in 1990s while the Nagas at the behest of NSCN (I-M) asserted their supremacy over the Kukis.

Nowadays most of the underground outfit of the Nagas and Kukis were in the peace process with the government. NSCN-IM, the main stakeholders in the issue were in the peace process since 1997 and other Naga separatists' outfits were also on the same line. From sovereignty to alternative arrangement, it had goes to a series of upheavals in its movements. In the meantime, apex Kuki body like Kuki Inpi said that though it has no objection in principle to the granting of alternative arrangement to the Nagas of Manipur, there has to be a top level official dialogue and agreement between the Kukis and the Government of India for a 'justified/deserved' and 'superior political solution' for the Kukis of Manipur. Outlining their argument, Kuki Inpi said that after "the British annexed Manipur kingdom in 1891 after a resistance, the Kukis revolted against the British administration for three years from 1917 to 1919 in the hill areas of Manipur. These historical events of the period clearly indicate that the administration/control of Manipur prior to the British rule had been in the hands of the majority Meiteis (plain areas) and the Kukis (hill areas)," argued KIM. Asserting that the term Naga is a connotative term to identify a collection/conglomeration of distinct/ separate tribal communities residing mostly in the present State of Nagaland, KIM said that there is no clear cut demarcation between the Naga tribes and non-Naga tribes, as the erstwhile Old Kuki tribes of Manipur now claim themselves to be Nagas. "In fact, the Kukis of Manipur are fully justified historically/politically for a superior alternative arrangement." Hinting its finger at the NSCN (IM), KIM alleged that the outfit embarked on a policy of ethnic cleansing of the indigenous Kuki population in Manipur in the early 90s and recalled the 'quit notice' served by the United Naga Council.

What is the historical/political basis (that is superior to other tribes in the hill areas of Manipur) for an alternative arrangement for the Nagas of Manipur, further questioned KIM. The apex body of the Kukis also asked "In the hill areas of Manipur, who are the Nagas and who are the non-Nagas ? Wouldn't it amount to gross miscarriage of justice, violation of universal human rights and State sponsored terrorism if the rights of the Kukis of Manipur are mercilessly ignored/violated and the aggressors rewarded with special Constitutional privileges."[14] As such claims and counterclaims persists in whole of the region, we need to revaluate that Nagaland was curved out from Assam to fulfill such aspiration but there emerge the issues of frontier Nagaland comprising of four districts of Mon, Kiphre, Longleng and Tuensang. And again, the unrest beyond the so called Bodoland, areas, demands of the Karbis, Dimasa etc. could not be easily subsided as it was always associated with territorial claims.

Deepening Democracy

The influx of population before and after the Independence across the borders was one of the primary reasons responsible for insurgency in at least two state of the region, Assam and Tripura. It is said that according to 1931 census, 95 per cent of the Tripura population is tribals. But after Independence, the demographic pattern had change as proportion of the tribals was reducing to the 28 per cent. The combination of the factors like diversity, history, geography, economy and demography had created fertile ground for outbreak of political violence in the region. At present in Meghalaya, Arunachal Pradesh and Mizoram, there is no any strong insurgency movement, though there is certain problem due to the 'spillover' of insurgency from adjacent or neighbouring states. Besides sharing commonalities ranging from communication bottlenecks to drug trafficking, illegal infiltration and insurgency, because of the rise of the insurgency in the region, most of the people tend to view the problem as a total issue of North-East India. Though if we analyze the root cause of the insurgency in different state of the region, it is necessary to take into account of the history and economy of each individual state.

In a democratic set-up, politics operated with existing categories of people and institution. In this process, categories of people change and so do the institutions. In a plural society like Manipur, particular ethnic groups have come to serve as the bases for political mobilisation by political elites which seeks to manipulate the identity of the groups. Therefore, identity of the groups tends to be consolidated. But politics is also about acquiring power and getting a share of the resources which are always scarce. This make the elites compete with one another in pushing the primary of the group they represent. In this basis that ethnicity manifest in its intensive forms resulting the bursting of conflicts in violent forms. It might be a process of political development, but we have experienced such development in different part of North-East India with unending violence.

The tendency of the governance to treat this extremely diverse region as one unit has resulted in the growth of totally incomplete and often misconceived notion where different histories and cultures and culture of the people inhabiting in this area. Today there seems to be the growing realization that the issues raised by the insurgents going on in different states of the North-East India can never be resolved by force but by a meaningful political dialogue. Since with development, we face the modern dilemma of scientific breakthroughs and dramatic technological revolutions on one hand, and the daily occurrence of human misery and tragedy on the other. It bring us closer the reality of conflict and violence, resulting in worst form of trans-border insurgency and genocide the persistent problems of inequality, poverty, ignorance, disease, destruction of environment and the depletion of non-renewable resources.

Nowadays, the region as a whole is subjected to a concerted insecurity at all the levels. The states of this region are victims of un-meaningful federalism. We know that India is a federation made up of many federating units and princely states beside some difference, like the formation of United States, Canada, Australia, USSR etc. Though, USSR was disintegrated in early 90s as it had the provision of right to secede from the union in its Constitution. In the United Sates also, there were turbulence to secede from the federation but all are in worthless and also because of the provision in the American constitution excluding some lists like defence, currency etc. all are in the power of the federating units. Therefore, it needs to change mode of the working of political processes. The emerging new types of protracted conflicts within our diverse culture, people, land, society etc. need to take steps on the road to deepening and cultivates the true spirit of representative democracy.

Concluding Remarks

Most of the people of the region believed democracy as one of the biggest business. Those marginalized people who were driven out from the mainstream day-by-day took up violence as a means for achieving their share. Here, one thing which appears in the scene is the development related scheme taken up by the government should directly reach to the people. The main issue for the deprived section of the people of the region is unemployment. Without employment there is no income. Different scholars, academician, social activist's and young researchers' argue that except Tripura, whole of the state of the region failed to meet and reach the target of the developmental scheme. But efforts have been initiated since Independence to improve the working of representative democracy which was obstacle with the loopholes in each and every sphere of state activity. So, the Government was more in favour of welfare State in order to ensure responsiveness to the needs of people. The adoption of Constitution, Fundamental Rights, Directive Principles of State policy, and Five Year Plans as the means of achieving social and economic development made the reorientation of the administrative machinery imperative. The governance structure and systems had to undergo a major revamping from revenue collection and maintenance of law and order towards socio-economic development, social welfare and citizens' satisfaction. In order to ensure responsiveness, several committees were set up which went into systematic review of the organizational structure and functioning of the government.

Owing to the geo-strategic location and poor governance, political violence becomes a common phenomenon in the region. The prolonged disengaged with neighbouring Myanmar which now becomes a launching pad for the outbreak of insurgencies in Assam, Manipur, Nagaland and Arunachal Pradesh is indeed a dilemma for security concern. Moreover, development and peace are both interrelated and the question of peace has risen in the region again and again. In the governmental perspective, peace should come first and development in the later as it is expressed by various Minister and high ranking official of the Centre and State government. But the people view is opposite to it. For bringing development and peace in the region, there needs good governance as it is the key for achieving the true spirit of democracy. Further, politics of Identity in the region has seen an experimental growth in the last two-three decades. It mobilized the marginalized section of people along the ethnic faultiness. Moreover, the creation of elite due to the neo-liberal economic policy among the hitherto marginalized social groups generates the feelings to demand a new identity for a greater share in the resource allocation. We need to redress the problem by realizing the claims of identity that have moved from exclusive cultural dignity to a new type of economic opportunities by claiming exclusive section of people. This would be very must at the behest of social inclusion which is an integral domain of representative democracy.

Notes and References

1. North-East Region Vision 2020; Ministry of Department of North-East Region and North-Eastern Council, 2007.
2. Sinha, Surajit, 'Social integration of the hill tribes and the plainsmen' in R. Mitra and B. Das Gupta (eds.) *A Common Perspective for North-East India*, Calcutta, 1967, pp. x-xvi.
3. From 1990s onwards, India adopted Neo-Liberal economic policy to enhance meaningful growth.

4. Caste and Community Based Labour Market Discrimination: A Pilot study in Noida, Working Paper Series 1, Vol. 1, No. 1, PSDE, 2009. New Delhi: JNU.
5. Strangers of the Mist; Tales of War and Peace from India's North-East; Sanjoy Hajarika; Penguin Books India (P) Ltd. 1994. New Delhi, p. 250.
6. *Ibid.*, p. 259.
7. See Udayon Mishra, *The Periphery Strikes Back*, p. 145.
8. *Op. cit.*, p. 74.
9. R. Brass, Paul; *Language, Religion and Politics in North India*, London, 1974, pp. 17-19.
10. See Udayon Mishra, *The Periphery Strikes Back*, pp. 156-157.
11. Horowitz Donald; *Ethnic Groups in Conflict, Berkley*, 1985, p. 626.
12. *Op. cit.*
13. *Op. cit.* Strangers of the Mist; Tales of war and peace from India's North-East; Sanjoy Hajarika; Penguin Books India (P) Ltd., 1994, New Delhi, p. 161.
14. *The Sangai Express*, Imphal, December 4, 2012.

7

Labyrinth of Neoliberal Crisis

Indian State and its Instrument of Peace

Malem Ningthouja

Peace is generally perceived as a state of tranquillity marked by freedom from war and conflict or absence of organised violence and disturbances. One of the predominant perceptions about North-East[1] is disturbance, i.e., a situation that act as obstacle to normal course of integrity, peace, security and growth. Global projection of North-East as disturbed area conjures up insurgency[2] as enemy to peace. According to this view insurgency stimulates a dissident culture and interplays with communal conflicts, radical assertions, militant agitations and protests. This perception is formulated in a discourse of disturbance. The discourse hegemonises Indian State to act aggressively to bring peace and security. *Ipso facto* Indian State pronounced its own interpretation of peace and initiate a peace process. The peace process involves both aggressive actions and tactical armistice. Media hype about armistice or ceasefire as peace or peace process becomes a dominant perception.

The chapter attempts to go deeper into historicising peace process in and around Manipur with special focus on the objectives and implications at the receiving end. I make due emphasise on the role of 'agency' in engineering historical course and question if the discourse of disturbance can be alternatively interpreted. My argument is that there has been disturbances that had not been revealed by the State and its discourses. What are being marked as disturbances can be differently interpreted as syndromes of a disturbing situation for which the Indian State has been largely responsible. To substantiate my point I have used Marxist methodology and argue for disturbance as integral to the structural crisis inherent in Indian capitalist path. My chapter also theorises the driving ideological current embodied in local dynamics of exploitation, misrule, dissent and concludes with alternative perception of peace.

Indian State, Disturbance and Peace Process

Perception is widespread about Indian State as rational. Its policies are being perceived as constitutional, democratic and axiomatic. Such perception eulogises Indian State, but overlooks its role as an agency subjected to the vested interest of those who directly control it and liable to commit errors, injustice and blunders in the course of actions. The perception about the State as rational becomes axiomatic; many personalise themselves with the State and defend it, but fail to mark out any distance between the ruler and the ruled. However, Marxists offer us with a different interpretation of State. According to Karl Marx the totality of the relations of production constituted the economic structure of society, the real foundation, on which arose a legal and political superstructure and to which corresponded definite forms of social consciousness.[3] In an economically stratified society the real architect of legal and political superstructures is the dominant class who rule upon the rest. The State functions as an agency (instrument). The question is who is the real ruler? According to Marxists contemporary Indian State functions within the framework of capitalist political economy controlled by big bourgeoisie. The judicial differential markers that juxtapose rational *vis-à-vis* irrational correspondingly referring to the State and its enemies have been the artwork of administrative technocrats to underpin bourgeoisie rule. The critique on contemporary Indian democracy can throw more light on it.

Common perception about Indian democracy is that it is the government of the people by the people for the people. This view is rejected by those who believe that Indian democracy is practically bourgeoisie totalitarianism. In this regards Engels' view on modern democratic republic can be referred to for an explanation. According to him, in the so called democratic republic, wealth exercises its power and state functions in the interest of the economically ruling class, which by its means becomes also the politically ruling class by means of universal suffrage.[4] Lenin also believes that democratic republic was the best possible political shell for capitalism, and, therefore, once capital had gained possession of this very best shell, it established its power so securely, so firmly, that no change of persons, institutions or parties in the bourgeois-democratic republic could shake it.[5] There is, of course, no denying that popular will (majoritarian consent) or public consent had been crucial in election, forming government and governance. But several question can be raised about the sanctity of popular will. Are public consents always formed on the basis of free and fair informed consent of those who would be affected by it? Are public consents immune from influences by networks of corruption, bribery, muscle power, misinformation and misguidance? Aren't there casual manufacturing of consent for specific issues primarily designed to camouflage bourgeoisie totalitarianism? Are we in a situation of 'spectator democracy,' to borrow the phrase of Chomsky[6] who had explained American context of controlling public mind? At the receiving end, according to Marx, "the ideas of the ruling class are in every epoch the ruling ideas... (they) determine the extent and compass of an epoch, it is self-evident that they do this in its whole range, hence among other things rule also as thinkers, as producers of ideas, and regulate the production and distribution of the ideas of their age: thus their ideas are the ruling ideas of the epoch."[7] Therefore, the ideology and objectives of the ruling class require closer scrutiny. Indian State's discourse of North-East disturbance can throw some light on it.

The discourse of disturbance depicts North-East within the domestic of Indian nationhood. The discourse camouflages bourgeoisie expansionism, but buttresses in construing or obtaining legal sanction of aggression in the name of peace and security. What appears to be legal has been politically framed and the political has economic background. To be more precise, historically, North-East inhabited by disunited and economically backward tribal and peasant communities, that could be easily occupied by any powerful external, apart from geo-strategic significance for India[8] had been important for: (a) labour, resources (water, uranium, oil, coal, precious stones, minerals, plantation, flora and fauna, tourism, carbon credits, and forest products), and market, (b) a buffer *vis-à-vis* presumed Chinese social imperialism, and (c) a military stockpile and commodity stocked for commercial expansion in South and Southeast Asia. For these reasons North-East was taken over. Annexation subjected many to the restructured economic order as primary supplier of labour, raw material, market, and military stockpile for subsequent capitalist expansion. Recalcitrance was expected and Indian State was doubtful about loyalty of North-East for various historical, racial and cultural reasons. Indian State also had to counter weight infiltration of communism, pro-mongoloid prejudice and pressure from China and Pakistan (East).

The discourse of disturbance, therefore, was formulated as a propaganda instrument. It had far reaching impacts. Firstly, the discourse camouflaged bourgeoisie aggression and buttressed the national hype about Indian State as harbinger of *ahimsa* (non-violence). Indian nation and *ahimsa* were being shown as integral to modernity, progress and peace. While construing *coevalness* in time and space respectively corresponding to modernity and national territory, India was being symbolised with peace and integrity. Insurgency was being identified with backwardness, atavism, internal disturbance and disorder. Secondly, the discourse objectified and misrepresented the context and ideology of dissent. It de-contextualised and dehumanised the insurgents by reducing them to few insistently repeated negative phrases, images and concepts. And since a connection was being conceptually built between North-East and disturbance, the criminality of the peoples of North-East was being taken as axiomatic; only the measures for controlling them needed to be worked out in deal. Conversely, the need to police, suppress and control them had the effect of making terrorists of them. The rhetoric about suspect became a pretext of punitive actions that placed the targets of attack outside the perimeter of human rights and democratic safeguarding. Militarisation was upheld, troops were deployed and repressive laws were enforced.[9] In the words of the then Union Home Minister Shivraj Patil, it was "our bounden duty to see that the morale of the armed forces also is not allowed to be attacked."[10] A soldier could suspect anyone and kill with impunity, thereby, promoted culture of impunity by other law enforcing agents in the long course. The trend has been continued till date.

The discourse of disturbance has been integral to a larger *carrot and iron* policy, i.e., to tame (domesticate) people or wipe out those who dissent. The policy involves two fundamental strategies of collaboration with loyal sections on one hand and on other hand armed aggression in which the loyal played important roles. Firstly, Indian State have established a layer of *rentier* bourgeoisie, i.e., subordinate ruling class composed of landlords-*cum*-contractors, commission agents, bureaucrats, traders, etc. that are dependent on the Indian big bourgeoisie for political and economic power. They play subjective role in the Indian capitalist order, do not directly create capital through investment in industry and capitalist productions units but play managerial role and accumulate wealth through misappropriation of public fund, bribery, corruption, usury and other forms of expropriation and exploitation. They remain authoritarian and deceiving. Secondly, Indian State adopted militarisation and several North-East areas were governed through governors and military officials for several years until reliable local regimes were installed through elections. The aggressive policy rely on a collusion of forces that operate in a very complex manner which may be broadly summarised as follows:

Firstly, the Army and paramilitary forces, who operate with impunity under AFSPA, occupy and convert several strategically important hilltops, tourist centres, grazing grounds, communal lands, institutional and religious campuses, etc. into barracks (including those in the residential areas). War hysteria in the operational zones had serious repercussion on the social mobility for economic livelihood. Troops impose typical war economy in the operation zones in the remote rural areas, e.g., forced rationing of supplies on the basis of quantity decided by them and Military Civic Action Programmes (MCAP). MCAP, not only undermine civil administration but also fail to bring qualitative transformation in economic production. On the contrary there has been militarisation of capitalist project (such as dams, mining, mining, oil drilling, forests, office buildings, etc.) to discourage protests. MCAP has been a mere cosmetic design to cover up military occupation, to divert away attention by creating a clique of beneficiaries who are being used as underpaid covert agents. Secondly, there are hordes of police, rifles, and underpaid auxiliary forces that are being recruited on contract basis (e.g., Village Volunteer Forces, Special Police Officers, Village Defense Forces, etc.) that operate under the unified command structures of the Indian army and enjoying certain amount of impunity. Several educated middle class youths are being recruited through bribery, i.e., normally at exorbitant price paid by selling off or mortgaging away properties. To recover the dues and lured by money and the prospect of promotion to higher rank, they indulge in widespread bribery, extortion, harassment and fake encounter. Thirdly, there are batches of criminal gangs allegedly operating either from jail or under the command of police or army. In addition there are communal warlords and conservative reactions who are stakeholders in the corruption nexus with the *rentier* bourgeoisie. In this scenario the number of people killed in cold blooded murder and fake encounter, convicted, intimidated, tortured, jailed, and forced disappeared as result of mistaken identity and for political ideology and dissent has been rampant. The collusion of forces has been responsible for counter-revolution, suppression of democratic dissent, violation of human rights and a state of confusion and disturbance.

Ceasefire and Paradoxes of Peace

The *Carrot and iron* policy had some spectacular achievements. Over the decades the policy had rooted out some insurgent parties and some had been brought under truce. The positive aspect of armistice is that it reduces armed conflict and casualty between the State and the concerned insurgent parties. However, some truces are temporary and in the overall analysis there are weak points as well. Firstly, policy of armistice has been selective and many parties are being left out from the scope of it. Secondly, the ongoing armistice does not ensure an end to armed conflict among the parties who had separately signed ceasefire with the State. Thirdly, among those who had entered into ceasefire, disillusionment led to factionalism, if not growth of new parties. Factionalism promote different set of conflicts and confusion. Fourthly, armistice does not ensure safety of civilians and terrorising assaults. Fifthly, the peace process in the larger context have been superficial as it do not address the root cause of political dissent and armed resistance. The chronology (1948-2011) listed below not only suggests the number of those that are being left out, but also the number of splinters and growth of new parties.

> Chronologically, Communist Party of Manipur (1948-51) was successfully suppressed and the cadres were given general amnesty. Successful repressive steps were taken up against democratic assertions of Revolutionary Nationalist Party (Manipur) in 1950s. Organisations such as Meetei State Committee and Revolutionary Government of Manipur were phased off without leaving much political impact. Naga referendum for independence conducted by Naga National Council in 1951 was not recognised by Indian State. In 1955, in Naga Hills and Tuenshang areas Naga National Council began armed protracted war to achieve Naga sovereignty and it began to spread in certain Northern areas of Manipur in mid 1960s. A peace mission was instituted in 1964 and a ceasefire came into existence. While suppression of or reconciliation with NNC was pursuing, in 1964 United National Liberation Front was formed to fight for Manipur sovereignty. Mizo independence declared by Mizo National Front in 1966 was invalidated and there was successful military assault using aerial bombing. In Manipur People's Revolutionary Party of Kangleipak (1977), People's Liberation Army/Revolutionary Peoples Front (1978/79),

Kangleipak Communist Party (1980) were formed to fight for Manipur sovereignty. In 1970s negotiations were carried out with NNC. A controversial Shillong Accord signed between Indian State and NNC in 1975 led to the split of the latter and factional war. It had considerably weakened the NNC. National Socialist Council of Nagaland (NSCN) was formed in 1980 to fight for Naga sovereignty. In 1984 Mizo National Front was brought to a negotiating table and on the basis of Mizo Accord of 1986 the Front laid down arms. In the subsequent years, dissatisfied with the outcome of the Mizo Accord, several parties such as Hmar People's Convention, Zomi Reunification Organisation, Hmar People's Convention-Democracy, Bru National Liberation Front and others were formed. In 1988 NSCN was split into NSCN (Isaac-Muivah) and NSCN (Khaplang) factions. The same year Kuki National Army, Kuki National Organisation and Kuki National Front (KNF) were formed to fight for *Zale'n-gam* or Kukiland. In 1992 Kuki Liberation Army (KLA) was formed to fight for Kukiland. In 1993 Zomi Revolutionary Organization (ZRO) was formed to fight for *Zogam* or *Zoram*. In 1994 Kanglei Yaol Kanna Lup (KYKL) was formed by merging UNLF (Oken), PREPAK (Meiraba Faction) and KCP (Ibo Pishak Faction) to fight for independent Manipur. In 1995 Hmar People's Convention-Democracy was formed to fight for autonomy and integrity of Hmar people. In 1997 Zomi Revolutionary Army (ZRA) was formed to fight for *Zogam*. ZRA became armed wing of ZRO. In 1997 Indian State and National Socialist Council of Nagaland-IM entered into ceasefire, which has been continued till date. Kuki Revolutionary Army (1999) and United Kuki Liberation Front (2000) were formed to fight for *Kukiland*. In 2004 Komrem People's Army was formed for integrity of Komrem people.[11] In 2005 Kuki National Organisation[12] entered into Suspension of Operation with Indian Army. On 23 November 2007 NSCN-Unification was formed by some deserters from NSCN-IM. On 30 April, 2008 United Naga People's Council was formed consisting of splinter group of NSCN (IM) to establish communal harmony by safeguarding territorial integrity and sovereignty of Manipur. On 20 May Naga based United People's Liberation Army was formed and it supported territorial integrity of Manipur. On 6 November a faction of PREPAK formed United

> People's Party of Kangleipak. The same year Manipur Naga Revolutionary Front was formed to defend territorial integrity of Manipur. In 2008 Suspension of Operation of operation was signed with Kuki-Mizo based umbrella organisation called United People's Front. In July 2009, following a coup on 21 June, a splinter group of KYKL formed KYKL-Military Defence Force. On 25 February Zeliangrong United Front (ZUF) was floated to protect Zeliangrong interests. In June 2011 a faction of PREPAK started operating under the banner PREPAK (Progressive). The same year Maoist Communist Party, Manipur was formed for national and social liberation of Manipur. Besides separate peace dialogue with the NSCN (Khaplang), Indian State had entered into armistice with selected groups. Between February and May, 2013 four insurgent parties viz., United Peoples Party of Kangleipak, United Revolutionary Front consisting of various Kangleipak Communist Party factions, (KCP- Lamphel) and Kanglei Yaol Kanna Lup (Military Defence Force) came forward for peace talks.

As discussed armistice has been significant from tactical military point of view. But there has been no indication of demilitarisation and reduction in the military budget. The number of recruitment to military, paramilitary, police, auxiliary forces and intelligence has been steadily growing and repressive laws remained functional. The failure to effectively address national question combined with the inability to resolve the structural crisis inherent in the neoliberal path have not created a conducive peace. The weakness of *carrot and iron* policy has been exemplified by the continuous cycle of conflicts centred on diametrical nationalisms, e.g., *India, Kangleipak or Manipur, Nagalim, Zale'n-gam, Zogam* agendas. Whether each of these projected national agendas suffers from theoretical anachronism and objective paradoxes can be discussed separately. But an overview of the situation is necessary to substantiate the argument for an ongoing conflicts. For instance *India* agenda continues with aggressive strategy to wipe out the enemies. On the other side *Kangleipak* (sic. Manipur) agenda concentrates on: (a) articulation of anti-colonial discourse directed against India and (b) formulation of one nation theory for Manipur that targeted divisive discourses formulated by *Nagalim* and *Zalen'ngam* agendas. But some of the parties had also entered into truce with Indian army. On the other hand *Nagalim* and *Zalen'ngam* agendas posited against one another over territorial control.

However, they are tactically united against *India* and *Kangleipak* agendas. But they are also separately engaged in armistice with *India*. They are tactically interwoven into one in construing divisive discourses between tribe and non-tribal. They identified Nagas and Kuki-Chin-Mizos with tribes and claimed for exclusive rights over the hills that comprise 90 per cent of the Manipur. They identified *Kangleipak* agenda with Meeteis who are being referred to as exploiters and oppressors of tribes. Holistically seen, the four set of agendas are contentious and militarily expressive in consolidating supporters and targeting respectively projected 'national' enemies. However, with the exception of *India* agenda the rest suffered from lack of homogeneity and unified command. Each of the three agendas are composed of different parties that are at times in violent conflicts. During internal conflicts some sought for tactical alliance with others by transgressing 'national' agenda barriers. In the overall scenario the dialectic of protracted armed struggle and violent conflicts had affected many economically, physically, socially and psychologically.

Neoliberal Context and People's Desperation

At the global perspective the Indian big bourgeoisie has adopted neoliberal path in which the State plays crucial role in providing security to private property and the reigning market forces.[13] Over the decades after the transfer of power certain degree of industrial development has taken place at a snail's pace which has led to the development of a medium level of capitalist development.[14] However, the Indian big bourgeoisie concentrated heavily on accumulation of wealth through collaboration with international financial capital and retarded the development of heavy industry, of the production of machinery by machinery in India. Therefore, India remained predominantly a market and an assembling warehouse of international capital and exporter of assembled commodities and agrarian products. To pave the way to penetration of international capital in assembling sectors, commercial complexes, transports and communications and mega projects such as dams and mining millions of tribes or rural village communities had been forcibly displaced from their homelands. Disinvestment in agrarian sector and maximisation of procurement of agrarian products to meet imperialist quota had severe impacts on peasants, agricultural labour and urban poor. All these are being carried out with an intensified offensive under the slogans of liberalisation and structural readjustment programmes. In this context the condition in North-East remains alarming.

In North-East aggressive policy by the Indian State and penetration by market forces have created an unfavourable situation. Casual cosmetic economic packages and limited job opportunities could benefit a small section of the population, but it had failed to address the larger issues of economic underdevelopment and political instability. In Manipur the instability situation is reflected in various levels of contradictions, which may be broadly categorised into three, i.e., contradiction between external and internal forces, contradiction among *rentier* bourgeoisie and contradiction among oppressed peoples. Firstly, the contradiction between external neoliberal forces and the oppressed population has not been resolved. With the exception of the *rentier* bourgeoisie who are in collaboration with external forces; assertions and agitations by desperate sections against the aggressive policy of the State, destructive projects, immigrations and infiltration of outsiders, etc. had been order of the day. Secondly, contradiction among *rentier* bourgeoisie had been largely centred on the control of political and economic powers. It had been temporarily resolved to some extent through creation of different vertical blocks and horizontal layers of institutions where they could find entry either through election or nomination or recruitment. However, most of them, particularly those competing or unsuccessful or newly emergent sections who posed counter-elites posited against the powerful, indulged in communal campaigns and sectarian assertions in their struggle for power and economic bargaining. Thirdly, contradiction among the oppressed had been predominantly communal, which has been largely orchestrated by the *rentier* bourgeoisie as discussed above. They invested in communal conflicts to divert away the attention of the oppressed people from exposing their parasitism. To some extents the communal overtones and sectarian rhetoric are being carried forth by certain sections of insurgents, civil societies and assertive intelligentsia. The objective is to become communal leader and enjoy certain degree of personal control over land, labour, fund and resources.

Disturbances or conflicts in Manipur are perpetuated in the context of the overarching neoliberal political economic practices. Firstly, insurgency has been largely a response to the aggressive national agenda and capital onslaught carried out by the Indian State. It remains unresolved. The *carrot and iron* policy has been bent on a superficial national integration trajectory without rooting out the system responsible for underdevelopment and disillusionment. Secondly, it has also become apparent that most of the insurgent parties who wage liberation war had been least critical of the existing political economy. They are yet to publicly articulate revolutionary political economic programme. Their confrontation or collusion with different sections of *rentier* bourgeoisie remain tactical based on issues, but all of them have commonality in sectarianism and communal orientation in certain forms or the other. Their polemics and articulations conveyed respectively formulated national euphoria, but most are apparently treading on the line of neoliberalism. The principles of national liberation and social emancipation had not been clearly informed to the public.

To sum up, there has been the clamour demanding basic democratic rights such as sovereignty, security and peace. Firstly, sovereignty has been deprived of in the circumstances when popular consents are being largely manufactured to serve the purpose of bourgeoisie totalitarianism. Secondly, peoples have misconstrued the State as source of economic, physical, social and psychological securities. These expectations have not been fulfilled. Aggressive offensive by neo-liberal forces have not only unattended to the basic democratic demands on economic, political and social issues, but also have caused physical torture, psychological humiliation, restive situation and hysteria at the receiving end. Thirdly, the aggressive peace process, bereft of providing a common democratic platform to spearhead a system of governance to be established on the principle voluntary unionism, has been counter-productive to the oppressed peoples. The desperation for a society free from subjugation, exploitation and suppression remains haunting.

Notes and References

1. A generic term collectively referring to present Arunachal Pradesh, Assam, Manipur, Meghalaya, Mizoram, Nagaland, Sikkim (since 1975) and Tripura states.
2. Ranging from those asserting freedom from India to ethnic or regional autonomy within India.
3. Karl Marx, *A Contribution to the Critique of Political Economy*, Progress Publishers, Moscow, 1977.
4. Frederick Engels, *The Origin of the Family, Private Property and the State*, 1884.
5. Vladimir Lenin, *The State and Revolution*, 1917.
6. Noam Chomsky, *Media Control,* Natraj, Dehradun, 2003.
7. Karl Marx, *The German Ideology*, 1845-46.
8. Statement by Shri Ari Bahadur Gurung and Rev. J.J.M. Nichols Roy in the Constituent Assembly of India, respectively on Wednesday, 23 November and Saturday, 19 November in 1949.

9. Such as the Assam Disturbed Areas Act 1955 and the Armed Forces (Assam and Manipur) Special Power Act, 1958 were imposed. AFSPA interplayed with other repressive legislations such as Land Acquisition Act 1894, Prevention of Seditious Meetings Act, 1911, Indian Penal Code and Criminal Laws, Unlawful Activities Prevention Act, 1967, National Security Act, 1980, Prevention of Terrorism Activities Act, 20029, and etc.
10. Statement by the Union Minister of Home Affairs Shivraj V. Patil in the Lok Sabha; 17 August 2004.
11. Comprising Aimol, Chiru, Kom, Koirem, Kharam and Purum communities.
12. Umbrella organisation of several Kuki-Chin-Mizo insurgent groups.
13. Under neoliberalism "if markets do not exist (in areas such as land, water, education, health care, social security, or environmental pollution) then they must be created, by state action if necessary" David Harvey, *A Brief History of Neoliberalism,* Oxford University Press, 2007.
14. '*On the Stage of the Indian Revolution*' in Revolutionary Democracy in its Vol. II, No. 1, April-May 1996.

8

Peace Process of Government of India and NSCN-IM

India's Successful Diplomatic Dancing and Democratic Initiation

L. Muhindro Singh

Introduction

Looking toward an amicable solution of Naga problem, political dialogue has been undergoing between Government of India and NSCN-IM[1] since 1st August, 1997. (First cease-fired was took place between NNC/FGN and Government of India in 1964) Government of India has been carrying down the demand of 'sovereignty' to 'alternative arrangement' and managing the various issues somehow. No further encounter in between Central forces and NSCN-IM is witnessing except confronting on area domination and possession. Violation of human rights, extortion or illicit taxes from the people and dual governance in the hill area are the another matter that has insignificance in India's integrity. In contemporary, many Armed Opposition Groups (AOGs) have been entering in electoral politics and politicians have nexus with them for mutual benefit. Such trends are seemingly very noticeable phenomena of electoral politics in the sense that both the Central and State government are also somehow managed it and claimed free and fair elections. They often made attempt to nominate their candidates who have loyal to them, eventually such coercive influence violates electoral rights of those aspirant candidate but it is positive result of the peace process of GoI and NSCN-IM. Ethnic Civil organisations supported by armed outfits are also actively involved in electoral politics in the hill areas with certain objective. The United Naga Council (UNC) in the State made clear that they would like to be part of a Greater Nagaland as demanded by the NSCN-IM and strongly involved in the electoral politics since NSCN-IM entered in to political dialogue with Government of India.[2]

Political Dialogue and Diplomatic Dancing

Both the counterpart (GoI and NSCN-IM) have no sincere in the dialogue though both claimed progress and sincerity.[3] The ground rules of ceasefire are often violated and the monitoring committees set up to implement the ground rules have remained callous in their approach. The government has been engaged in talks with the NSCN (IM) for the last sixteen years and managing conflicting issues somehow but there is still no concrete acceptable resolution. The so called 'violence' is controlled but the outfit has continued all its activities with impunity. From organised extortion to narcotic smuggling to arms running this outfit feeds and raises other smaller groups to expand their area of control. Therefore, 'talks' ensure certain legitimacy to the underground activities of these groups across the spectrum.[4] Samir Kumar observed that "the primary objective of peace dialogue is to bring warring groups in the negotiating table, set forth potentially agreeable ceasefire terms and conditions and offer alternative ways of settling conflicts that beset the region".[5] In regard to success of peace process Kishalay observed[6] that "those some AOG started with a vision for sovereign state are seemingly deferred to the local issue and ethnic cleansing and rather emphasising federal relations."[7] Significantly, NSCN-IM deferring their demands from sovereignty to federal autonomy and even alternative arrangement within Naga inhabited areas in India's North-East. Indian Government has had some success in achieving stability in the region, using tactics from negotiations to military operations to root out militants.[8] In such pandemonium situation the dynamics of peace process and subsequent effect in different ethnic groups in India's North-East is wider day-by-day. On the other hand Suspension of Operation with some minor AOGs in Manipur is indeed success and failure of one and the other. Initiative of the government is somewhat success, but its ramification is rather developed a conflict within different ethnic based AOGs. Thus, the ongoing peace process has been advancing with no significance achievement in terms of mutual agreement or acceptable but coercive nature of GoI is a plenty and widening ethnic divide while trying to manage conflict on the way what the Central government want *'wait and watch'* which is success of the one side and loser of the other, it is indeed a ***diplomatic dancing***.

Successful Democratic Initiation

Obviously, elections in the hill and remote areas are witnessing abnormal election where many electorates could not enjoy the right to franchise. Moreover some civil organization who loyal to insurgent groups have been acting like a political party and imposed does and don't to the electorates and intending candidates. The problem of factionalism also casts its shadow over the operation of electoral processes as one Naga underground outfit does to promote its interests by involving in elections, so also other outfits.[9] Besides, political elites have nexus with insurgents and using them for mutual benefit. Perhaps the conflict situation may compel to do so. Politics in the North-East are not based on democratic norms as understood in the western-model democratic system observed by Ved Marwah, former Governor of Manipur.[10] During elections political leaders seek support of the AOGs in the form of muscle power. The entire political system in the region has grown around these unscrupulous politicians.[11] In the hill districts, under the imposition of parallel *diktats*, intimidations, forces from different underground factions, the voters remain helpless for free exercise of their voting right. The imposition is often exercised through frontal Naga NGOs, Naga political parties, etc. It has its beginning after 1997 which was the year in which current ceasefire agreement was inked between Government of India and NSCN-(IM).[12]

It may be noted that general strike/ban on the polling day in Manipur were also very common which is totally violates electoral rights but all the concerns seem to consider it as a result of conflict. NSCN-IM boycotted the Seventh Manipur State Assembly Election and 12th (1997) and 13th Lok Sabha Election (1999).[13] The NSCN-IM's call for boycott was stringently observed by some of the over-ground Naga organizations under the banner, "We want solution not election".[14] In the Seventh Assembly Election of 2000 the number of Kuki MLA's had outnumbered the elected Naga MLA's.[15] The people of Ukhrul had no other option, but to abide by the *diktat* of the NSCN (IM). But this time, the people of Ukhrul have not only participated in the Assembly elections defying the boycott call by the NSCN (IM), but also ensured the defeat of a person, who had reportedly close links with the underground group. The United Naga Council (UNC) in the State made clear that they would like to be part of a Greater Nagaland as demanded by the NSCN-IM; for the Meiteis and other ethnic groups, this became a question of defending their territory. This divide has its impact on the political set-up in the State, including a realignment in the political parties, the electioneering process and, possibly, on the outcome of the polls.[16] In the Eight Assembly Elections, 2002 and the 14th Lok Sabha Elections 2004, NSCN-IM decided the fate of the Naga mainstream politics, right from the selection of the candidate to their election.[17] The line of divisions between the various communities in Manipur can no longer be treated as a fall out underground politics with the submission of a Memorandum by Naga MPs and MLAs of the state to the Prime Minister openly supporting the NSCN (IM)'s concept of Nagalim on 27 May, 2005.[18]

Ethnic Organizations for Peace and Naga Unification

On the eve of elections, many Naga NGOs and frontal organisation of Naga Armed Opposition Groups have been trying to make more unite and close cooperation by organizing traditional functions and even campaigned door-to-door in the entire hill areas to convince and support sponsored Naga candidates on the backdrop of Naga integration. Some Naga politicians and social organization claimed that the word "Manipur Integrity" is against their aspiration of Naga Unification though some sections of Naga community do not have much interest on the integration demand. Taking the opportunity on this diabolic situation most of the politicians in hill and valley have often been made a great deal on ethnic or communal politics. NSCN-IM, on 13 July, 2005, and ANSAM asked all the Naga MLAs and Ministers in Manipur to resign, declaring that Naga identity and dignity can't be safeguarded under the present arrangement of Manipur State under any circumstances. Only for their political gain politicians often insisted many innocent electorates to condemn the ruling government charging betray or neglect them in any field on communal line. Even former Chief Minister, MP Rishang Keishing himself claimed "Meitei Betrayed".[19]

In the 9th Manipur State Assembly Election 2007, a faction of the Naga rebel group, while considering it as an opportunity of strengthening the ongoing peace process for securing the aspirations of the "Naga people for a united Naga Homeland" involved in a big way. The UNC, its constituent Tribe Councils/Hohos and the Naga civil societies have decided to define the objectives with which the Naga people must approach the same for securing representatives through whom the voice of the Naga people can be articulated loud, clear and consistently.[20] The UNC appeals to the Nagas of Manipur to choose/elect only those candidates who have no party affiliation whatsoever, who enjoys the confidence of their respective constituencies who are God fearing and who subscribes to the following four objectives to work unitedly with his/her other fellow Naga representatives elected in the same manner.

- to fulfil the inherent and democratic aspiration of the Naga people for unification of all homeland;
- to mobilize the peoples' fullest support of the ongoing Indo-Naga political dialogue for an honourable solution;
- to provide leadership to society in nation building; and
- to promote the common interest of all ethnic communities in the state.

The UNC appeals to the Naga people of Manipur through their respective tribal council/Hohos, churches, intelligentsia, professionals, women, youth and student's organisations to rally behind the goal to mutually strengthen for the unification of the Nagas. (*Ibid*)

> "The Nagas of Manipur have to go beyond the immediate compulsions of personal gains; family, clan, village, and tribal interests and political opportunism. We must ensure the return of responsible candidates with clear visions who will represent the Nagas aspirations and carry forward our struggle for peace, justice, and freedom. It is an uphill task but we must do it because we know what awaits us if we don't," it further says. *[UNC]*

The NSCN-IM has also joined the fray by attacking the candidates of various political parties.[21] The UNC has fielded 11 independent candidates in 2007 Manipur State Assembly Elections in the four-Naga dominated districts of Manipur under the United Naga Democratic Front (UNDF) with the twin objectives of intensifying their agitation for the integration of Naga-inhabited areas under one administrative unit and mobilising support for talks between the GoI and NSCN (IM).[22] The UNC took a resolution (3 August, 2006) wherein Naga candidates had been instructed against contesting the 9th Manipur State Assembly Elections under any national political parties and intimated to all the sitting Naga MLAs.[23] In the UNC sponsored meeting of the all the intending Naga candidates for the Manipur State Assembly Election 2007, 60 Naga intending candidates signed the Eight Point Declaration.[24]

> I willfully support the ongoing Indo-Naga Peace talks for a negotiated and honourable Solution. On being elected I will steadfastly defend the interest of the Naga people for the integration/Unification of the Naga Areas; That I will resign from the Manipur Legislative Assembly if called upon to do so by the Naga people represented by the UNC. I declare that I will accept without any reservation whatsoever, the candidature of the particular person who is determined by the Naga people represented by the UNC to be the consensus candidate; I shall not defect/split/merge to any political party without the approval of the Naga people represented by the UNC. Failing to fulfill the above Commitments and Declaration, I and my witness shall be made liable to any measures adopted by the Naga people.

In another meeting of the UNC held on 28 December, 2006 at Senapati resolved to totally ban and restrict the political party affiliation of whatsoever and holding of political parties' conventions and campaigns in the Naga areas.[25] The UNC had afterwards served ultimatum on 24 January, 2007 to all those candidates who had not been nominated by the UNC to withdraw their candidates.[26]

Insurgency Involvement on Election

From the above analysis it is very cleared that NSCN-IM and its frontal organizations strongly involved in the electioneering activities. It is indeed positive way of peace process for bringing them in the mainstream politics. On the contrary the NSCN (K) had alleged the UNC and All Naga Student's Association Manipur (ANSAM) of directly monitoring the 2007 Manipur Assembly Elections allegedly at behest of NSCN-IM and further added that NSCN-IM had selected its own pick and choose persons as the independent candidates. It also stated that the course of action taken up by NSCN-IM, UNC, and ANSAM was "not election but selection." It also warned that the two organizations would be held solely responsible if any untoward incident takes place resulting in the loss of human lives and properties on account of undue interference by them.[27] For this analysis, let see some data collected from five hill districts collected through structured questionnaire. Altogether 66 samples were collected from five hill districts (as Chandel-13, Senapati-12, Churachandpur-14, Ukhrul-14, Tamenglong-13) Most significantly, it is to insight the emerging modus operandi of insurgency involvement in electoral politics in the hill areas where even armed opposition groups are often attempted to nominate their nominee who have loyal to them.

Threat to Party or Candidate

Threats or intimidations to follow their AOGs diktat to the particular candidates or party are not an exception in this state in the particular hill areas. It is witnessed by various reported news and appearances: National Congress (INC) has alleged the Naga People's Front (NPF) of using insurgents/armed opposition groups (AOG) in their favour and resorting to all sorts of election related crimes in the recently held Manipur state assembly elections 2012.[28] The Kuki militant groups, which are under Suspension of Operations (SoO), and the NSCN-IM, which is also under peace-talks with the Centre were openly involved elections. The Kuki militants openly supported the INC candidates, while Naga People's Front (NPF) was supported by the NSCN-IM. When we look in to the matter seriously base on the available data, it is proved that many respondents said intimidation or threat to candidate/party are mostly came from AOG which is 50 per cent while miscreants/local goons 20 per cent (see the following).

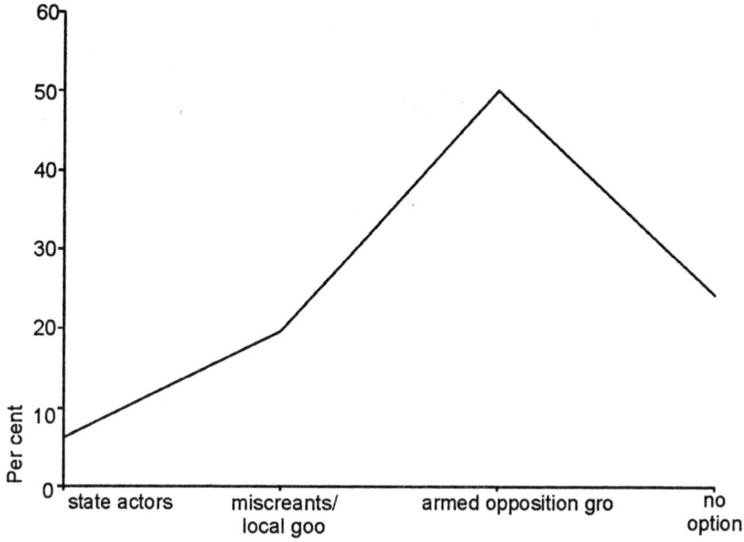

Fig. 8.1: Did you Hear Intimidation/Threat to Party or Candidate from any Quarter?

Bullying to Electorates

Bullying or intimidations on particular elector or electorates were also a plenty on the eve of elections. The *modus operandi* of intimidation might be any act of bullying or coercive force to make behavioural change of electors, for instance, intimidation to support or not to support particular candidate or party, or not to involve in any electioneering activities which is attempt to curve freedom of electorates on the one hand but the success of India's peace process. Such intimidations often appear in many parts of Manipur though the frequency is accordingly different. Trinamul Congress president Kim Gangte said "Voters in the hill districts failed to get their franchise ... had been paralyzed and manipulated by militants".[29] One executive member of Senapati District Congress Committee was severely assaulted by NSCN-IM on 26 January, 2012. Amidst the threat of NSCN-IM, a peace rally was staged at Chandel on 19 February by womenfolk demanding that they be given the freedom to freely exercise their franchise without threat and intimidations.[30] Naga National Council (NNC) charged the Isaac Muivah leadership of shrieking their responsibility owed to the "Naga Nation." It alleged that the formation of UNDF was at the behest of NSCN-IM. It also alleged that the Nagas in Manipur are not only forced and threatened to vote for the UNDF candidate, but the IM leaders have also been abducting public leaders from Tamenglong and Ukhrul district areas for raising objections to the NSCN-IM Stances.[31] The data also insist that 60 per cent respondents agreed that AOG threat electorates to support or not to support particular candidate while 21 per cent respondent support it that 'might be'. See the following:

Table 8.1: Electorates awareness of any threat to support or not to support particular candidate/party?

		Frequency	%	Valid (%)	Cumulative (%)
Valid	no	11	16.7	16.7	16.7
	yes	40	60.6	60.6	77.3
	might be but can't say	14	21.2	21.2	98.5
	no option	1	1.5	1.5	100.0
	Total	66	100.0	100.0	

Concluding Remark

Thus, from the above analysis and findings shows that the NSCN-IM and other hill based ethnic AOG are also involving in the electioneering process. Yes, their involvement with coercive influence is violation of electoral rights. Significantly, it is positive result or so to say advancement of India's peace process in the sense that they are also entering in the mainstream politics to follow the democracy. As the primary objective of peace dialogue is to bring warring groups in the negotiating table, set forth potentially agreeable ceasefire terms and conditions and offer alternative ways of settling conflicts their involvement on the electioneering process is positive. That is the main reason for why the Central Government kept silent when they noticed threaten of NSCN-IM on election. We all agreed that Manipur is clear example of flawed democracy where elections are totally in servitude. Electorates of this state cannot decide their franchise instead influenced by various factors. More or less, *modus operandi* on the eve of election in particular in the hill districts whether it may be against electoral integrity or not, but it is indeed positive way and advancement of peace dialogue. NSCN-IM and frontal organizations like UNC want to nominate their nominee through election so as to fulfil their aspiration whatever it may be.

Notes and References

1. In 1975 when Th. Muivah stayed at China, under the leadership of Angami Zapu Fizo an accord was signed between Naga National Council and Government of India. By denying such Accord the then V.P. of NNC Isak Swu along with Khaplang and Th. Muivah formed another revolutionary group in the year 1980 under the banner of NSCN (National Socialist Council of Nagalim) as Isak-President, Khaplang—VP, and Th. Muivah—General Secretary has been generating movement for Naga independent against Government. of India. After some years, conflict and different views between the leaders were coming up and formed another faction as NSCN–IM (1988) by Isak Swu and Th. Muivah. Since then both the Naga underground are on side by side as enemy and confronting each other as they have different ideology.
2. The emerging trend in elections observed in Naga areas of Manipur is shaped by Naga ethnic politics. In other words, the ethnicisation of electoral politics in Naga areas of Manipur is responsible for the emergence of the present trend in elections. It has its beginning after 1997 which was the year in which current ceasefire agreement was inked between Government of India and NSCN (I-M). The present trend may continue in near future. Benjamin,

G., 2013, Impairing Free and Fair Election: The Emerging Trend Observed Among the Naga Tribes of Manipur, in L. Mhunindro and G.T. Haokip, (ed.), Emerging Electoral Trends and Violation of Human Rights: A Paradigm of Exacerbating India's Democracy, New Delhi, Mittal Publication.

3. Muhindro, L. (2008) Political Dialogue of NSCN-IM and Government of India: an Introspection, *South East Asia Politics,* New Delhi, Vol. 7, Issue. 6, pp. 21-24.
4. Kishalay Bhattacharjee, (2011) 'Peace Talks' in Assam's Post Election Scenario, IDSA comment, 16 May, (Online) available at: http://www.idsa.in/idsacomments/PeaceTalksinAssamsPostElectionScenario_kbhattacharjee_160511, accessed on 10 February 2012.
5. Samir Kumar Kumar Das, (2007) Conflict and Peace in India's North-East: The role of Civil Society, East-West Center, Washington, Policy Studies 42, Washington, D.C.
6. Kishalay Bhattacharjee, (2011).
7. Besides NSCN-IM Secretary Th. Muivah and Chairman Isak-Swu diverted/reversed their demands of sovereignty to the Greater Nagalim within the Indian union by disintegrating territory of other neighbouring states in North-East including large area of Manipur and even some parts of Myanmar, make immense influenced to the Naga political leaders and Naga social organizations though some Naga leaders condemned NSCN-IM decisions after devoted many lives on the long way.
8. Bibhu Prasad Routray, Manipur Assembly Elections: Divergence of Ethnic Interests, Institute for Conflict Management, http://www.ipcs.org/article/military/manipur-assembly-elections-divergence-of-ethnic-interests-703.html, accessed on 23 October, 2010.
9. Benjamin, G., 2013, Impairing Free and Fair Election: The Emerging Trend Observed Among the Naga Tribes of Manipur, in L. Mhunindro and G. T. Haokip, (ed.), Emerging Electoral Trends and Violation of Human Rights: *A Paradigm of Exacerbating India's Democracy*, New Delhi, Mittal Publication.
10. Ved Marwah, Former Governor, Manipur and Jharkhand delivered a lecture on Ethno-Political situation in India's North-East, at Centre for Strategic Analysis, Tamilnadu, 19 May, 2010.
11. The growing nexus between the undergrounds and the over ground political leaders and the civil servants is directly related to the lure for easy money. As the people do not trust the state police to protect them, the different ethnic groups have organized their own armed militias. They need funds to maintain these armed, which they secure by extortion and pilferage of government funds practiced on large scale. Ved Marwah, Former Governor, Manipur and Jharkhand delivered a lecture on Ethno-Political situation in India's North-East, at Centre for Strategic Analysis, Tamilnadu, 19 May, 2010.
12. Benjamin, G., 2013.

13. The Naga Members of Legislative Assembly (MLA)s sent emissaries to negotiate with the NSCN-IM when the later issued a directive to all Naga MLA's in Manipur to resign their seat by December 31, 1994 in protest against the Central and State Government's alleged assistance to the Kukis in their conflict with the Nagas. This shows the NSCN-IM had a considerable hold on Naga MLA's.
14. The issued NSCN(IM)'s note of appreciation jointly signed by both Isak Chisi-Swu and Th. Muivah, dated 10 February, 1998 expressed appreciation and thanks to UNC and others for "their outstanding decision to disallow the imposition of Indian election in Nagalim. It says,
"The Collective Leadership acknowledges here its profound gratitude to the Naga people for their outstanding decision to disallow the imposition of Indian elections in Nagalim. We would particularly like to thank the Naga Hobo Summit, United Naga Council, Naga Peoples' Movements for Human Rights, Naga Students' Federation, Naga Mothers' Association, Naga Village Chief's Federation Concerned Citizen Forum, Naga GB' Federations, Political parties and the Church leaders for their decisiveness in asserting the national rights of the Naga people. Your momentous endeavour is unprecedented since the time of 1951 Plebiscite under your bold pilotage the Naga people have come forward all the more, taking the firm political stand at a crucial moment such as this one. History is more securely in our hands now. It is indeed your timely efforts and unsparing sacrifices that have proved beyond doubt the unconquerable power of the people in different dimension. Now, no one on earth can deny this fact. Thanks be to God, now no force under the sun can hold the Naga people back. We are committed to the national cause heart and soul."
15. Media miss Manipur polls, editorial, *Oriental Times*, NEN, 2 (37-38) 7 Mar.-21Mar. 2000 (Online) available at http://www.nenanews.com/OT%20Mar%207-%20Mar%2021,%2000/editorialC.htm, accessed on 22 April 2002.
16. Bibhu Prasad Routray, Manipur Assembly Elections: Divergence of Ethnic Interests, Institute for Conflict Management, http://www.ipcs.org/article/military/manipur-assembly-elections-divergence-of-ethnic-interests-703.html, accessed on 23 October, 2010.
17. Aheibam Koireng Singh, Some Reflections on Land Questions and Ethnic Crisis in Manipur, paper presented in National Seminar on *Land Problem and Ethnic Crisis in North-East India*, sponsored by Maulana Abdul Kalam Azad Institute for Asian Studies (MAKAIAS), Kolkata, orgd. by Dept. of History, Manipur University, 27-28 July, 2005.
18. *North-East Sun*, Delhi, 15 July, 2005.
19. *North-East Sun*, Weekly Magazine, Guwahati, (7) 15: 2005.
20. Koireng Singh, A. (2011) In the Whirlpool of Delhi Bandits' Skulduggery and Insurgency: Manipur Electoral Politics, paper presented on two day UGC sponsored National Seminar on Emerging Electoral Trends and Violation of Human Rights: A Paradigm of Exacerbating India's Democracy,

held on 25 and 26 November, 2011, at S. Kula Women's College, Nambol, Manipur.

21. According to the former Chief Minister, Reishang Keishing, two candidates from the party contesting the Chandel and Tengnoupal seats have already been forced to withdraw their nominations by the NSCN-IM.
22. The common front floated by the United Naga Council (UNC) has been christened as the United Naga Democratic Front (UNDF) with Kho John as its convenor. In its manifesto, it pledges to mobilize the people for fullest support to the on-going Indo-Naga political dialogue for an honourable solution; to provide leadership to society in nation building; to fulfill the inherent and democratic aspirations of the Naga people for the unification of all the Naga Homeland; to promote common interest of all the ethnic communities in the State. *The Sangai Express*, English local daily vernacular, 7 February, 2007.
23. *The Sangai Express*, a local English Daily vernacular, 03 November, 2006. With it a verbal spat erupted between the Congress MLA, RK Theko and UNC When a newspaper cited the former saying that the NSCN-IM is attempting to wipe out the Congress organisation from the Naga areas through the UNC. It can be recollected that RK Theko was the President of UNC at a time when it issued Quit Notice to the Kukis in 1992. Spat of resignation by Naga MLAs took place ahead of the 9th Manipur assembly Election in which five sitting legislatures namely Samuel Jendai, Henry Paotei, Danny Shaiza, BD Behring and Wungnaoshang Keishing resigned from the Manipur State assembly in support of the ongoing GoI—NSCN-IM peace process and "to fulfill the inherent and democratic aspirations of Naga people" for "unification of all Naga Homeland". [*North-East Sun*, Delhi, 16-31 January 2007].
24. *The Sangai Express*, English local daily vernacular, 12 January, 2007.
25. *Ibid.*, 12 January, 2007.
26. *Ibid.*, 2 February, 2007.
27. *Ibid.*, 23 January, 2007.
28. Hueiyen News Service, Congress presses ECI to disqualify NPF candidates, The Hueiyenlanpao, Manipur, 8 February, 2012.
29. Hueiyen News Service, TMC demands re-poll in hill constituencies while BJP wants re-poll in Thoubal AC, The Hueiyenlanpao, Manipur 31 January, 2012.
30. *The Imphal Free Press*, English local daily, 20 February, 2007.
31. *The Manipur Mail*, English local daily, 21 February, 2007.

9
Regional Security Council for a Viable Peace Process in North-East India

B. Angousana Sharma

Introduction

The word PEACE is worth to the sensible beings, so called human beings, or the beings who are in the built-up societies, where understanding prevailed. At the same time, the wave of violence also can be prevailed, in the same society where the socially cultured people are living together. At the same time, a third culture is developed very slowly, into the society. That would be the phenomenon of tussle of violence and non-violence. The result of the tussle of the two acts of violence (Anti-social) and non-violence (Social) creates a new atmosphere in the society. That is the cause of REVOLUTION. Both acts have own synthesis of TIME. The time is wave carrier, and dream of the POSITIVE and NEGATIVE results. That is REVOLUTION.

In reality, revolution would be of the TIME; Revolution does not mean to be an act or reaction of a theory or theology. Therefore, the needed act of non-violence or peace become common desire of the people, when, the act of revolution enforced the society to think over the situation. That would be the synthesis of the acts of REVOLUTION in the societies of the North-East states of India. That would therefore, the administrations of the North-East states are facing the hot wind of violence acts of the rebellions, extremist outfits, unlawful organisations, under the circumstances of killing people; kidnapping, torturing, harassing the people; collecting funds unlawfully; extortion, loot, forceful endorsement of own power into the society by threat; damaging the property of the people and the Government; demolishing private and Government properties; etc. were found to be destructive culture, are assertive. On the other hand the apprehensions of the government forces, of police, Armed Policemen are taking high advantage of Armed Forces Special Powers Act (AFSPA) in the region. As a result the people are under crush in between the unlawful forces and law handling forces of the states.

What is the necessity of Mass killing, mass annihilation? None of the killing elements can explain. But it is a presumption of the selfish leaders that; the acts of violence are either show of existence of violence or show of supremacy over the administration which is selfish, rather insensible. At the same time, to the similar acts of the insurgents the government forces with armed had been trying to suppress the Armed Insurgents without being heard the voice of the outfits. Crux of the time for the sensible human being is: fighting a guardian with the children who are already committed crime, instead of searching mechanism to deal with the misappropriated outfits. Too much waste of time with the acts of gun culture is leading the innocent people in trouble.

The government is to wake-up; the people have to be sensitized; the political dialogue should not waste time; nomination of the interlocutors should have been sincere with the inclusion of more members of the team of interlocutors from both sides and from the intellectuals of the North-East States. One man interlocutor cannot bring the solution of the causes of different issues. For example, Naga issue in the North-East is taking prolonged duration on table; within 13 years period 3 (three) interlocutors have been changed; but, no way out to resolve. Because, Monkey judgement system has been inducted for peace for the issue, which is bad luck to the states of the North-East. Naga insurgents are happy with the dream to bring sovereignty in the Hills. But the time pulling diplomatic tactics of the bureaucrats are not comprehensible to the Nagas. Government of India could not interpret the real meaning of the INDEPENDENCE, FREEDOM and SOVEREIGNTY. Government of India has no bold responds to the illegal demands and the issues. Government of India is not ready to dig at the real issue of the Nagas as well as the issues of the other outfits. Government of India is not ready to feel the pain of the peoples of the states of the North-East. Government of India has no interpretation of INTEGRITY in the true sense. Therefore, the protracted fights with issues and demands are carrying chronic situations in the states. Because of unsolved, unending and neglected issues in front of the youths of the region are compelled to come on the fore (leaving the education) to join the war of no destiny. Youths are disgruntled; people are deprived of; administrations are corrupted; bribe becomes source of employment; police become popular service in the society; public leaders are very busy to attend small functions in the locality. Public leaders are not thinking of plan for future generations; leaders are behind fund and self engaged into the jobs of self financial benefits e.g. contracting small works in the name of relatives; and keeping interest in the small employments in the departments.

Leaders are not caring for educational institutions, like schools, colleges, staffs, maintenance of buildings. Leaders are not caring the public health and Public Health Care Centres. Governments of the states of the North-East have no provision of discussion over the issues of the region. For example: The interstate overlapping boundaries; the international border pillars; the geo-politico inter relationships between states; socio-religious inter-community relationships of the states of North-East as well as between the mainland states are rarely enshrined to interlock for the sake of the upcoming generations. Indeed, every tomorrow is a better dream of the generation.

Democracy is the slogan, autocracy in application; Union is written theory, diversity is primary factor. Besides, sectarian thoughts in the minds of the leaders advantaging to divulge own decline from the mainstream of democracy. As a result the innocent peoples of the region devoted to the leadership, divert their faiths from the democracy, became follower of the individual leadership. Such thoughts and theories become main cause of creation of the theory of REVOLUTION. The revolutionary theories of the world are derived from ECONOMY, CULTURE, REGIONAL and COMMUNITY based, generally caused by exploitation of the mainland administration. Therefore, in the democracy, the system of administration is normally lenient and flexible in the course of situation. Also the specific character of the multi-party parliamentary Democracy of India is more flexible than the other systems of democracy of the other countries. Therefore, India is the largest democratic country, of its kind, in the world. But, due to the loaded thoughts of the leaders, taking share of thoughts from the visionless politics of the nation the leaders of the North-East could not brush own thought on toward self-determination. As matter of the fact the States administrations in the North-East become self-centred business cells; where, only the matter of funds discussed; where, no proper plan of the budget year discussed, so that, the people in the North-East could not open-up the avenues of developments in the States.

As matter of the self-cornered administrations in the States, as well as the selfish leadings of the revolutionary parties in the region, the people of the states have been made insecure; the private, public and government properties have been left insecure, the integrity of the people of the states are alarming. Peoples of the North-East States are moving without leaders and without proper directions. No one is worrying for the morrow year. Everyone is busy to fetch an opportunity. Thus, peoples of the East are compelled to learn cunningness instead of exhorting to correct the mistakes committed by the individuals. But, the self-securities of the people become question mark today; rather security of property and institution for integration are all away from the sense of the administration. The administrations in the region are behind offence/defence theory. But, no one has considered upon security of the people, property and integrity which is now placing in front of the people and the government for necessary discussion for immediate promulgation of the theories in application, so that, the people shall maintain peace in the region.

Therefore, it is the great hope of the people that a "Regional Security Council" of the North-East Region shall bring peace to the normal citizens of the region; also hope that the security of property and safeguard the integrity shall maintain in the states. Besides, dialogues of the Naga issue, other issues of the States due to insurgency problems also shall carry on, according to the political provisions, into the ambit of the National Policy, into the ambit of the National Policy.

What is Freedom?

Freedom has high sense of meaning which does not fit to an established society. Freedom is first of all has different senses and interpretations according to the situations of a place, according to the thoughts of the people of a particular society, where administration would not be concerned over the existence, due to either very highly civilized or not controlled by an administration. In the sense, the highly civilized society has own responsibilities of the people; of the responsibilities with the people have spontaneous acts into the society, administered the government without having push of the administrator. Say, there is the government, but no complain. In like manner, there is a kind of beings having free movements living in the out-senses for whom the sensible people have no interest to disturb as he/she is free in the society. Or there are some live stocks whom are preserved in the Amazon valley without disturbing their lives which are inaccessible to the modern society, which are called freedom from the society. They are free on look but not free because of fights in different groups. Therefore, question of FREEDOM is vague and unanswered.

What is Independence?

The term independence is adorn to the society of a democratic, republic, socialist, secular; having dignity of lives of the people with Duties and Rights of the people; indeed justice systems of the law over shadowed the society, over and above the systems of administrations and individual(s); where too, the executive whip is under administrative control; rather system of economics links to the plan programme of the governance. Thereafter, also the boundary of the independence, the phenomenon of the different cultures and systems also guarded with the troops of Defence on the ground, in the air and in the sea. Therefore, independence has the boundary, not free. A system of the society established in the independent group of the peoples. Therefore, such system of administration has been imposed into the society, where, the peoples of the societies can act independently. But, when the human civilization upgraded to form a group of society; for the society an authority was required. For the authority a strong Arm was necessary. For the Strong Arm a competition, a challenge has been committed. After the successful challenge a strong, bold, dominating personality was nominated as ruler of the society, so that, the people of the group of the society can be protected; can be administered; can be solved the problems of the society; also has to maintain a boundary of the administration. That was a King.

A king became authority of a boundary of administration. There were wars and fights, killing, arrest, slavering, occupying land and tributary system have been established. But, such jurisdictions of administrations have been considered not satisfactory and limited to the human boundary of thoughts. Such thoughts extend to socialistic patterns of society. Such society has to have equal status, equal education, and justice to the people which is ahead to the administration of the king, where social justice was dark, where only the king and his descendants were independent. Therefore, such pattern of society was found to be people friendly and an advance system of administration. Which of the systems of the critics will be dealt with the various departments of Legislative, Administrative, Executive, Judiciary, Defence, Environment, Natural Resources, Communications, Civil Societies, Education, and Women Forum etceteras to be dealt with different necessities?

Thereafter, more defined culture of administration was searching into the society which will be more democratic, more open, more avenues for the generations; more institutions for more technology and redefined institutions for the administrative authorities also have been taken into account of the government, so that, a never rusted crank with a chain can be arranged to pull the huge societies of administration with full of commitments, with full of avenues and full of hopes and dreams of the people can be solved and turned to reality. That is INDEPENDENCE. Therefore, the meaning of independence would be beyond freedom, kingdom or merely existence of an administration. For example: when, the *Bharatavarsha* became free from British Rule there were more than 630 small kingdoms altogether. Therefore, to make Union Government of India was facing problematic task to form the New BHARAT. In the meantime some small kingdoms have been voluntarily merged into the Union Bharat. Moreover, the new Government has endeavoured to merge more territories into the new Bharat.

India could arrange to form an Union Government as well as could write a constitution till 1949. India declared as INDEPENDENT, DEMOCRACTIC, REPUBLIC country on 26th January, 1950. The jurisdiction of the constitution has been elaborated DEMOCRACY with the verse of multi-party parliamentary democracy, in which, duties and rights of the citizens of the country has been deeply considered and promulgated the constitution in all over the country with full confidence. It is for the reason that DEMOCRACY is the path of INDEPENDENCE. No democracy, no independence. Therefore, there was no applicable terminology as independence before commencement of DEMOCRACY.

Qualifications and Characteristics of Independence

The qualifications and characteristics of Independence shall be considered as follows:

1. Must have a boundary of the sovereign territory, demarcated; bilaterally and unilaterally be accepted.
2. Must have sufficient population according to the area of the land, so that, defence forces can be deployed for safeguarding own space.
3. Must have an administration, comprising of a ruler and various departments so as the Government can fulfil the demands of the population.

4. Must have the Ruler who is authority of the land.
5. Must have a language so that inter-communication, International communication can be established.
6. Must have own currency or coin, so that exchange of trade and commerce with the other countries can be established.
7. There must have diplomatic relationship with other countries.
8. Must have a National Emblem.
9. Must have a National Flag.
10. Must have a system of administration; either Parliamentary or President or Empire.
11. Must have a Constitution, so that, the law of the land can be initiated on the basis of the Constitution.
12. The sovereign must be recognized by the United Nations Organisation.
13. The overall requisite qualification of an independent country would be considered upon the economic status of the land as well as of the citizens.

Sovereignty

Therein upon, Sovereignty termed to be extremity of independence like a king. Of course, it is true the king was independent, which already mentioned earlier. But, sovereignty is not the independence. Sovereignty has been termed the Ruler on super imposed status, which does not assert independence. It is also true that; there should not have external intervention of the administration while the king with the helm of the kingdom. Therefore, Sovereignty or independence both so wrongly conceived to the innocent people of the particular states where indoctrination of the selfish doctrines of the outlawed leaders, which would near rounded the corner when implementation of a righteous theory of democracy prevail into. Therefore, to remove the thorn of misconceived theories into the people an anti-dot element would be required. That would be "The Regional Security Council" of the North-East States of India. It is also true that; Government of India had neglected the North-East States of India. It is obvious, also nature of the Indians had not been studied by the then Government. The Indian mainland has been widely accessible for better administration. The inaccessible North-East has been treated as dark cornered stone for long. The North-Eastern Frontier Agency (NEFA) now Arunachal Pradesh and Naga Hostiles activities of the Naga Hills had given tough time for development. Government of India could not deal with the Naga problems as well as the lack of communications of the East.

When the war of 1971, i.e. Bangladesh conflict enforced the Indian Mainlanders to reach the East. The influx of Bangladeshis in 1945 has been neglected; the refugees of 1971 became headache to the Assam and neighbouring States. Administrations in the North-East States were sleeping. Insurgency problems in Mizoram and in Manipur, till then, exhibits the high tone and tenor of internal turmoil which reacts to the territorial integrity of the country; security of the people and property by the time Bodoland, Tripura insurgency also swung into the region. In the meantime Government of India had singular mechanism, of dealing with Armed Forces; enhancement of Armed Forces Special Powers Act (AFSPA) which brought harmful to non-violence; broken the peace of the people. The legislators, bureaucrats and civil societies had no idea to deal with the situation. Neither the authorities concerned over the circumstances (which was already delayed) to put effort for peace, nor, the Government of India has full scale elements to deal with the problems of the States. Thereinafter too, the concrete directives of the States administrations had not been stressed to control over the boiling states of the East. Such inactive government has perturbed the citizens of the region; had felt to secure the youths into the region.

Besides, the missionaries could have footed into the far flung interior, remote areas where the government agencies are not active. And therefore, Missionaries had given spiritual education as well as the basic social education to the peoples of the states, like, Manipur, Mzoram, Nagaland. For such Christian Missionaries working into the deep and tough terrains are found to be appreciable. For example, Arunachal Pradesh (NEFA) was under Monasterial Administration before reaching the political agents. Also Ram Krishna Mission in Arunachal Pradesh has done tremendous human services. Therefore, missionaries had hand to hand practical services with the people for development of education, health, social and human development.

These are all about narratives of the sovereignty, Independence and freedom. Proper interpretations of the terms have to be institutionalized to the people, so that, thereafter, there should not be any more confusion.

The Ceasefire Agreement between NSCN-IM *Vs* Government of India: A Disclosure of Conspiracy in the Ceasefire Agreement

Resting on the standoff 15 days Shiroi village, sealed by the Assam Rifles w.e.f. 19th January, 2009 to 2nd February, 2009 after the unlawful perpetration of the NSCN-IM and in this connection a hand out of the Imphal Free Press released of 16/03/2009 and 17/03/2009 was found to have been dealt with the Government of India and NSCN-IM with the following facts:

That, the agreement so far been underwent, came to the notice of the people which reflects to be preparatory plan to suppress Manipur by infusing divide and rule, injection into the Manipuri tribes and Meiteis with a deliberate tactics to squeeze the territory of Manipur. The report of the ceasefire monitoring group was further tried to misinterpret thc Constitution of India with the phrase of the "Union in form and federal in nature". The report was tried to twist the constitutional terms of Union and Federal Characters. There was also no question of not protecting the territories of the State by the Constitution. Here, the Constitution is very clear on the part of the protection of the territory. The term Federal in nature cannot be changed even being tempted the paras of the articles of the Constitution of India.

Therefore, simply similarity of cultures of the two neighbouring communities of the two States will not be interpreted to be administered under a single umbrella, nor it has the provision to be administered by a single particular community in a state; but there is provision of Unity in Diversity, not Diversity in Unity. Therefore, as per the report collected from the reliable sources, published in public; if been not incorrect the system of secrecy, confidentiality while building up of a pragmatic reasonable structure the agreement in between the Government of India and NSCN-IM in which the elements represented and rendered the responsibilities as:

1. The ceasefire monitoring group
2. The fact finding team
3. The DGMO
4. The NSCN-IM
5. He PRO Indian Army
6. The PRO Assam Rifles
7. The Secretaries of Home Ministers
8. The reaction of the Government of Manipur
9. The telephonic version of the Chairman CFMG
10. The GOC in C Eastern Command and the field officers crushing into the circumstances, would be accountable to damage an integrated body.

Here again, in the executive summary of a fact-finding report by a group of lawyers has particularly mentioned about "working of the cease-fire in Naga areas" which tried to mould the situation to bring into the knowledge of the Home Secretary as on 3rd June, 2005 at 11.30 hrs in his chamber; which found to be differed today, in which, it was mentioned about interaction with the DGMO and GOC-in-C Eastern Command by the Secretary Home. Moreover, Lt. General R.V. Kulkarni in his letter, spoke to the DQMO on 15/6/05 stated confirmation should be awaited. Again on 16/6/05 spoke to the DQMO as the new location of the NSCN-IM stands approved with two conditions which are not ignorable to the Meiteis.

1. NSCN-IM would refrain the valley based groups (mean for insurgent groups or rebellions in the valley) in Manipur,
2. No more camps would be considered hereafter.

But for what location or the nomenclatures of the locations meant to be designated camp have not been told for which Shiroy (in Ukhrul district) has been considered to be taken by NSCN-IM is a matter of conspiracy and confusion. And what matters have been received, the MSCM-IM been conveyed by the retired General also not known, not declared. Thus, the language of the bureaucrats have more underlying meanings could be used for safeguarding the people; could also be used to hack down the development of an unfavourable to the Government or unlikely culture of a state.

Thereafter, the disclosure of the inapplicable ceasefire proposal to extend into the Naga settled areas of Manipur perhaps fixed to be inapplicable. The conversation, the version, the interpretation seems flammable to the ground realities. Either Government of India has suppressed the reality of the agreement after 18th June, 2001 mob in Manipur or the Government of India could not give a proper direction of the agreement underwent, for pacification. Therefore, unfloored initial agreement to be publishable has been kept in the save custody. Hence, as to how such irresponsible decision could have been made. It might consider to have been granted the designated camps inside the unauthorized territory of Manipur. On the other hand under what circumstances such flammable, reactable, inapplicable documents are long been maintaining in the administration of the Government of India in spite of removing the doubts from the minds of the people of the country. Such delaying tactics is sufficient matter of befooling people of the country.

It is astonished, on hearing the statement of the new Chairman of the Cease Fire Monitoring Groups Lt. General Mandhantha that his jurisdiction of work is up to Nagaland only, not up to Manipur. Therefore, it is crystal clear that the cease fire agreement is meant for Nagaland or the agreement has been prepared for Nagaland, and applicable in Nagaland only, not in Manipur; is an indirect declaration of the new General as the boundary of agreement would be in between Government of India and NSCN-IM for Nagaland and Ministry of Home, Government of India is logic, not beyond Nagaland. On the other side the documents which are invisible to the Government of Manipur to the people of Manipur would not encroach the boundary, of Manipur. Because, the CFMG has no jurisdiction into Manipur. The telephonic versions communicating after four years of the commencement of the agreement in public sought to be exposable, rather disposable. The actionable, reactionable matters, integrity matters and operational would not so easily disclosed to the public as the administration has own boundary of administration in the top secret bags. Because, the dealing with the agreement is meant for Nagaland, not meant for Manipur. Also, the matter of territorial integrity if breached with the neighbours would have been discussed with the intellectuals, politicians of Manipur. Otherwise, to pick up the matter of territory without consulting the administration of Manipur would not be wise steps of the Government of India.

In context of the cease fire agreement came into act with the steps taken by India was not found satisfactory to the people of the North-East The nomination of an interlocutor of Shri K. Padmanavaiya, IAS, retired Home Secretary as one man commission for negotiation with the NSCN-IM was the first wrong step taken by the Government of India. GoI could not form a team of interlocutors including the names of the intellectuals, the political pontiffs, historians, the bureaucrats and geographical concerned persons from the North-East. Simply holding the NSCN-IM has jumped over the executive culture of the administration. GoI has not considered to invite the insurgent groups of the North-East region, since number of, rebellions were operating in the region termed to be larger in number. The momentum, the eventualities, the circumscribable dictations had not listened to the Government being guardian of the Country. Simply deploying forces in the region could solve the problem of the North-East is known to the innocent peoples of the North-East.

Today, people wanted development in the region, for that, no gun culture would be successful. But youth had been compelled to lift the guns due to ineffective administration and plan of the country. The

Government should know that the development will appear in good governance only. So far the Indian democracy is concerned any party in majority does rule in the parliament has the culture of direct interfering to the State Government instead of discussing the directive principles. The party politics have lost the Preamble of the Constitution. The meaning of the DEMOCRACY turned to DEMOCRAZY "the meaning of SARKAR turned into SAARKHAR". There is neither Government nor administration. Money is determination for all power crazy politicians. Manipur become Moneypoor. Even rebellions have been fragmented into pieces for the sake of money and power. The cause of the rebellion is not known to the people, but only panicky is "demand letters" from the outfits and fake outfits. Therefore, to bring the scattered fragments into the main stream on negotiating table of the Government by giving up the confuse making and divide and rule ideology of the Government of India and fueling communalism into the small groups of the people in the name of secularism would be the right step.

The action of the army PRO Major Shamser Jung, the prompt reply of the PRO the Assam Rifles and further reaction against the cease fire extension into Manipur was a real positive reflection of the force as the agreement communicating in between NSCN-IM and GoI had been read delude; due to the reason the application of the agreement also surfaced as wrong. As a result the local peoples are also misled, local administration also cramped to lose the muscle of the administration for a while, before being disclose of the real interpretation of the agreement. In the meantime the Central Government used to throw small-small package into the region, so that, the innocent peoples would able to forget the big problems of the State, as well as the dependable State Government will be running behind the whirlpool of the coins instead of removing the vagues. This is all about the misinterpretation of the agreement of the Government and the simple overt senses have been sprinkled on the eyes of the people as a golden dust became material of arson and communal fire. There, people of the region should try to understand the true lies in the text of the publication of the Government of India. Thus Peace process in the North-East India is in the shape of incomplete due to conspiracy in the agreement.

Peace Process in the North-East

1. Peace is the hidden gem in chaos and in the war. To trace it in the human intent is the system of administration.
2. Peace is earned after cessation of the unlikely atmosphere.

3. Peace is like that of correct solutions of mathematical problems.
4. Literature of peace is description of the advent, rather struggle to attend liberation.

Peace Process

1. Peace Process why? Because there is chaos (according to the ideological term); or because of war (according to the fatal term). Therefore, to posses peace is the birth right of the human civilization.
2. Both terms of chaos and war are different courses of ideologies and sufficient causes, of overt or covert scientific war of the century. Both ideologies of the different terms have different amount of synthesis of violence in the human civilization. As early human civilization flourished physical tussle, occupation, invasion was nature of war as ideological doctrination come into force to day. That is violence in human mind. But to remove the remote culture of war an ideological, philosophical and logical discourses are required, so that, the habituated war or unrest in the human society can be replaced by peace and harmony. But, to deal with war for war, chaos with chaos; and armed with armed will never bring peace; nor will solve the problems forever. Therefore, to remove unrest or chaos from the minds of the people of the region with the act of a perfect organisation with proper induction of correct elements will surely embrace peace very soon.

Decades gone by, the Government of India is endeavouring to pacify the region; whereas, the British India was affording to expand her Empire into the region. When freedom arrived on 15/8/1947; thereafter, republic in January 1950 promulgated the Constitution of India with the preamble of SOVEREIGN SOCIALIST SECULAR DEMOCRATIC REPUBLIC and Secure to all its Citizens.

JUSTICE: Social, Economic and Politics
LIBERTY: of thought, expression, belief, faith and worship
EQUALITY: of status and of opportunity and to promote among them.
FRATERNITY: assuring the dignity of the individuals and the (unity and integrity of the nation).

Development/Welfare

Above all assurances and preamble of the Constitution of the Republic Parliamentary Democracy in the country the Government of India has brought the North East Council (NEC), which is purely civil and open for all citizens. Thereafter, another Minister also designated DONER (Development of North-East Region) for the development of the region. However, violence does not come down due to the reason as:

1. Armed Forces Special Powers Act (AFSPA) 1958 is decade old Regulation designed by the British Regime is found to be unfit in this century.
   (a) But, AFSPA could not be removed from the region so soon because, there is no alternative or replaceable Act in the hand of the Government.
   (b) Until AFSPA has been lifted from the North-East Region by reforming a replaceable institution and grooming a negotiable atmosphere of the North-East Region, the chaos and turmoil cannot be doctored, the Government shall not ready to lift AFSPA which is unfortunate for the citizens of the North-East States of India.

   By the time, behind AFSPA Armed Forces personnel is taking undue advantages inside Civil Population which causes more violence. For example Fake encounter is heinous crime in the human Civilization, but it became tool of the administration. In the advantage of insurgency and pseudo gangs operations in the states the Governments of the region could model the district police, admixing the enrolment of Armed Police in the name of Commandos, which is an ugly look. Such commandos used to move on Motor bikes and in Gypsys. Commandos used to arrest the outfits and unidentified civilians, picked-up and killed the persons arrested in the name of encounter, which is called fake encounter. However, the acts of fake encounter have been noticed under scan of the Government of India for killing more than 2500 youths in Manipur alone. Whereas, the real Commandos use to smash the camps of the enemy with the capacity of 150 to 1000 manned, by 2 or 3 Commandos. Whereas, such sophisticated commandos killed one by a section of police men with motor, cars, Jeeps and such acts defamed the name of commandos, should be re-inchristened as Special Task Force (STF).

2. On the other hand the decade old Naga insurgency problem would be the origin of the creation of UNREST and CHAOS in the East. Hence forth, Government of India for 60 years unable to break the chain of violence committed by the outfits as well as by the Armed Forces Acts, one after another; the name of the outfits can be mentioned as NNC, NSCN, (IM), NSCN (K), PLA, UNLF, KYKL, PREPAK, KCP, KCP (MC), KNA, KNF, ULFA, NDFB etc. More than 40 insurgents groups are operating in the region. Lifting, collecting funds from the people, from the transports; business cells and service people; besides, price of the commodities are shooting double price due to invisible taxes. Direct and indirect taxes paying from the economically backward states in the region. These are of illegal taxes which are causing economic drain and chaos in the North-East States of India.

Now the Peace Process Why

Consequent upon uprising of the fatal ideology and Armed struggle groups the State Governments are unable to design a negotiation table; even been tabled with the political discourses the unscrupulous situation is overtaking the State Governments. The system of the existing machinery of the Governments are yet to stance a defensive priority in the states against the outfits, despite NEC/DONER like extra constitutional establishments have been introduced into the region for the welfare and developments programmes with the grant of 10 per cent of the Union budget, shared from every Union Ministers. Moreover, the people of the East have been down trodden, deprived, legal privation exhibits, rather facing uncomfortable due to lack of right machinery for peace, and due to lack of institution and non-installation of machineries for the security of personnel, security of property, security of integrity. Therefore, it comes certain to highlight the reason for the vagarious phenomenon and outputs of the violent atmosphere prevailing in the region; due to what reason, what step wrongly taken, while dealing the indigenous people of the East is a matter of discussion today.

Peace Process in the North-East

The peace process is as old as the human civilization come into existence. As of the same process of the human civilization the British India and Republic India or before, Naga nomenclature entrusted for the indigenous people of the region into the Hills had the prolonged, protracted practice to break the village laws (so called customary laws) particularly into the Naga Hills; on the other, Nagas on defensive trench. Because, to educate the tribals to remove the mind sets of war in between villages (they called countries) would be the prime objectives of the administration. Jawaharalal Nehru presumed and stated; since 1819 till 1880 the British tried to break through Naga Hills. The "Excluded Area" status declared in the year 1834; has been decreased when Indian Act 1935 come into existence.

As of then when Naga (Approx. 3000 in nos.) had been employed during 1st world war in the labour corps from 1914 to 1918 in France which had given exposure to the Nagas about war of the villages in savage and war in the big countries in the wider spectrum. But, the concept of war could not be erased from the minds of the Nagas. Because, they were born in war have seen war, remained in war.

Political Outsources

A political light glimpsed in Naga Hills that establishment of "The Naga Club", Sir John Simon visited Naga Hills and could feel the political future. It was influential that Naga is going for self-identification. Nagas approached to the British Government with the memorandum to keep Naga Hills under direct administration of the British Empire. But the crude facts of war in between states and communities are nothing, but ethnic culture and religiously motivated and differences appears between the neighbouring states. British concede the proposal for a separate state from Assam, of India. On the other, Manipur had the princely administered state; where all kinds of administrations and systems are different. Because, the king of Manipur was crowned ruler; as matter of the facts maintained a State Assembly (*Darbar*); even taken by British India deputed an Assistant Commissioner to supervise the State. Therefore, Naga Hills has been included in Assam in 1837, till then Tuensang area was termed unadministered. During Second World War (1939) Naga Hills remained as battlefield.

On 1st April, 1945, an institution in the name of Naga Hills District Council was formed. In the mean time Lord Atlee came into power in England with his Labour Party. As soon the Atlee's news reached, NNC organised Wakha conference 1946. The Maximum Propaganda blown in the Naga Hills, as it had not ever been conquered by India; British India invaded or conquered etc. Therefore, the innocent people of the Naga Hills had the phobia of war; believe that India is on foot to conquer Naga

Hills. In the mean time the opportunist leaders endeavoured to warm up the situation, so that, the protracted war of clandestine ideology could have floated into the people.

The then Phizo was fully aware that Naga Hills about the scattered population of Nagas had no administration due to non-existence of rulers. The same situation was also known to S.C. Jamir the then Chief Minister of Nagaland and 3rd time Governor of different states in India. He tried to persuade underground squads but futile. In turn Jamir has been ambushed and called betrayer. As of the situation of Naga Hills during 1946 the British was ready to give freedom; but the fact was that Nagas found no ruler in Naga Hills. As a result Sir Adhrew Collin the Governor of Assam and later Sir Akbar Hydari the Governor of Assam, in India had tried to bring Nagas under persuasion as well as through legal bindings. Also gave 10 years time for improvement as interim period; for up gradation of thought, economy, education, technology and social status. But Nagas evade the doctrine of democracy. On contrary Nagas disregard the legal formulation.

Instead of following the norms of the democracy NSCN (IM) leaders had visited United Nations Clandestinely. The President of the NSCN (IM) had the conference in UN during 1993 to represent indigenous peoples meeting of the UN in Geneva; tried to convince the flagrant violation of Human Rights of Nagas by deploying Armed forces into the Naga Hills by the Government of India. He tried to refer ULFA, Bodo outfits, Khalistan and their supports for Nagas on the path of independence also referred the diplomatic relations with New York, Dhaka, Islamabad, Bankok, Nepal and Myanmar with NSCM (IM). They (NSCN-IM) represent UNPO (unrepresented Nations People organisation) during his presence in Geneva in 1994; he explained about the Kuki extremist, backed by Indian forces. From 20th to 26th January, 1995, in the UNPO General Assembly held at Hague, Convener of NPMHRs reached Geneva and spoke and communicate the situation in Nagaland.

Thus, situation in the North-East India became sorrowful to the future generation. But, to tackle the situation through which positive acts of implementation of the Government programmes into the deep villages and areas could have been guided affectively, but the impact of democracy without education has brought negative impact with bribe and corruption into the far flung areas, taking the shape of wild fire into the people's mind. To control over such wild fire and establish a stable democratic society will take time. It is for the reason that our father/mother of democracy had not considered education of basic requirement of the people. This was of the fact, different ideologies of the different missionaries could reach into the deep habitation without hesitation; thereon, they put their institutions according to their own wish which was not considered the principle of *Sanskar, Parampara* of the domestic behaviour; but their aim was to achieve the goal of their ideology. But its results will be appeared in the coming generation as negative to the plan, policy of the States.

It is not deniable to the thinkers and social lovers of the nation that there was something wrong in the administration because, the factors responsible in the administration; nook and crony of diplomacy, the *summum bonum* of democracy and adaptablity of the administration to the people have not been considered.

As there was no ruler in Naga Hills for administration the Centre had no idea of the eligible leadership for the North-East states. As a result the problem is facing today. Perhaps Sardar Ballav Bhai Patel could not properly handle the problems of the North-East due to short lived. At the same time, divide and rule of the British Empire also would be a factor of cropping the ideological, ethnical and religious attack upon the Democratic sociology. It is because British had no belief or dream to quit the Empire from India. Besides, no idea about the fabric of integrity in the Indian soil, looming a stronger anchor to pull out India from sinking. The strong nerves of the Indians were not measurable to the British. Sepoy Mutiny of 1857 educated the rulers of the day.

These are all history of Union India, not for division of India. India has own culture and *Dharma*; the *Dharma* is far beyond religion, which is the cause of fear and panicky to the established missionaries. Because, to reach *Dharma Shastras* or philosophy of *Sanatana* (*Vedas*); analysis with the *Vedantas* which based on wisdom was found to be unconquerable by any kind of attack. This was known to British; therefore, it is also the factor a plan to divide Naga Hills by sanctioning Independence, but not succeeded the new establishment of the Government of India.

Tussle in Between Democracy and Separatist Theory

The local concept of Nagas was first war, and then conquers upon the neighbouring village (so termed to be a country). Therefore, annexation theory of India Act 1935 from "EXCLUDED AREA" 1837 was strongly objectionable according to their mind sets of war, battle and combat. On the other a 10 years interim period of observation for the improvement of education, improvement of social status and to upgrade in various faculties of civilization, had not been utilised by Nagas in the proper institutions duly provided by the Government for future of the Nagas. Nagas were behind Armed, war and attack education. Therefore, development into Naga Hills is not visible as per expectation. In the mean time the then MNF (Mizo National Front) leader Laldenga could establish coordination with the then Chief Minister of Mizoram Mr. Lalthanhoula, established contact and brought understanding with the Central Government during the time of the then Former Prime Minister Shri Rajeev Gandhi. Laldenga surrendered with his cops with the Arms, became Chief Minister of Mizoram. Lalthahoula was happy. Remained lie-low, Lalthanhoula revive with stronger will; after Laldenga's expired at Landon. MNF could not retain longer. Lalthanhoula returned. Thereon, Mizoram had taken advantage of education, political mileage and improvement in the state. Therefore, leaving Sikkim rest of the states of the North-East has bypassed by Mizoram with positive culture of the civilization.

Notwithstanding the MNF there were insurgents groups operating in the North-East but controlled, e.g. Tripura is one of them. Tripura, after 1971, the Bangladesh conflict had faced tremendous problems of refugees as well as the influx populations into Tripura from Pakistan from 1945. After Elections 1979 CPM came into power in Tripura with full determination to establish a stable Government and maintain equilibrium. The State Government had the plan of protection of the indigenous tribal areas as well as concentration upon the illegal influx of population on the border and administration thereon. Although Assam Students' movement 1984 also reached Tripura, huge massacre caused alarm. Tripura in the year 1985-86 tackled the situation carefully. At the same time Assam had the tough time during 1984 till the overthrown of the Hiteshwar Saikya Government and arrival of Assam Gana Parishad (AGP) regime. AGP could no longer retain the Government; could not provide a stable Government. Hiteshwar Saikya returned and Prafullo Mahanta retreated. Another era of United Liberation Front of Assam (ULFA) led by Paresh Baruah comes to the State with violent act in Assam. Moreover, functioning of ULFA disconcerted the people of Assam. Surrender of ULFA activist appeared very shortly. But the sections of people of Assam in Karbi-Anglong and Dimasas in the North Cachar Hills Districts have become problematic to the Government. Demanding Statehood, but overlapping territories in the two segments of indigenous peoples of Assam compelled Assam to constitute a negotiation table. The tripartite negotiation/agreement is inviting in the region.

The tripartite negotiation of Bodoland in between Assam and Government of India is on progress of negotiation table over the demand of Bodoland for autonomous state, totally separate from Assam. On the other hand, Assam Government is trying to pacify with the grant of autonomous administration of Bodoland. But Bodos are not ready to stop their movement before sanctioning a separate state. The Government of India is on deep thinking on the conscience of the Assam Government. In the meantime hundred and ten years old Gorkhaland demand is another headache to the Government, though Gokhaland is an autonomous Hills district of Bangal Sarkar. As if the problem of Gorkha movement for an autonomous state is partially affecting the North-East Region, the term of identity as a bonafide citizen of India as well as to remove deprivation or legal privation in the Gorkhas in Bangal Sarkar seems to be strongly determined.

Therefore, to discuss upon the peace process in the North-East would be optimistic on the part of demand of the segments of the people of the East. Demand should be based on security of people, security of property and security of territorial integrity. Therefore, it would also be kept in mind of the people of the North-East that we are brethren of India. Government of India is our centre; the Constitution of India is our gospel.

But, Nagaland is still on the dock to open the intellect with the remote politics of armed struggle. Still the youths of the Nagas are in puzzle with the procrastinated connotations of political dialogues in the foreign countries. The British as well as India were better knowing the weight of the term sovereignty than the Naga people understand. The Government of India is aware of the qualifications of sovereign country which is not aware to the Naga people. Thus, the NSCN (IM) is losing the opportunity of the Naga Children. Who will be responsible for the negative impact of the Naga struggle? AZ. Phizo had realised and kept mum himself for long 30 years till his death. The then Prime Minister of Union of India exerted to educate Naga Delegates in the year 1945. His henchman, Sir Akbar Hydari, the Governor of Assam in front of the then Deputy Commissioner Pawsey persuade the Naga leaders to improve Naga Hill under the mainstream of the Constitution of India. Nehru further educates the Naga delegation in 1956. Nehru told them that Nagas were independent because they were part of Independent sovereign, and Democratic India. And therefore, assured that maximum autonomy will be given to them within Indian Union under the framework provisioned of the country; but prior to this step peace must be restored there and Hostile activities should stop. It was conceived by the Pro-Indian Nagas. But outfits are not ready to hold peace. But back to war and conquer principle, which was already outdated in the twentieth century. This was all about war. But when BJP came into power under the leadership of A.B. Vajpayee brought Naga on the negotiation table. Naga force has been under cease-fire till the time Kuki movement has been commenced; due to ethnic culture in Naga, particularly in Manipur Hills where different types of Hills tribes settled; among the tribes Kukis are also one of them. Kukis have been driven out from Ukhrul district, during 1992 till 1995 innumerable Kuki houses have been burnt down. Kuki retaliates. All the Hills of Manipur gripped under communal fire.

Besides, Naga politics tried to demolish the neighbouring territories. The leaders are indoctrinating the Naga ideology into the neighbouring States, which is damaging to the administration. Manipur is serious victim of Naga Politics and indoctrination. Assam, Arunachal Pradesh is targeting the next Naga strategy. But, the people are still puzzled into the whirl wind of the extremist culture in the North-East. Therefore, to rescue from the poisonous political wind the duty of the conscious citizen of the country would be active and alert to understand the theory in implying into the region. Therefore, to construe and cement the regional administrations with logic and scientific resolves would be called of the TIME. Otherwise the younger generations in the region would be belated to hold the torch of civilization. At that time of delay to reach solution no one will be ready to take responsibility for the damage occurred in the region.

Therefore, to initiate the right directives will only possible for establishing of an institution, in which personnel security, security of property, development of integrity with optimistic tune can be administered. Education for all categories of people also can be given; such INSTITUTION which will build democracy into the region; such institution shall redirect the misappropriated peoples, such Institution shall de-doctrinate the indoctrinated principle of war, attack, invade etc. Such Institution would be the asset of the Nation. Such Institution will be a Rising Sun in the East. Such Institution will be guardian of the people of all categories of people of the North-East. Such Institution shall be guide liner to democracy. Such Institution must be the MESSANGER of PEACE.

Such Institution will be nothing more than safeguarding the integrity of the region. The INSTITUTION would hereby propose to be named as "REGIONAL SECURITY COUNCIL" of the North-East of India, headed by the Prime Minister of India. It is true enough to emphasize the Security Council should also remember that there is National Security Council for the Country. But the Regional Security Council would be smaller in size but larger in responsibility. It is because this council would be purely extra constitutional budgetary organisation for the region to be implemented in practical manner. Such Security Council will be constituted comprising of the following as under:

Components of the Security Council

Security Council is the Institution of the people of the region, represented by a Skeleton body consisting of the following:

1. *Chancellor*: The Existing Prime Minister
2. A Secy. General will be nominated by the Prime Minister (should not be nominated from the cadre forwarded bureaucrats).
3. *Executive Members*: Chief Ministers of States.
4. *Legal Advisors*: Advocate Generals of the States.
5. *Women's participation is important*: Chairpersons of The Women's Commissions of all the States in the North-East will participate the Council in all respect; provided facilities and enhancement of power of the women in the nation will be applicable.
6. The Civil Societies of the Nation are important on the part of the security of the Nation. Therefore, Security Council has to effort to involve the civil societies of the states on any occasion.
7. *Field Executives*: DGP of States and DG, AR and GOC Eastern Command.
8. The Home Guard, the Civil Defence, Fire fighting units and Natural Disasters Units of the states will be involved in any kind of operational occasion, wherever the units would be fit to induct.
9. *Technical Advisors*: I. Architect, Engineers.
10. *Medical Advisor*: Director of Medicals.
11. *Council Secretariat*: IAS (1), Senior Advocate (1), Medical Officer (1) Accounts Offier (1), Section Officers (3), Junior Account officers, (3), Comp. Operator (5), Head Asst. (2), Medical Staff (5) Clerks (10), Peons (10), Orderlies (5), Caretakers (3).
12. A liaison officer will be appointed whose qualification will be at least MBA (HR) to deal public grievances, assisted by a team

of officials from the States, i.e. eight assistances, one from each State of the North-East.

It is further define the Constitution of the Institution does not include the Member of Parliaments. But the Parliamentarians of the region will take part with passive manner, in the Council.

(a) Because Parliamentarians have their own responsibilities in the Parliament.

(b) Parliamentarians representing Parliamentary Democracy in India are party based leaders. Therefore, their responsibility in the Regional Council seems to be lighter to some extent. Therefore, to create unity of MPs will not be possible due to party based. Whereas, Chief Ministers are victim of the circumstances in the region and their responsibilities being member of the Council would be more accountable in the States as well as in the council. Therefore, keeping in view of the above circumstances and time-to time phenomenal appearances in the region the MPs and CM have been properly considered to be included or excluded as the member of the council. However, exclusion from the membership of the council does not mean MPs are not important, CMs are more important. Both are equally responsible in the National duties. The legal experts as already mentioned in the proposal of constitution of the council, who are from legal cells, will be responsible person to compile the points to be considered while constituting a relevant law for the institution, as well as legality in the Council.

Aims and Objectives of the Council

A. 1. To safeguard the citizens of the region; of education, of health, of liberty, of expression; and to remove deprivation, resentment, suppression.
2. To upgrade the Social status of the people in the region.
3. To check and upgrade economy of people and give guidelines for enhancement of economy of people of the region.
4. To restore peace from the social violence and to make up deficiencies of the society with the help of the states as well as with the centre.

5. To safeguard people from the illegal forces.
6. To streamline the out tracked people of the region who are unable to improve.
7. To safeguard the people from exploitation.
8. To check the institutions.

B. 1. To safeguard the natural properties like: Hills, Rivers, Lake, Streams, Woods, Herbs, Fish, Animals, Birds and valuable Medicinal Plants and Herbs in the region.
2. To preserve the ancient monuments and to protect destruction of nature.
3. To check the imbalanced ecological destruction and construction of unplanned, unapproved activities like: Cutting woods, Cutting earth from the Hills as well as from the reserve areas.
4. To check siltation of lakes and artificial earth filling into wetlands and diminishing cultivating lands.
5. To preserve the religious centres and to preserve and discover the likely tourism spots for development without disturbing ecological balance.

C. The most important but a defensive strategy required in the region is invisible ideological inputs, the war of wits, the war of words, the psychological warfare.

The psychological war is planned war through particular agents into the society, so as enable the people to divert the philosophy of the constitution into the newly planted concepts without weapon.

Therefore, loss of integrity is loss of the Nation, rather maintaining the integrity is success of the Government. Therefore, a team of unarmed soldiers to fight such war of wits has to be arranged in the Regional Security Council, so that, to protect, to preserve and to create the sense of belongingness, sense of responsibility in people of the region which is the object.

Duties and Responsibilities of the Regional Security Council (Responsibilities and Functions)

The Security Council will be equivalent to the office of a Union Minister of India.

1. The Chancellor is the Supreme Authority of the Institution, but He/she will act the power of the President of India in the council.

2. The Secretary General shall hold the power of the Chief Executive of the Institution. Also shall be equivalent of the Union Minister as:
   (a) Secretary General is supreme authority of his staffs.
   (b) Secretary General shall be administrative Head of the Institution.
   (c) In absence of the Secretary of the staffs, i.e. an IAS Officer, the Secretary General shall hold the office with the official order; shall thereafter look after the duties of the Secretary.
   (d) Leave and salary of the staffs shall grant by the Secretary General, leave of Secretary staffs too shall grant by the Secretary General.
3. Policy matters of the institution shall approve by the Chancellor. In absence of the Chancellor Secretary General shall deal the matter in anticipation to the Chancellor.
4. In absence of the Secretary General the senior most Chief Minister of the States shall hold the office of the Secretary General with the approval of Chancellor.

Duties (Dos)

1. The Council shall establish communications with all the States of the North India and also shall establish communication with the centre.
2. The Council shall establish coordination to all relevant elements and members.
3. The States Chief Ministers and Field Executives shall keep understanding on the duties and responsibilities of the Regional Security Council.
4. To scan, to enquire in regular to all events/occasion into the society, so that, no loop hole in the services of the Council will be occurred.
5. To conduct conferences of the Council members as per schedule of council.
6. To maintain discipline of the Council (According to the CCS conduct Rules).

Duties (Don't)

1. The Council is Scare of the Judiciary, Defence and Finance. Council shall not interfere the three of the Government of India

as well as of the Government of the States at any cost, unless security matters of the Regional Security Council is involved.

2. Council shall not interfere the civil administration without being necessitated.
3. Council shall not interfere the legal duties of the District or Central Police organisations.
4. Council shall not argue the Legislative Assemblies and Parliament without being concerned the Security of personnel, security of properties, security of National or Regional or of the State, or of departmental integrities.
5. Council shall not interfere the family or personal duties which does not interfere the norms of the Security Council.

Duties and Responsibilities of the Secretary General

1. Secretary General will be the nominal head of the Security Council under the Chancellor, i.e. the Prime Minister.
   (a) He will be coordinator, convener or head of the staffs of his/her secretariat.
   (b) He will remain in the Office for 4 years to 6 years.
   (c) He will Sanction, approve the Bills to be involved the matter of the Council in anticipation to the Chancellor, prior to the approval of the Chancellor.
   (d) He is responsible for maintaining the discipline of the Council.
   (e) He can remove, enroll, and suspend the staff's prior information to the Chancellor, except the Secretary of staffs. In case of Secretary of staffs Secretary General can initiate the disciplinary action as per provision of the Constitution.
   (f) According to the financial budget of the Council approved by the Chancellor; he will be authority of expenditure of the Council.
   (g) The Secretary General will be the authority of the Council, in absence of the Chancellor from duty. Rather Secretary General can exercise/impose power to implement the rules/regulations of the Civil Service Conduct Rules (CCSR) while administering the Regional Security Council.
   (h) A periodical audit of the expenditures of the financial year shall be conducted by a registered Chartered Account (CA). The same Audit Report will submit to the Minister of Finance every year during March.

The matter of formation of a Regional Security Council for the North-East States of India shall be submitted to the Government of India for kind perusal and the necessary approval of the institution, mean to be the institution of the people of the North-East States. For such responsibility the Government of India is requested to invite the responsible person/ persons who deserve to hold the office of the Secretary General of the Council. So, that the long been anxiety of the people of the North-East and the dreams of the people to bring a new Sun Rise of peace can be fulfilled. At such juncture of transition period of violence and non-violence in the States full co-operation from the Chief Ministers of the States is expected.

The Government of India is therefore, requested to please extend suggestion to establish such an institution, so as enable to build a new horizon of administration in the institution of the Regional Security Council. Hope the inspiration of the patriots of the nation shall bestow upon the Head of the administration of the Government of India with a new dream for the people of the North-East. It is further clarified that the function and the responsibility of the Council shall not interfere/ intermingle/intermix the issues of the insurgents and the responsibilities of the NEC (North East Council) and the DONER (Development of North-East Region). The Council shall deal with the Security matter of the people, of the property and of the integrity of the North-East. To safeguard the territory of the North-East and to maintain integrity of the people the North-East States is the motto of the Regional Security Council. (The Regional Security Council Headquarter shall be fixed at the Regional Capital City of Guwahati. For such the Council shall approach to the Government of Assam for acquiring of land as per requirement of the Council under intimation to the State Government, and approval thereof.)

Conclusion

We are already in the late hour rising States. We have to exercise own franchise to wake-up the sleeping senses. We should not believe or not to keep faith upon the precarious dreams. We have to sensitize the innocent people in the deep inaccessible villages who are keeping faith upon the opportunist heroes in the name of politician. God is there, where right use of time is there. God is there, where Truth exists. God is there, where doctrine of Rationalism flown. God is nowhere but exist in your true senses. Where there is true sense there is peace. Peace exists in truth. So, define Peace; we are in search of it. If we want peace we have to give-up violence. Violence is enemy of peace. Unveil peace which is behind the dark curtain of violence. The dark curtain is in the shape of opportunism, selfishness, personality, ego and unwanted property.

Call of the time is peace, off the way to violence clean-up the hiding principles of WAR, CONQUER, INVASION and OCCUPATION of a land in unauthorized manner. The weapon of violence is not merely armed in hand but also provoking against integration, indoctrination and practice of the leaders of the society to insinuate the human skill with the purpose of deviation, according to the own will. Try to resist propagation, provocation, indoctrination and communal ideologies of hate, instigation and insinuation to destine violence, which is against the Regulation of the Government. We shall appear peace. Peace is not away from us. Peace exists in optimistic culture of the society.

Peace is not away from us. Come and join together to institute peace.

10

The Fifty Four-Year Indo-Naga Conflict A Question of Internal Indian Ethnic Conflict or a Conflict between Two Nations?

Kaka D. Iralu

Introduction

1. In the light of modern political developments, the author will first try to develop a conceptual understanding of the word ethnic identity and national identity in relation to Nagaland and India. The first section will also point out the striking differences between the ethnic and national identities of Nagaland and India in the light of history, race, culture, religion and other factors.
2. In the next section, the author will give a brief history of the development of how different and even diverse ethnic identities merged into modern nation-state in the modern world. These modern phenomena began in the thirteenth century and culminated in the twentieth century. The author will trace the history of this development as it started from Europe in the twelfth century and finally took over both Americas in the eighteenth century and on to Asia and Africa in the twentieth century.
3. In the third section, the author will trace the development of this concept of the modern nation-state as it developed in Nagaland and India in the twentieth century. This development will be described with the words, *from ethnicity to nationality*. Interwoven with this concept will be the development of Naga

nationalism and Indian nationalism as they both struggled for freedom from the British yoke.

4. The chapter will end with a statement of what the Nagas strongly believe are their lands and their rights which had been suppressed by India and Myanmar for over half a century.

SECTION–I

Conceptual Understanding of Ethnic Identity and National Identity

The Chambers Twentieth Century Dictionary defines "*ethnic*" as "*concerning nations or races.*" The Oxford Advanced Learners Dictionary defines the same word as: "*connected with or belonging to a nation, race or tribe that shares a cultural tradition.*" The word ethnic has its origin in the Greek word "*ethnos*" which literally means nation. In ancient times it was used to denote a tribe or city-state because of the nature of its independent political systems. In ancient times Nagas and Indians also lived in the pattern of the ancient Greek City States. For the Nagas, their villages were their worlds. Every village was a sovereign democratic republic with its own set of laws for the governance of the village. In Naga history, no village ever ruled over any other village or any tribe over any other tribe. In the case of India, it was in the form of Princely States. Even as late as 1947, India was comprised of five hundred sixty two Princely States. Broadly speaking, both the political and ethnic identity of the Indian citizen was then confined to the Princely State concerned. The citizens of the Princely State owed their allegiance only to the Prince or Maharaja of their State.

One cannot be too dogmatic here and insist that the Naga world and the Indian world were similar in all respects. In fact as later details will show, whatever similarities their worlds may have, the Naga worldview and the Indian worldview were poles apart. For many hundred and thousands of years, the two Naga and Indian worlds existed in their respective patterns. However, with the dawn of the modern era, drastic changes overtook the world political scenario. In the cataclysmic changes that swept over the pages of human history, old political words changed their meanings from the ancient to the modern. In the process old words with narrow meanings suddenly developed broad meanings. In many cases entirely new words also came into the fray, sometimes swallowing up many old concepts into themselves. The word "*ethnic*" is one such word, which developed a much wider meaning in the modern era. For example fifty or so years ago when a Punjabi talked about his ethnic identity he would be talking in the context of his Punjabi race, culture, and customs, etc. But now in the modern world, he has to talk in the much wider Indian context. What developed in the modern world therefore, was a dual identity. Today citizens of many modern nation-states have to live with these two identities. In my case I am an Angami by tribe, but I am also a Naga by nationality. Politically, the only way I can describe myself is to say that my ethnic identity is Angami and my national identity is Naga. Here I must remember that while I am an Angami, all Nagas are not Angamis. In the case of Indians while a Punjabi is an Indian all Indians are not Punjabis. In my case there are cultural factors that are peculiarly Angami in nature. Similarly, there are cultural factors which are peculiarly Lotha (another Naga tribe) in nature. These peculiar cultural factors are found in the form of dialect, customs, dress, mannerisms etc. However, in spite of these peculiarities, there are also common cultural factors like democratic polity, system of law, clan affiliations etc which binds the Naga family together. One can put it this way; that the "*peculiar factors*" come under ethnic identity and the "*common factors*" come under the national identity. I believe this fact is also true of the Indian Punjabi and the Indian Marathi. This fact is also true of almost all-modern nation-states in the world.

Differences in the Ethnic and National Identities of Nagas and Indians

We have just concluded that there are similarities in the patterns of the ethnic identity and national identities of both Nagas and Indians (as well as other nationalities). However, we must remember that similarity in pattern does not mean similarity in essence too. As far as the national identities of the Nagas and the Indians are concerned, they are worlds apart. What I mean is that the "*Naganess*" of a Naga is totally different from the "*Indianness*" of an Indian. Please do not get me wrong here by accusing me of racism. What I am talking about here is the national identity differences of different nations. These differences are an undeniable universal fact. It is true that at the human level, irrespective of our different nationalities, there are many common human factors that bind all human beings together into a common humanity. These common human factors are factors like a common sense of right and wrong, truth and falsehood, justice and injustice etc. At this level we are all citizens of the world and the UNO is a symbol of that common humanity. However, at the level of our ethnic and national identities, there are undeniable differences. These differences are based on historical, political, racial, cultural and religious factors. To deny their existence is to imperil our own peaceful co-existence as nations. In the case of Nagaland and India, various attempts have been made to deny the existence of these truths. Not to talk of a denial of its existence, even military force had been used to impose the Indian national identity on the Naga identity. Hence, there is political conflict between the two nations.

Therefore, in order to understand the Indo-Naga conflict, we must put these differences into black and white so that both sides know what they are talking about. Now, the Indo-Naga ethnic and national identities are different because of the following facts:

1. While racially, the Indian people mostly belong to the Dravidian and Aryan races, the Nagas in contrast belong to the Mongolian race.
2. Religion-wise, except for a very small minority of Christians and other faiths, the bulk of India's millions belong either to the Muslim faith or the Hindu faith with its multifarious offshoots like Buddhism, Jainism or Sikhism etc. By contrast, the Nagas were all formerly Animists, but are now mostly Christians. There is not a single Naga Hindu or Muslim to date.
3. In the Linguistic category too, the Indian languages belong to the Indo-European group of languages with Urdu and Sanskrit as its main languages. In contrast the great variety of Naga languages belong to the Tibeto-Burman group of languages.

Because of these striking differences in race, religion, and language, the cultural by-products and the national identities of both countries are strikingly different. Now, nobody can deny that the cultural ethos of a nation is the visible and practical expressions of a nation's "*worldview.*" A nation's worldview is in turn based on the nation's religious or philosophical beliefs. To put it in mathematical equation, it will be Religious and Philosophical beliefs + Worldview of a Nation = Cultural Ethos of a Nation. The laws of a nation and the character of a nation are all influenced and shaped by this formula. Keeping this formula in the back of our minds, let us now briefly summarise the Indian worldview and the Naga worldview.

The Differences between the Indian Worldview and the Naga Worldview

The Indian worldview: The Indian worldview has been deeply influenced by Hinduism and Islam. Islam has its different sects with slightly different theologies. On the other hand, Hinduism, besides its pantheon of gods and goddesses, also has its many offshoots like Sikhism, Jainism, Buddhism etc. In all these offshoots, there are myriads of Gurus, Monks etc. Now, nobody can deny that these religions have influenced and shaped the Indian national identity. The cultural history of India as a result of these influences has a history of Kings with divine right to rule; Brahmins with divine authority to dominate and exploit and some Emperors with no hesitation to kill anyone according to their whims.

The Naga worldview: The Naga worldview, on the contrary, was devoid of any such religious so called divine rights to dominate or rule. Prior to the coming of Christianity in the late nineteenth century, Naga conscience was the only Naga religion. In fact prior to 1875 there was not a single religious or historical manuscript in the possession of any of the Naga tribes! However, solely on the basis of the dictates of their conscience, the Naga forefathers evolved a very pure form of democracy that could put to shame many religion-influenced Democracies or Monarchies in the world. Captain Butler, the British anthropologist and soldier wrote in 1875 that the purest form of democracy exists among the Nagas. In Naga history no one has ever ruled over any other one.

As a result of these totally different worldviews, Nagas and Indians not only think differently and live differently, but they even eat differently and smell differently! (The Naga definition of meat, by the way, is "*anything that moves*!") To stretch the difference to its logical conclusion is this: An Indian culture can never produce a Naga mind neither can a Naga mind ever produce an Indian culture. What I am talking about here is not racism, but the simple yet undeniable fact of racial differences. These racial differences are a global phenomenon. It is also a biological and anthropological fact. It is therefore, both a social and scientific truth. To superimpose the Indian national identity on the Naga identity and say that they are one and the same thing is unthinkable and therefore, utterly unacceptable as far as the Nagas are concerned. Imagine what would happen if the Chinese would claim "*Africans are Chinese and Africa is China*!" No nation on earth can even imagine that such an experiment could ever be possible. "*Hindustani bhai, bhai*" (all Indians are brothers) may make sense to a Gujarati or a Marathi or a Punjabi because whatever their differences they all share a common racial, lingual, and religious background. But "*Hindustani bhai, bhai*" is total nonsense to the Nagas.

Some arrogant Indian Hindu politicians and social thinkers think that the Hindu Pantheistic umbrella can swallow up even other nations into the Indian belly. I have often sat arguing with Hindu intellectuals including Army Officers who just cannot understand why I refuse to be swallowed into what they call the Indian mainstream. They would argue "*after all the Indian nation is a multi-diverse nation of various ethnic groups, linguistic groups and religious groups.*" The fact is, whatever the multi-diversity of the Indian polity may be, I simply do not belong to any of them historically, politically, religiously or culturally.

To conclude this section, allow me to describe in a few words my political and economic status as a citizen of Nagaland. I am from Khonoma village of the Angami tribe. My political status and identity as a Naga starts from that village level. As stated earlier, here the reader must remember that every Naga village is a sovereign democratic republic with its own sets of laws governing the village. Now within the village, I belong to the Iralu clan. The Iralu clan in turn belongs to the wider clan group called the Meyasetsu clan. (The Meyasetsu clan is comprised of five minor clans). The Meyasetsu clan in turn belongs to the still wider and larger clan group called the Merhüma Khel. (The Merhüma Khel is comprised of three major clans). The Merhüma Khel in turn is one of the three major Khels that make up Khonoma village (The other two major Khels are Semoma and Thevoma). The Khonoma village in turn belongs to the Angami tribe and the Angami tribe in turn belongs to the Naga nation. My sense of political identity therefore, starts from the Iralu level to the Meyasetsu to the Merhüma to the Khonoma to the Angami and ultimately to the Naga national level. At every level of my political identity, I have hundreds of my clansmen, khelmen, village men, tribesmen and fellow Nagas who have the obligation to protect me as a Naga. I, in turn owe the same obligation and allegiance to all these levels of my political identity. This is how the Nagas, though they are a very small nation, had defied the mighty British Empire for over a century and India for over half a century. In actual political reality, no Naga stands alone. Hence, if any foreigner harms a Naga, they will find themselves pursued by hundreds of the victim's clansmen crying for their blood! Land ownership of an individual also spreads across all these various levels of clan, Khel, village and tribal lands. The Naga sense of both political and economic sovereignty exists and functions in this way. Every Naga therefore, is a man with many clansmen and many lands. In conclusion, if I were to write all my affiliated surnames it would go like this: Kaka Iralu, Meyasetsu, Merhüma, Khonoma, Angami, and Naga.

As far as I am concerned, these ethnic and national identities are precious to me. They in fact define my political existence as a man with a country to call his own. As such I can never surrender this birthright to India or any other nation on earth.

SECTION–II

A Brief History of the Development of Ethnic Groups into Multi-Ethnic Nations States (13th-20th Century)

The process of the formation of ethnic groups begins with a single-family unit. With the passage of time the descendants or offspring of this one single-family unit develop into clans. With further passage of time, these various clans merge themselves into tribes. Tribes, in turn, form themselves into nations as history progresses. This multiplication of families into clans into tribes and on to nations may take hundreds of years. This process is a universal phenomenon that applies to every nation inhabiting the planet earth. Here, the Bible provides the clearest answer to this universal phenomenon. The Bible states that the history of humankind began with the creation of Adam and Eve, the first male and female of the human species. From these two first human beings, the nations of the earth evolved through the passage of human history.

There are also of course other so called scientific and mythological theories about the origin of man and nations, but none of them conform to historical reality as we know it. On the one hand, Darwin's theory of evolution remains unproven even after 150 years of extensive scientific research. On the other hand, mythological theories of man, having crawled out of caves or from stones or trees or the sea are matters of pure fiction and superstition. An investigation into past human history reveals that the evolution of nations follows the pattern mentioned above. For example, today's modern German nation-state evolved from the Germanic tribes of past history. Similarly, the modern nation-state of Great Britain is a conglomeration of various ethnic groups like the Iberians, Celts, Nordic tribes and Anglo Saxons etc. of past history. In fact all modern nations were formerly savage tribes and head hunters! It is also a universal fact that in ancient time and even as late as the twentieth century, nations were mostly ruled by Kings and Monarchies. Today with the exception of a few kingdoms most nations follow the modern nation-state pattern. The Nagas, with the exception of some Chieftain systems like the Konyaks and the Semas, never had any King to whom they bowed. When the British first encountered them and asked them about their King, they thrust their spears into the ground and said: *That is our King.*

In the modern era of human history a new phenomenon overtook the human race in the form of the formation of modern nation-states. The history of this new phenomenon will be briefly outlined here tracing its history right up to the point where it also overtook both Nagaland and India in the late 1940s. In this new development, different and even diverse ethnic groups began to merge together to form new nation-states. It is difficult to pinpoint one single event in history as the søle cause for this new development. However, in the Western world, this phenomenon began to develop towards the beginning of the thirteenth century with the signing of the Magna Carta in 1215. In this epochal event, the paramount authority of the King of England (John) was curtailed by the English Nobles. This event paved the way for Constitutional form of Government. Following a series of similar changes in France, Italy, Germany etc., by the end of the First World War in 1918, the concept of modern nation-states under Constitutional form of Government was firmly established in the Western world. By the end of the Second World War in 1945, this phenomenon had become a global reality effecting even Asia and Africa. One important factor to be noted here is the fact that beginning from the Sixteenth century and on to the first half of the twentieth century, for nearly five centuries, the Western world marched out from their cities and forts to conquer and rule most of Asia, Africa, the two Americas, Australasia and the South Pacific. Along with these conquests, the concept of modern nation-states and Constitutional form of Government came with these Western conquerors. The Western nations owe the insights and principles of this modern nation-state concept to Martin Luther's reformation of the sixteenth century. In this reformation, besides the religious reformation of salvation through Christ and not the Church (Papacy), Martin Luther also set the ordinary citizen free from the clutches of the political powers of both the King and the Pope. The new political development that emerged was "*sphere sovereignty.*" Sphere sovereignty was founded on the Biblical principle that the state was divinely instituted by God to control and curb the evil actions (lawlessness) of fallen men. However, sphere sovereignty also brought into glaring focus the fact that the laws of the state are not sovereign in themselves, but subject to the sovereignty and authority of God who is the ultimate lawgiver of the universe. Under Martin Luther's reformation, everything under heaven—the King, the law, the state, the church and every citizen within the state was brought under the sovereignty of God. "*Coram Deo*" the Latin words meaning "*in the face of God*" was the catchword of the reformation. In this way, every facet of human existence was brought under the sovereignty of God.

The founders of the American Republic of 1776 incorporated these concepts into their Constitution by clearly defining the separate powers of the Judiciary, the Legislature and the Executive. This model was based on the Biblical teaching that God is our Judge, Lawgiver and King (Isaiah 33:22). What emerged was a Government of the people by the people, and for the people based on the rule of law which was in turn based on the word of God—the lawgiver. Martin Luther's Bible-based reformation thoughts were further developed by Christian intellectuals like John Calvin in the sixteenth century and Samuel Rutherford in the seventeenth century. Samuel Rutherford wrote Lex Rex which means Law is King. Samuel Rutherford's main thesis in Lex Rex was that the rule of law (rather then the law of the ruler) was supreme. He was asserting that the law stands even above the King and that the King is also subject to it like all other citizens. All these preparatory steps and the subsequent events of Western imperialism from the sixteenth century to the first half of the twentieth century eventually led to an explosion of modern nation-states in Asia and Africa by the end of the Second World War. In today's Eastern world of modern nation-states, whether we acknowledge it or not, it is still an undeniable fact that our Constitutions are based on Biblical principles which have their roots in the great Protestant reformation of Martin Luther in the sixteenth century.

Acknowledging this fact of the dominance of the Western and Bible-based British common laws in the Constitution of India, noted Indian Jurist, Nani Palkhivala wrote thus in his book: Let us not pretend that the rule of law is a concept which can be regarded as a part of the Indian psyche (*We the People*, p. 212). The fact is, no such concept of the rule of law exists anywhere in the *Vedas*, *Upanishads*, *Ramayana*, *Mahabharata*, the *Bhagavad Gita* or the *Puranas*.

SECTION–III

The Development of the Concept of Modern Nation-States in Nagaland and India in the Twentieth Century

Prior to 1947, neither Nagaland nor India were independent sovereign states in the pattern of modern nation-states. Nagaland was then a country of more than fifty-four tribes with the British having suzerainty over only eight tribes. India, on the other hand, was then a sub-continent of five hundred sixty two autonomous princely states besides the provinces under British rule. The spirit of nationalism that swept across Asia and Africa in the twentieth century affected Nagaland and India only in the earlier half of the twentieth century. This spirit of nationalism took some concrete shape and direction for both Nagaland and India only in the 1920's. Now, some Indian historians would argue that the Indian independence movement started from the Sepoy Mutiny of 1857. This assertion is disputed as exaggeration of actual historical facts by historians, many of them Indian. We will come to these details later on. For the moment, we will separate the two country's historical developments. In the case of Nagaland, we will begin with a brief account of Naga history.

The Development of Ethnicity to Nationality in Naga History

Ancient Naga history—The Nagas are an ancient people whose forefathers migrated into their present habitat from Central Asia. Their forefathers belonged to the Sino-Mongoloid race that came in waves from South-East Asia in the B.C. era. Their entry points to their present lands were through the Himalayan region and the Burmese corridor. Their forefathers migrated from Mongolia in 2617 B.C. and after migrating across Turkistan, Tibet and Mongolia, they finally arrived in Eastern Yunan Province of China in 1385 B.C. Many of them again migrated from China and entered South-east Asia and on to their present habitat in 1225 B.C. Whether in historical records or oral traditions passed from one generation to the other through word of mouth, there is no mention whatsoever of the Nagas driving away some former inhabitants of the land to make the lands their own. The fact is one where their forefathers, like any other nations in the world, at some specific time in history migrated from more populated regions of the Asian continent and settled down in their present lands and made it their land. Their continuity as a people inhabiting their present lands is an established historical fact. In historical records, the first mention of the Nagas as a people inhabiting their present lands was made by Claudius Ptolemy, the Greek historian and geographer in AD 150. In his records Ptolemy mentions the Nagas as Nagaloi [Claudius Ptolemy, *Geographia,* Vol. VII, (ii), p. 18]. They were again mentioned by Hiuen Tsang, the Chinese traveller who spent 15 years in India between AD 629-645. Hiuen Tsang visited Kamrup the capital of the Varman King, Bhaskar Varman in AD 643. From Kamrup in Assam, in his accounts "*Si-Yu-Ki*" he writes about the Nagas saying: The east of this country is bounded by a line of hills, so that, there is no great city to the kingdom. The frontiers are contiguous to the barbarians of South-west China. These tribes are in fact akin to those of the Man people in their customs. (Thomas Watters, *On Yuan Chwang's Travel in India*, Vol. III, Part II, Varanasi,

1903, p. 11) Quoted in Visier Sanyü, *A History of Nagas and Nagaland*, p. 7.

Besides these records, the Nagas are also mentioned in the Royal chronicles of the Manipur kingdom in records like Chietharol Kumbabu and Ningthourol Kumbabu (AD 663-763 and AD 906-996). They are also mentioned in the chronicles of the Ahom kings who came from upper Burma and the Western Unan provinces of China and settled and ruled in Assam for 600 years beginning from the thirteenth century. Naga resistance against intrusions and raids from these two neighbouring kingdoms and also other kingdoms like the Burmese, Tripuris, Dimashas and the Cachar kingdoms from the thirteenth century to the eighteenth centuries are all there in recorded history. As for their encounter with the British in the nineteenth century and their resistance against British rule for one hundred fifteen years (1832-1947), numerous accounts are found in the British colonial records. It is said that the battles the British fought with the Naga tribes in the nineteenth and first half of the twentieth centuries far outnumber all the frontier battles fought with the Indians in the great Indian sub-continent. Even in spite of all these battles, the British were able to subjugate only thirty per cent of actual Naga territory. (The actual Naga ancestral domain would be around 120,000 sq. km). In British colonial accounts, the unconquered 70 per cent territories of the Nagas were recorded as unadministered territories or excluded area. Even in the thirty per cent lands that the British administered, they never laid any claims to the lands they were administering. In fact C.V. Aitchinson in Treaties, Engagements and Sanads clearly records that: No written treaties or agreements have been made with any of the Naga tribes. (Vol. XII, 1931, p. 91). Also following the submission of the Naga memorandum to the Simon Commission in 1929, where the Nagas had refused to be included in the reformed scheme of India, the British Government in recognition of their demands put the Naga Hills under excluded area in the Government of India Act, 1935.

Modern Naga history—The submission of the Naga memorandum to the Simon Commission in 1929 by the Naga Club was in a sense the first Naga action in the transition from Naga ethnic identity to Naga national identity and ultimately towards the realisation of a modern Naga nation-state. The Naga Club was formed in 1920 by the Nagas who had returned from their First World War experience in Europe. By February 2, 1946, the Naga Club of 1910 had metamorphosed into the Naga National Council (NNC). One of the first important actions, taken by the NNC was to submit a memorandum to the British Cabinet Mission which came to India in 1946 in the light of the impending transfer of power between India and Britain. In the memorandum, the NNC declared that the future of the Nagas would not be bound by any arbitrary decisions of the departing British Government if such decisions were taken without the prior information and approval of the Naga people. This memorandum was submitted to the Cabinet Mission on April 9, 1946. This was followed by the submission of another memorandum to the outgoing British Government and the incoming Indian Government, entitled Memorandum of the case of the Naga people for self-determination and an appeal to Her Majesty's Government and the Government of India. This memorandum was submitted on March 27, 1947. Copies of the same memorandum were also sent to Clement Atlee, the then Prime Minister of Britain, Members of the House of Lords and also Winston Churchill. Getting no favourable response from either the British Government or the Indian Government, the NNC next met Lord Mountbatten, the then Governor-General of India with the proposal that the new Indian Government act as the guardian power for a period of ten years after which the Nagas would be free to determine their own political future. (Full contents of all these lengthy memorandums can be found in the appendix section of my book: Nagaland and India, the Blood and the Tears with a sub title A historical account of the fifty two year Indo-Naga war and the story of those who were never allowed to tell it, five hundred forty three pages. The book was clandestinely published by me since no publication company was willing to take the risk of publishing it).

Meanwhile, a British scheme of forming an independent North-East Agency on the pattern of a Crown Colony comprising all the eastern peoples between Burma and India was offered to the Nagas. If the Nagas had accepted this scheme, a British Crown Colony with over 200,000 sq. km could have come into existence with Chittagong as its sea outlet. The colony would be comprised of people like the Nagas, Kachins, Karens, Mons, Shans, Khasis, Assamese, Mizos etc.—a people who were then more devoted to the British than their own citizens. The lands were also very rich in oil and other mineral deposits. If the Nagas had acted selfishly, they could easily have gotten the lion's share in such a scheme. Knowing that the Nagas were politically the most advanced tribe, this scheme was thoroughly discussed with the NNC leadership during its formative years. However, the NNC leadership rejected this offer on the grounds that they could not betray the eastern peoples right to their respective freedoms. It was evident that a "*Yes*" from the Nagas could have resulted in all the eastern peoples being condemned to many years of subjecthood to a British

Crown Colony. Another obvious reason was the Naga love of their own freedom, which they were sure the British would not treacherously betray into the hands of the new emerging Indian Government.

Subsequent events would however show that the Naga sense of integrity and honesty and also the recognition of other people's rights would be betrayed and trampled by both Britain and India.

Besides these events, many other important representations and actions were made by the NNC and the Nagas to clearly declare and demonstrate their political will to become a free nation again when the British left their South Asian Empire. Up to 1947 six different memorandums and representations were given to the British Government before they handed over power to India. One possible reason for the apathy and indifference shown to the Nagas by the British may be because of their rejection of the British Crown Colony scheme. Or perhaps Britain was too exhausted from the Second World War and the mood of the British was to retreat homeward from their empire. What was so desperately important for the newly emerging Naga people did not impinge on a people weary of their world responsibilities. They left behind a legacy Nagas could not accept. In turn, their later rejection of the legacy produced the Indo-Naga conflict.

As for India, the NNC made many representations to the Indian leaders before India became a free nation on 15th August, 1947. Among those many representations and actions, when the Indian Constituent Assembly constituted a Sub Committee for the North-East region in 1946, the then NNC President T. Aliba walked out from the meeting at Shillong saying: We the Nagas cannot sign our names to be under India. He further said, I cannot return to my people as a traitor. Saying thus, he resigned from the committee and came back to Nagaland. At that time the NNC had a Constitution of their own and refused to be under any other Constitution. Even when the Constituent Assembly Sub-Committee again visited Kohima in May 1947, the NNC still refused to join the Indian Union. In that confrontation in 1947, the NNC stated its position that it was willing to co-operate with India only under the ten-year period of an interim agreement, details of which had earlier been submitted to Her Majesty's Government and the Indian Government on March 27, 1947.

A further proposal was offered by the Governor of Assam, Akbar Hydari, called the Nine Point Agreement on June 27, 1947. However, even though the NNC was willing to co-operate with India under the provisions of the Nine Point Agreement, a dispute arose over the ninth point as to whether Nagas could choose their own political destiny at the end of the ten-year agreement. The proposal was later unilaterally abrogated by India. The NNC next met Mahatma Gandhi on July 19, 1947 at Bhangi Basti in Delhi. After a thorough discussion of all the political and historical facts about Nagaland and India, Gandhi assured the Naga delegation that Nagas had every right to be a sovereign independent nation. Gandhi even promised the Nagas that in case the Indian Government tried to forcefully annex the Naga territories into India, he would be the first person to lay down his life in opposing the annexation.

Assured by the father of the Indian nation, the Nagas came back and declared their independence on 14th August, 1947—one day prior to India's declaration of her own independence. A cable was also immediately sent to the United Nations on the same day and an acknowledgement was received from Salt Lake, New York. In order to further consolidate their intention in the light of India's indifference, the NNC further conducted a national Plebiscite on 16th May, 1951 where an overwhelming majority of the adult Naga population (99.9%) gave their verdict that they would not join the Indian Union of 1947. Prior to the Plebiscite, information and invitations were also given to the Indian Government to come and see the conduct of the Plebiscite with their own eyes. India never responded to the invitation. The result of the Plebiscite was sent to both the Indian Government as well as the United Nations. The result of the Plebiscite along with a long letter was given to Jawaharlal Nehru on December 29, 1951. In the letter Phizo, the NNC President had written:

> ...With the verdict of the Naga adult population embodied in the Plebiscite papers go our sincere feeling of goodwill to the Government and people of India. It is the prayer of the Naga people that the Government of India will respect the desire of the Naga people for having their own independent state, separate and sovereign. To allay the fear and suspicion of India, Nagas on their part will agree to accept an Indian national to be the President of independent Nagaland for a stated period...

(Please note that, the Nagas far from trying to violently oppose India, offered themselves to be even governed by an Indian President for a stated period. This was in 1951. The Nagas took up arms to defend themselves only when, as B.N. Mullik put it in his book: troops moved into Tuensang by October 1955, and the war (*of invasion*) with the Nagas started from then). Italics mine.

When the NNC leaders later met Jawaharlal Nehru at Delhi on March

11, 1952, in the short interview given to them, Nehru banged his fist on the table and screamed:

> Whether heaven falls or India goes to pieces and blood runs red in the country, I don't care. Whether I am here or any other body comes in, I don't care. Nagas will never be allowed to become independent.

Phizo, leading the delegation, replied: "Well, Pandit Nehru, you seem to know even more than God about our future. Goodbye." The delegation returned to face the might of the Indian Army, which Nehru sent to suppress the Nagas. The Nagas on their part, in order to consolidate their position and also in accordance with legal norms of establishing a modern nation-state, established the Naga Supreme Court on July 4, 1954. On January 14, 1956, the Naga Constitution (Yehzabo) was approved and on March 22, 1956, the Federal Government of Nagaland was established. On the part of India, by November 15, 1954, Assam Armed Police and other Paramilitary Forces like the Assam Rifles had started killing innocent Naga civilians. This was followed by full-fledged Indian military troops moving into Nagaland by October, 1955.

To cut a long story short, I will here again quote B.N. Mullik who was then the Personal Secretary of Nehru.

> ...Troops moved into Tuensang by October, 1955 and the war with the Nagas started from then...

About the number of troops deployed at this stage he writes:

> ...Ultimately nearly two divisions of the Army and thirty five battalions of the Assam Rifles or Armed Police were in operation in the Naga Hills and Tuensang Frontier Division and in the adjoining areas...and though there were nearly one security troop for every adult male Naga in the Naga Hills Tuensang area, there never was a time when it could be claimed that the Naga guerrillas had been broken into submission...
> (B.N. Mullik, *My Years With Nehru*, 1948-1964, Allied Publishers, India, pp. 308, 312, 313)

These Indian troops (fifty four thousand in total) between 1955 to 1956, burnt down to ashes six hundred forty five Naga villages out of eight hundred sixty one Naga villages existing in those days. All the village granaries were also burned to ashes and within one year over one lakh Nagas died from bullets, aerial bombardments, rape, torture, murder, starvation and disease.

On June 30, 1956, a totally devastated Phizo through his Ministers (Kilonsers) sent a long and desperate message to the Prime Minister of India. I quote here a few excerpts from that letter:

> ...People are being killed without ceasing. Houses and villages are being burned daily. What justifiable necessity impelled the Indian Congress Government in directing the Indian Army to start killing our Naga people and burning all our houses, we do not know. If these barbarous cruelties are meant to compel the Nagas to accept the Constitution of India and be a member unit within the Indian Union, these acts of conscience-less inhumanity are highly improper. Village after village—has been surrounded and the people compelled to give their fingerprints as a token of loyalty to India and acceptance of the Constitution of India. Nagas as a people and the Naga Government strongly condemn your policy now being put into practice in Nagaland.
>
> Our Naga position must be understood. Naga people made the position of our country very clear to the Government of India from the very inception of the emancipation of the Indians and the starting of the Government of Free India. Nagaland belongs to the Nagas only and nobody else. We cannot feel ashamed to state this simple fact, or be frightened to stand on our national rights and defend our honour.
>
> We wanted to part in a most friendly atmosphere with your goodwill, but failed. The controlling reasons for the Nagas to remain as a distinct nation, and thus enjoy national independence, need not be explained to the most eminent champion for the freedom of the dominated people and nations in Asia and Africa. The great author of "*Discovery of India*" and of "*Glimpses of World History*" knows that the Nagas are no more a peculiar people or unreasonable than any other virile nation.
>
> We should not be misunderstood. And your great Government should not attempt to make this simple issue of the Naga case as having political or constitutional complications with the Republic of India.
>
> You knew very well that Nagas did not participate in the Indian

> election. Your Government have been fully informed of our Naga position, either by telegram or through letters, on all the appropriate occasions.
> Firstly, Nagas are not Indians, and we do not want to become Indians.
> Secondly, Naga territory is not and has never been a part of the Indian territory. And we cannot give you our country. This is the actual position...
> ...If the Congress Indian Government is determined to wipe out the Nagas from the face of this earth, WHAT CAN WE DO? You have the capacity to do so. But is not killing people a horrible thing to do in spite of disagreement with you? Is it not contemptible to resort to terrorism for the usurpation of other people's land? The ORDER TO KILL TEN MEN in each village, and to wipe out big villages, have been already made known to the Nagas...
> ...The ORDER and directives for DECIMATION and ANNIHILATION must be immediately called off, without delay. Bombardment with 3-inch mortar shells against our people's camps and people in the fields continues daily. Shelling the villages with cannon (type EXR.CE 9719. C.Co/2/44) started on June 28, 1956. All these must be stopped.
> If killing the people, sniping the workers in the fields of cultivation, raping and molesting women and girls, and burning houses and villages are stopped, YOU MAY BE SURE that our Naga people, and our Home Guards, will full heartedly respond in real faith, as these are what we are against.
> We are wholly and absolutely at your mercy. And, in the name of humanity, we submit this appeal to you to stop tears and bloodshed...
> (An appeal to the Prime Minister, India, Urra Headquarters, June 30, 1956)

What happened afterwards is a story of blood and tears, sacrifices and heroism as a small nation fought against overwhelming odds for over half a century. As for A.Z. Phizo who wrote all the above words, he was first offered the Chief Ministership of Assam. When he refused, he was next offered to become a Minister in the Central Cabinet. This was followed by another offer to become the Ambassador to Malaya. He was next offered to ask anything from the Indian Government including any amount of money. This offer was brought by Shri Prakasa, the then Minister of Natural Resources and Scientific Research. Phizo in his letter to S.C. Jamir from London dated October 31, 1963 wrote that he declined all these offers because he loved the Naga people more than anything else in the world. (S.C. Jamir, *Reminiscences of Correspondences with A.Z. Phizo*, p. 21). When all these efforts to buy the Nagas with money failed, the Indian Government tried to militarily impose Indian nationality on the Nagas. When even this failed, the Indian Government again offered Phizo to become the next President of India in the early 1960s. Full details and a systematically chronicled account of many of the above stated facts can be found in the afore-mentioned book written by the author of the present article.

The Development of Ethnicity to Nationality in Indian History

It is not within the scope of this chapter to give even a summary of the ancient history of India stretching to over five thousand years. We can therefore, only begin with the colonial British period for the purpose of our analysis. It must however be noted here that the development of ethnicity to nationality in India also began only during the colonial British period. This development began with A.O. Hume when he started the Indian National Congress in 1885. But though A.O. Hume had started the Indian National Congress in 1885, it took almost thirty years for true Indian nationalism to take root in Indian hearts. One possible reason for this very slow development of Indian nationalism may be because of the fact that prior to 1885, for more than four thousand years, the Brahmins of India had kept all of India's intellectual, philosophical and scientific knowledge locked away in the Sanskrit language and texts. All the repository of Indian literature, science, medicine, law and religion were kept locked away within the Brahmanical sect. The Brahmins monopolised all these knowledge through the caste system by making it a sin for other lower caste to read or understand the Sanskrit language. Had it not been for nineteenth century Christian missionaries like William Carey and Alexander Duff, the Indian masses would still have been denied their own history and achievements even in the nineteenth century. Christian missionaries like William Carey, Alexander Duff and many others translated these sacred Sanskrit and Urdu texts into English and threw open India's past greatness to the Indian masses. As one Indian Christian writer, Vishal Mangalwadi had argued in his book India, the Grand Experiment, long before the British colonisation of India, the Brahmins had for centuries so colonised the Indian mind that the seeds of freedom, progress and development could not sprout and grow.

I personally believe that had this reservoir of Indian knowledge been released even a thousand years earlier, perhaps India and not Europe or the West might have led humanity's march into the modern world. After all it is partly true that while the Europeans were still nomads, the Indian mind had already analysed metaphysics to a very high level. The Indian zero (0) was also already in Indian mathematics from that time. (Unfortunately the Brahmin caste strangulation of Indian society was so complete, India stayed stagnant within this great zero for centuries!) Coming back to the British colonial era, the Indian Congress was from the beginning, ridden with suspicions and prejudices of high caste and low caste feelings. The *Dalits* and the Muslims were always suspicious of the Hindu hierarchy that dominated the Indian National Congress. As a result of all these suspicions and prejudices, even though the British had by August 20, 1917 promised Indian self-rule, even as late as November 11, 1917 the Indian National Congress was expressing its full loyalty and support to the British Government. These facts and resolutions can be found in their November 20, 1917 meetings in Bombay. There were of course some extremist and violent nationalist movements prior to 1917 in the persons of people like the Chapker brothers, Savarkar and Bal Gangadhar Tilak etc. These movements were however confined to Hindu religious groups rather then a universal Indian national movement.

No doubt, the early sparks of the development from ethnicity to nationality in India, had begun with the likes of Bipin Chander Pal and Gangadhar Tilak, but it took Mahatma Gandhi to awaken India to a consciousness of her national soul. Things began to move with vision and direction only when Mohandas Karamchand Gandhi came back to India in 1914. However, here too it took many years for India to come to a clear stand for the demand of sovereignty and independence. The first great movement was launched by Gandhi in 1921 in the form of the Non-Co-operation Movement. But this mass movement was suddenly withdrawn in 1922 after the incident of Chauri Chaura in Uttar Pradesh. And though the movement continued through radical nationalists like Ram Prasad Bismil, Bhagat Singh etc., the national movement in a mass manner picked up momentum again only in 1930. This came in the form of the Civil Disobedience Movement. However, in spite of all the Round Table Conferences from 1930 to 1931, the momentum was once again dropped in 1933 when the movement was again suspended. It was only nine years later in 1942, that on July 14, the Quit India Movement was finally and decisively launched. This final decision and mass movement finally led to the Indian Independence Act of July 18, 1947, and the declaration of India's independence on 15th August, 1947.

Some Interesting Observations in the Naga and Indian Journeys from Ethnicity to Nationality

1. Both Nagas and Indians were ruled by the British imperial power in modern history. The national souls of both the nations were awakened by this British rule. In the case of Nagaland, their first encounter with the British imperial might was in 1832, when Captain Jenkins and Pemberton marched across Naga country from the Manipur kingdom to the Assam kingdom *via* Zeliangrong and Angami regions. The British came with seven hundred troops and eight hundred coolies. This first British expedition into Naga country was met with fierce resistance from the Angamis and Zeliangrongs and the British lost several soldiers and many were injured. The Angamis and Zeliangrongs too suffered heavy casualties in this, their first encounter with guns. After this initial survey expedition, many other military excursions were undertaken by the British to subdue the Nagas. But in all these excursions, all the various Naga tribes relentlessly fought the British intrusion from 1832 to 1881. Khonoma village alone fought the British for thirty-five intermittent years (1845-1880). After the verbal peace treaty of Khonoma on 27th March, 1880, the British were able to control about thirty per cent of Naga territory from 1880-1947. This sixty-seven years of British suzerainty over thirty per cent of Naga territories, was however, interspersed with many confrontations against the British administration. As for the seventy per cent Naga territories that remained outside the British administered area, they continued hostile activities against British administrators up to 1947. Many punitive raids also had to be carried out by the British into these unadministered areas throughout their suzerainty over the thirty per cent Naga territories for sixty-seven years. In the light of these facts, it can be said that the Nagas defied British rule for one hundred fifteen years in the nineteenth and twentieth centuries (1832-1947). The primary concern of the British throughout their many years of Anglo-Naga association was to protect their subjects in Manipur and Assam from the marauding raids of the Nagas.

In the case of India, the British entered the Indian sub-continent from the early part of the seventeenth century (1611). In the first British victory,

Bombay surrendered to the British East India Company in 1668. By 1757, in the battle of Plassey, Robert Clive with nine hundred British soldiers backed by one thousand five hundred Indian mercenaries routed the Nawab's Army of over sixty thousand soldiers. Following this victory, Robert Clive colonised a population that was larger than England. From the battle of Plassey the British went on to rule the whole of India for over two hundred years.

2. The first Naga defence of their land against British intrusion was in 1832. This preceded the Indian Mutiny of 1857 by twenty five years. Anywhere the British stepped into Naga territory they were consistently met with Naga hostility and defence until 1880 (or as stated earlier up to 1947).

3. The Naga Club was formed in 1920, after the First World War. This was done solely on Naga initiative alone. In 1929, the Club submitted the important Naga memorandum to the British Simon Commission. In April 1946 C.R. Pawsey, the Deputy Commissioner of the Naga Hills, established the Naga Hills District Tribal Council (NHDTC) to help the Nagas to rebuild their Second World War devastated economy and villages. Within nine months, on February 2, 1946, the members of the NHDTC had transformed themselves into the Naga National Council (NNC). The NNC, besides, the numerous important memorandums submitted to the outgoing British Government and the incoming Indian Government, went on to declare Naga independence on 14th August, 1947, and also conducted the Naga Plebiscite on 16th May, 1951. By July 26, 1960, its President A.Z. Phizo, after escaping the Indian dragnet was addressing the world press in London on the atrocities committed by the Indian Army on sovereign independent Nagaland.

On the part of India, though as early as 1885, A.O. Hume had established the Indian National Congress in order to train Indian intellectuals to give them political and administrative training in self-governance, it took until 1931 (forty five years later) for Mahatma Gandhi to finally reach London to attend the Second Round Table Conference. In fact there were many opportunities for India to have gotten her independence even as early as the end of the First World War. The British Government's post- First World War intentions had been clearly stated by Secretary of State for India, Edwin Montagu on August 20, 1917. This was followed by the Government of India Act 1919. Had India seized these opportunities in a united way, she could have gotten her independence three decades earlier then August, 1947. At the risk of blowing our own trumpet too loudly and also at the risk of offending some of my genuine Indian friends, I have made these comparative observations. However, I have done it because I have met too many arrogant Indians who think their own history is glorious as compared to ours.

SECTION–IV

Towards a Resolution of the Fifty-Four Year Indo-Naga Conflict

In this solution-seeking section, I want to state the Naga position regarding their right to sovereignty and independence very clearly. Here, I do not need to say anything about Indian independence because India has already achieved her Independence on 15th August, 1947. The two nations—Nagaland and India—though incomparable in size and population awoke to their respective national destinies at more or less the same period of history. It took both the nations many years to evolve from ethnic backgrounds into multi-ethnic nations. However, the tragedy for Nagaland was that, India, that giant nation on receiving her freedom after two hundred years of humiliation, turned and trampled her tiny neighbour Nagaland into the dust. Today Nagaland's cry for freedom and Nagaland's rainbow and star (national flag) lies crumpled and blood soaked in the battlefields of the fifty-four year Indo-Naga war. Compared to India's national martyrs of a few thousands, more than two hundred thousand Naga martyrs lie fallen in the various battlefields stretching to over half a century. But Nagaland has not suffered alone. India too has paid a terrible price both in loss of human lives and financial expenditures. This war must end, but it will never end as long as India refuses to recognise Nagaland's right to her own sovereignty. So, here then is a summary of what Nagas believe to be their national and geographical rights which can never be surrendered.

The Naga Lands and the Naga Rights

No nation on earth, no individual in human history has come into existence without a concrete geographical reference point. This is to say no nation on earth, no individual in the world has fallen into earth from outer space. All political histories of every nation have their origin from some concrete geographical lands. Within the boundaries of this geographical land the people of the land develop their national identity, their cultural identity and their political identity. The inhabitants of the land call the land their land. The Nagas, like any other nations on earth, call their geographical land Nagaland. Corresponding to this fact, there is a geographical land called Britain for the British, a geographical Russia for the Russians and a geographical India for the Indians. The Nagas on their part are not covetous of even an inch of anybody else's lands.

But by a tragic twist of history, Nagaland in the twentieth century was severed in two through a treacherous betrayal by the British Government. Burma was gifted with half, and the other half fell under Indian dominion. Those areas that fell under Indian territory were further subdivided into four fragments, namely—Assam, Manipur, Arunachal Pradesh and Nagaland. Thus, within the Indian territory, large chunks of Naga lands and Naga people were put into three other states against the wishes of the Nagas. This was done to reduce the Naga political issue to the smallest possible geographical area. The present Indian State of Nagaland is comprised of only 16,557 sq. kms with a population of hardly over two million people. However, in actual fact, the greater Nagaland including those areas in Myanmar is comprised of over 1,20,000 sq. kms. This area is located at 25° 60′ and 27° 40′ latitude North of equator and between the longitudinal lines 93° 20′E and 95° 15′E. The total population of the entire Naga people of the actual Nagaland would be about four million. Thus, the actual Naga territory for which all Nagas have been fighting for, for all these fifty years is almost five times the size of Israel with a population of about four million people.

Throughout their history the Nagas had defended their lands against foreign invaders and aggressors. As far as her relationship with her neighbour India is concerned, prior to 1947, not to talk of Indian Kings or Princes having ruled the Nagas, no Indian King or Prince had ever even set foot on Naga territories. Also, prior to 1947, Nagas had no affinity with India whether racially, historically, politically, culturally, religiously or any other wise. Therefore, Nagaland is not part of Indian Territory neither are Nagas Indians. Another point to be noted in this connection is that since all Naga territories never came under British suzerainty, the British had absolutely no right to hand over such territories to India or Burma after their departure from their South Asian empire in 1947. Similarly, India or Burma also has absolutely no legal right to claim these territories as their territories.

Even Jawaharlal Nehru understood this fact very clearly. On August 19, 1946, in connection with the proposed British Crown Colony plan, he described the Naga territories as:

> The tribal areas are defined as being those long frontiers of India which are neither part of India nor Burma, nor of Indian States nor of any foreign power.
> (Quoted from Phizo's letter to Rajiv Gandhi, May 10, 1986, p. 6)

How these long stretches of frontiers (which were neither Burmese nor Indian territories) could simply disappear into India and Burma after 1947 is the issue that has caused the fifty four year Indo-Naga war. What Nagas have been asserting and fighting for, for fifty years is exactly what Nehru had described. When we say, we are Nagas and not Indians, we also mean we are neither Burmese nor Russians nor Africans; for our people and our land had never belonged to India or Burma or any "*other foreign power.*"

As far as the Nagas under Indian dominion are concerned, Nagaland is not in India, but India is presently in Nagaland by invasion and subjugation. All these historical and political facts showing that Nagas were not Indians and would not join the Indian Union were conveyed to India, Britain and the world by the Nagas long before the emergence of the present Indian Union in 1947. Also when India and Britain did not take notice of these communications, the Nagas declared their independence on 14th August, 1947—one day prior to India's declaration of her own independence.

The Nagas have been waging a war of self-defence for their geographical land for the past fifty-four years with India and Myanmar. This is because this land is their land and they want to live in their land without fear or domination as free citizens of a free country. The Nagas are fighting for their lands because they have no other lands on the whole face of the earth besides these 1,20,000 sq. kms. Therefore, the question of surrender or retreat or migration to another country does not arise simply because they have no other land on the whole face of this planet earth. To retreat or run away from their land and occupy another land would be to claim other people's land as their own. Hence, the Nagas have no alternative, but to stand and fight, even if to do so, could mean sure death. They have been fighting against India and Myanmar with courage born of desperation and against overwhelming odds for half a century.

Nagas not secessionist:

Contrary to India's allegations, the Nagas neither consider it

> criminal nor their actions unlawful activities when they fight in self-defence for their sovereignty. The Nagas had never volitionally joined the Indian Union when it was offered to them prior to 1947. Their acts of self-defence are therefore, not acts of secession. They are also neither guilty of breaking any Indian laws and thus deserving to be branded as perpetrators of unlawful activities by the Indian Government. As far as the Nagas are concerned the defence of their motherland is a moral and political duty. They owe it to themselves and their children and all future generations of Nagas to defend their God apportioned land with all their strength and might.

For them not to do so is tantamount to reducing themselves to refugees without a country to call as their own.

Hence, they can never surrender their lands to India or Myanmar or any other nations on earth. India on her part must understand that Nagas are not secessionists or terrorists. The Nagas have absolutely no ill intentions of trying to destabilise India or create any problems for India. On their part they want to live in Peace with India as the most friendly neighbour.

References

Ao, Tajen, 1993, *British Occupation of Naga Country*, Naga Literature Society, Nagaland.

Colson, Charles and Pearcey, Nancy, 1999, *How Now Shall We Live*?, Tyndale House Publishers, Inc., London.

Elwin, Verrier, *The Nagas in the Nineteenth Century*, Oxford University Press, London, 1969.

Jamir, S.C., 1998, *Reminiscences of Correspondences with A.Z. Phizo.*

Iralu, Kaka D., 2000, *Nagaland and India, The Blood and the Tears*, Kohima, Nagaland.

Iralu, Kaka D., 2001, *How Then Shall We Live*?, N.V. Press, Kohima, Nagaland.

Langer, William L., 2000, *An Encyclopaedia of World History*, Surjeet Publications, Kamla Nagar, Delhi.

Mahajan, V.D., 1960, *Ancient India*, S. Chand & Company Ltd., Ram Nagar, New Delhi.

Mangalwadi, Vishal, 1996, *Missionary Controversy, Letters to a Post Modern Indian*, Nivedit Good Books Distributors, U.P., India.

Mangalwadi, Vishal, 1997, *India the Grand Experiment*, Pippa Ran Books, U.K.

Mullik, B.N., 1972, *My Years With Nehru, 1948-1964*, Allied Publishers, India.

Palkhivala, Nani A., 1994, *We the Nation, The Lost Decades*, UBS Publishers Distributors Ltd., New Delhi.

Sanyü, Visier, 1995, *A History of Nagas and Nagaland*, Commonwealth Publications, New Delhi.

Scott, Rev. Michael, The Naga Case—India's Problem or the World's? (Unpublished article).

Watters, Thomas, 1904, *On Yuan Chwang's Travel in India*, London.

11

Indo-Naga Peace Process

Critical Observation

Yaronsho Ngalung

Many of you have spoken about the peace processes in North-East India from various perspectives and understanding. In this chapter, I am presenting some of my views and observations about the ongoing Indo-Naga Peace process that was started on 1 August, 1997 between the Government of India (GoI) and the National Socialist Council of Nagalim (NSCN) led by Isak Chishi Swu, President and Thuingaleng Muivah, General Secretary of the NSCN political organisation. Government of India has also signed a Ceasefire with Khaplang group in April, 2001. Let us mention some words about the Nagas before we discuss about Indo-Naga Peace Process.

The Nagas

The Nagas are an ancient people whose forefathers migrated into their present habitat somewhere before the Christian era of AD 1. The Nagas belonged to Sino-Mongoloid race. Forefathers of the Nagas entered into the present Naga lands were through the Himalayan region and the Burmese corridor. The Naga, who pierced their ears to accommodate big wooden plugs and other ornaments, were given this name while they were passing through the Burmese territory during their migratory stage. The term "Naga" is derived from the Burmese word "Naka", meaning "people with perforated ears". Whether in historical records or oral traditions passed from one generation to the other through word of mouth, there was no mention whatsoever of the Naga driving away some inhabitants of the land to make the lands their own (Kaka D. Iralu, 2002, pp. 34-35). The fact of the matter is the Nagas have migrated from more populated regions of the Asian continent and settled down in their present lands and made it their own land. Accordingly, the Nagas are settled in their contiguous geographical locations in Nagaland, Manipur, Arunachal Pradesh, and Assam in India and Sagaing division and Kachin State in Burma/Myanmar covering an area of 120,000 square kilometres.

The Nagas as 'a group of people' have constituted themselves as an organised political community like other people of the world. It is a fact that Nagas are not Indians historically, culturally, politically and racially. Thus, Nagas are groups of people or a nation having political aspiration. They have been struggling for their collective right to Self-Determination through their mass-based political movement. The Naga political movement is conducted within the framework of Naga nationalism, politics and Universal principles of human rights and freedom. The Naga political movement indicates the co-existence of modern and traditional features of nationalism (Yaronsho Ngalung, *Dissertation*, 2003, p. 1). Naga political movement's ideology has been indicated as "National Socialism" of its own brand. The Naga politics is conducted *vis-à-vis* India's democratic political system and Government of Burma. The Naga political movement can best be understood from the statement of Isak Chishi Swu and Th. Muivah when they said, "The struggle of the Nagas was not only 'to defend Nagaland's independent existence', but also 'safety from the doom' of silent invasion of Indian and Burmese capitals and cultural conquest" (Isak Chishi Swu and Th. Muivah, 1993, pp. VI, 10, 15-18).

The NSCN defines the Indo-Naga conflict as an Armed Conflict within the meaning of the Geneva Conventions. Protocol II of the 1949 Geneva Conventions defines an armed conflict as those conflicts "which take place in the territory of a High Contracting Party between its armed forces and dissident armed forces or other organised armed groups which, under responsible command, exercise such control over a part of its territory as to enable them to carry sustained and concerted military operations and to implement this Protocol. The NSCN believed the Indo-Naga Conflict as an armed conflict within the meaning of the Geneva Conventions because the Organisation is a well disciplined national resistance with an armed wing, under responsible command, exercising control over all Naga areas between India and Burma, and it is able to carry out sustained and concerted military operations" (*The Legal Status of Naga National Armed Resistance*, GPRN, January 8, 2001, p. 4).

The philosophy of the NSCN can be understood by the following sentences: "In this world of bitter history where powers and unruly ambitions make life insane, the only way for a people to hold out their salvation is to cling to their freedom, because it is freedom and the love for it that give meaning to life. Therefore, freedom the very precious most, shall on no occasion be yielded to whatever guests history may still afford. We shall hold fast to our freedom, for what remains when it falls! Yes, we will never back down from our principles; they are all the world to us. This is our treasured philosophy. The fate is decided, it is in our hands. We shall live only in freedom." (*A Brief Political Account of Free Nagaland, Nagaland for Christ*, GPRN, pp. 45-47). With the objective of achieving the Political Freedom or Political Sovereignty, the Nagas have been fighting against the occupation of Naga territory by India and Burma since the launching of Naga political organisation in the 1940s. The struggle to achieve the right to Self-Determination of the Naga people is still on through peace process with the Government of India. The question of whether both the political entities—India and the Nagas transformed the conflict during the ongoing peace process is yet to be seen. Now, let us briefly discuss some of my observations about the ongoing peace process between the Government of India (GoI) and the Nagas.

Indo-Naga Peace Process: Critical Observation

The present Ceasefire or Indo-Naga Peace Process was not easily signed or initiated. It was a hard-earned kind of initiative by both the parties. It has taken a lot of diplomatic measures and political steps on the part of GoI to sign this Ceasefire with the NSCN. The Nagas have been refusing to engage with GoI due to historical juncture and trust deficit of the past. The NSCN leadership have made a point that without recognising the issue as political issue, they will never come forward for talks with India. Historically, Government of India failed to recognise the Naga political movement as political in nature. It is this attitude that GoI termed the Naga Political Movement as "Law and Order" problem or Insurgency or Separatist or secessionist Movement. However, the Nagas political struggle has been often 'misunderstood and misquoted' according to A. Lanunungsang Ao. (A. Lanunungsang Ao, 2002, p. 5) by the Government of India and Journalists writings. "The question of secession from India did not arise because the Nagas never thought in lines of being an Indian" as according to Udayon Misra (Udayon Misra, 2000, p. 26).

Taking Kashmir as an example of conflicting interests between Pakistan and India, Diethelm Weldemann observed that Pakistan politicians and columnists sometimes seem to live in a world of their own perceptions, which is not always congruent with the reality. But at the same time the dominating Indian perception to assess the Kashmir question merely as a law and order problem or as unconstitutional attempt to secede from India, is explicitly narrow-minded, incorrect and full of grave consequence (Diethelm Weldemann, 1997, p. 6). The impression of the civil societies is that, it is true that the Naga question has always been perceived in the same fashion by the officials and the policy-makers of the Indian State for the last more than five decades. So, many writers and Institutes in India have also failed to come out of the statist's perception while explaining the Naga political movement. However, in contrast to the policy-makers, journalists and various Institutes, former Army General, Shankar Roy Chaudhary realised that the Naga Movement is not terrorism nor can it be equated as such. He said, "Military solution is not possible. We have realised it. It is the time for India and the Nagas to talk across the table" ('*Conflict Managers or Conflict Mongers*', NPMHR, 2002, p. 9). Former Indian Security Commissioner, A. Murkut Ramunny, in his writing said, "Nagas do not kill civilians". One of the earliest Indian Generals who recognised the Indo-Naga conflict as not of law and order problem, but of political problem requiring political wisdom for a solution was General K.S. Thimmaya. Among the Indian politicians who recognise the Indo-Naga conflict as political issue are Jaya Prakash Narayan, Narasimha Rao, H.D. Deve Gowda, I.K. Gujral, Atal Bihari Vajpayee, Dr, Manmohan Singh, Ms. Sonia Gandhi etc. (See *NPMHR*, April 2002, p. 9, *Souvenir*, 2005 and also see A. Lanunungsang Ao, *From Phizo to Muivah*, p. 91). It is with this political realisation on the part of the Indian leadership that the present peace process was able to take off with the Naga people.

As mentioned earlier, after more than five decades of military operations against the Nagas, three Generals of the Indian armed forces acknowledged that a "Military solution is not possible: the Naga issue is a political one requiring political solution. After long intensive low-key negotiations, a landmark meeting was held in June 1995, in Paris between the then Prime Minister of India, late P.V. Narasimha Rao and the Collective Leadership* of the NSCN, Isak Chishi Swu and Th. Muivah wherein various substantive issues were discussed. During the talk, Mr. Rao stated, "I believe in a political solution. We must solve the problem through political talks and dialogue. We should be patient enough and tolerant in tackling the problem" (*Nagas: The Pilgimage for Self-Existence and Quest for Dignity and Peace, GPRN*, November, 2005, p. 19). As stated earlier, the recognition of Indo-Naga problem as a 'political' one paved the way for talks through peaceful means. It created a congenial atmosphere of understanding and patience for peace talks. Subsequently, series of meetings were held with various functionaries of the Government of India. The political initiatives were further strengthened when in February, 1997 Mr. H.D. Deve Gowda, the then Prime Minister of India met the NSCN Collective Leadership in Zurich, Switzerland. The Prime Minister of India assured that "We believe in peaceful means. We must seek a political solution" (*Souvenir*: 25 Years of NSCN and GPRN (1980-2005), NSCN/GPRN, 2005).

All these significant meetings that unfolded through this delicate process entered into a new phase of formal negotiations when the present Indo-Naga Ceasefire Agreement was declared in Indian Parliament by the then Prime Minister of India, I.K. Gujral and Chairman, NSCN, Isak Chishi Swu at the *Unrepresented Nations Peoples Organisation* (UNPO) Headquarter, The Hague, the Netherlands on 25th July, 1997 for a period of three months with effect from 1st August, 1997 (*Souvenir*, 2005, p. 17).

The Agreement reads:

> "For securing a peaceful political solution discussion had been held between the Government of India and the National Socialist Council of Nagalim leadership. It has been mutually decided to Ceasefire for a period of three (3) months with effect from the 1st of August, 1997 and embark upon political level discussions" (*Souvenir*, 2005, p. 17).

As congenial environment were necessary to hold political negotiations, therefore, the NSCN and GoI formulated certain modalities for peace talks known as 'Ceasefire Ground Rules' that will be abide by both the parties. Accordingly, the Ceasefire Ground Rules were finalised between the GoI and the NSCN on 12th December, 1997. The three guiding principles, on which the Ceasefire Agreement was bilaterally agreed upon, were that:

(i) Without any Condition (Unconditional);
(ii) At the Highest Level i.e., Prime Ministerial Level; and
(iii) In a Third Country.

It was based on these principles and understanding that the peace process has began for bringing a political solution to the 60 years of conflict. Both the parties appoint Interlocutors or Emissaries to represent their respective Governments from time to time. Interlocutors such as Swaraj Kaushal, K. Padmanabhaiah and RS Pandey from GoI side and V.S. Atem, Retd. General from the NSCN side in the Indo-Naga Peace Process were cited as "Track One and a Half" diplomacy by some experts.

Now, let us make a critical assessment of the negotiations that have crossed 17 long years. The Naga leadership have made it clear to the Indian leadership that for an amicable and honourable solution to fructify, historical and political rights of the Nagas be respected while at the same time Indian democracy and its security concern be respected by the Nagas. It may not be wrong to mention here that Government of India has understood the stand and aspirations of the Naga people. The only question is GoI seems to be failing in its political wisdom and commitment to solve the problem. The Congress-led UPA Government has not been able to resolve in its talks with the Nagas. UPA Government has been making several promises to the Nagas, but such promises have never seen the light of day and such promises have become a far cry for Congress led UPA Government as a new Government has already installed under the leadership Mr. Narendra Modi of the BJP-led NDA Government.

In fact, people have failed to see much sincerity and commitment from the Government of India during the talks. The GoI has on several occasions violated the principles of talks. We have also witnessed a number of Naga cadres being killed by the Indian Security forces while having a ceasefire. More than 100 Naga Armed cadres have been killed in the peace process. These killings can be executed by using the power of Armed Forces (Special Powers) Act, 1958. This AFSPA has a notorious history of committing grave human rights violations not only in North-East India but also in Jammu and Kashmir in the name of the so called counter-insurgency.

We have seen how the Interlocutors were replaced one after another. Swaraj Kaushal resigned as Interlocutorship for the alleged sinister campaign against him by the PMO, for his inclination to solve the Indo-Naga Issue earnestly as reported. The Former Home Secretary represented as Interlocutor to the Prime Minister of India until July 22, 1999. Likewise, K. Padmanabhaiah was also removed because he understands the aspirations of the Naga people. Moreover, the last Interlocutor, R.S. Pandey resigned from interlocutorship and joined the BJP party because GoI refused to listen to his views and ignored him on the Naga political questions. And, before a new Interlocutor was appointed election process has overwhelmed the UPA Government. Now, it is upto the new Government to resume the stalled peace talks if at all a solution has to find. Some of the threats to the peace process may be mentioned for our perusal. One can classify the threats to Indo-Naga peace process into two, 1. The contentious issues between the two entities, and, 2. The external factors, especially from non-entities to the Indo-Naga peace talks. Certain incidents have also brought numerous apprehensions on the Nagas that Ceasefire might be broken. Moreover, the arrest of Th. Muivah in Bangkok in 2000 and protests by certain communities opposing the extension of ceasefire coverage to all Naga areas have also brought unexpected developments in the peace process.

The 1998 Election boycott call by the NSCN was made due to lackadaisical attitude of the Indian Government to the peace process. However, GoI reacted sharply. The ceasefire nearly broke down, but both the parties overcome the challenge. One of the most contentious issues was the coverage of the ceasefire "without territorial limits" in all Naga areas. This was agreed in Bangkok on 14 June, 2001. However, GoI deleted the words after the protest in Imphal turned violent on 18 June, 2001. In 2000, S.C. Jamir's book '*Bedrock of Naga Society*' has created a lot of controversy because the booklet defended the 16-Point Agreement which was a total contradiction to the Naga vision for their society. In a way, according to Naga Civil Societies, Jamir has played a negative role to sabotage the ongoing peace process.

It is very uncalled for that leaders of the NSCN who have been involved in the peace talks have also been arrested and detained in Indian jails by National Investigating Agency (NIA) on this or that ground. Example, Anthony Ningkhan Shimray who was on his way to attend peace talks in New Delhi was arrested in Kathmandu Airport by the Indian Government with the help of Nepal Government in 2010. Many more related events have contributed to the peace talks. Apart from the threats to the peace process, many more positive events have also witnessed. Many Naga civil societies, Indian civil societies and International civil societies and many people including various political parties have supported the ongoing Indo-Naga peace process. It is to be noted that NSCN has become a member nation of UNPO on 23th January, 1993 at The Hague in its Third General Assembly. As part of its diplomacy, NSCN has also participated International Conference organised by Parliamentarians for National Self-Determination (PNSD) held at Houses of Parliament, Westminster, London, on May 11, 2006. Naga civil societies such as Naga Hoho, Naga Students' Federation (NSF), Naga Mothers' Association (NMA), Naga People's Movement for Human Rights (NPMHR), United Naga Council (UNC), All Naga Students' Association,

Manipur (ANSAM), Naga Students' Union, Delhi (NSUD) etc. have played their positive role in support of the peace process. The peace process has been consistently supported by the Naga people at large for which the Naga leadership could have engaged the Indian leadership thus far.

Forum for Naga Reconciliation (FNR) since 2008 has also been trying to reconcile the various factions among the Nagas. Recently, Lenten Agreement was singned on March 28, 2014 among three Naga Political Groups, namely, NSCN-IM, NSCN-KK and NNC/FGN in Nagaland for establishing Naga National Government. However, it is learnt that FNR has failed to condemn in letter and spirit the 16-Point Agreement which created Nagaland State, Shillong Accord which has brought national disaster in terms of surrendering to the Constitution of India etc. to the dismay of Naga people. The initiative of FNR is appreciable in so far as it is doing its works for reconciliation among the Nagas. However, it is reminded of the fact that various Church leaders in the past have played negative role in the process of the Naga political movement. For which, it is emphasised that any political act or behaviours of civil society group(s) should have a political connotation for such acts to be fruitful and meaningful.

In the run up to the 17 long years of peace talks, it was the BJP-led NDA Government under the able leadership of Atal Bihari Vajpayee that officially recognised the "Unique History and Situation of the Nagas" on July 11, 2002 at Amsterdam. ("Joint Communique" of GoI and NSCN, Amsterdam, July 11, 2002). The Nagas are very much happy and confident that an honourable solution acceptable to both the parties could be brought about by the move of the NDA Government. However, the Congress-led UPA Government has neglected this recognition in its talks with the Nagas. Nevertheless, it is very important to note that Government of India which has officially recognised the Unique History and Situation of the Nagas in its approach towards resolving the Indo-Naga political issue. This recognition is important as far as Indo-Naga engagement in the last 60 years is concerned. It can be said that he basis for solution has been laid by the then NDA Government which was neglected by the UPA Government. Nagas still believes that Indo-Naga issue can be resolved by recognising each other historical and political rights. While doing so, NSCN still upholds the May 16, 1951 Plebiscite where 99.9 per cent of Nagas voted in favour of Naga Independent from India and Burma. It still does not believe the creation of Nagaland as a complete unification process of the Naga people. NSCN was formed in 1980 after the rejection of the infamous Shillong Accord as a total sell out of the Naga Nation. As such, the Naga leadership are of the position that an amicable and honourable solution acceptable to both the parties should be based on the recognition that has accorded to the Nagas by the Government of India on July 11, 2002. The recognition of the "Unique History and Situation of the Nagas" simply means that India and Nagalim will exist as separate entities where a cordial relation is established. Recognition of the "Unique History and Situation of the Nagas" simply means recognition of the "historical and political rights of the Nagas". In such relations, it is envisaged that Naga people find themselves living in one political system in the amalgamated land of their own unlike the present. In such political arrangement, subjects of common interest may be jointly looked after for peace, security and regional stability. At best, both the parties should recognise each other's history, culture and identity for democracy, justice and the rule of law.

The new Government at the centre has a new role to play in the Indo-Naga peace process. The new Government headed by Narendra Modi has the moral responsibility in translating what was recognised in 2002 into action by transforming the Indo-Naga issue with commitment and political wisdom. At the same time, it is also equally important that Nagas play their part in areas such as, diplomacy, political activism, harmonious relationship with all including neighbouring communities etc. in strengthening the hands of the leadership of both GoI and the NSCN. In the process, democratisation and sensitisation on the importance of transforming one of the world's oldest conflicts is initiated at all levels. The role of civil societies, intellectuals, media and the public at large have become very crucial in fructifying the peace process. The basic idea to be reminded us all is fairness, justice and freedom are more than words, they are perspectives. The popular slogan "Give Peace a Chance" should be waged by all with full commitment. Let us not miss the opportunity to resolve/transform the hard-earned peace process between the Government of India and the Nagas. It is hoped that good wisdom prevails upon the leadership of both India and the Nagas.

References

1. Kaka D. Iralu, "Is Underdevelopment the cause of Insurgency in Nagaland?" In *Naga Journal of Indigenous Affairs, A Biannual Review of Indigenous Peoples*, Naga People's Forum Publication, June-November, 2002, Vol. 1, No. 2.

2. Yaronsho Ngalung, Dissertation, "Evolution and Nature of the Naga Movement", 2003, Submitted to Centre for Political Studies, School of Social Sciences, JNU, New Delhi.
3. Isak Chishi Swu and Th. Muivah, 'Free Nagaland Manifesto', NSCN: Dated Oking 22-11-1993.
4. *The Legal Status of Naga National Armed Resistance*, Published by Publicity and Information Service, GPRN, January 8, 2001.
5. *A Brief Political Account of Free Nagaland*, Nagaland for Christ, Published by the Publicity Department, GPRN.
6. A. Lanunungsang Ao, From Phizo to Muivah—*The Naga National Question in North-East India*, Mittal Publications, New Delhi, 2002.
7. Udayon Misra, *The Periphery Strikes Back: Challenges to the Nation-State in Assam and Nagaland*, Indian Institute of Advanced Study, Rashtrapati Nivas, Shimla, 2000.
8. Diethelm Weldemann, "The Interaction of Conflict Perception and Conflict Resolution-Basic Requirements and South Asian Context" in Talat Ayesha Wizarat ed., *Conflict Resolution in a New Era: Lession for South Asia*, Deptt. of International Relations, University of Karachi and Hanns Seidel Foundation, Germany, 1997.
9. "Conflict Managers or Conflict Mongers" Issued by Naga Peoples Movement for Human Rights, Kohima, Nagaland, 4th November, 2001, in *NPMHR*, Vol. 6, No. 1, Quarterly Publications, April, 2002.
10. *Nagas: The Pilgimage for Self-Existence and Quest for Dignity and Peace*, Oking Publicity and Information Department, GPRN, November, 2005.
11. *Souvenir*: 25 Years of NSCN and GPRN (1980-2005), Silver Jubilee Souvenir Editorial Committee (ed.) NSCN/GPRN, 2005.
12. "*Joint Communique*" of GoI and NSCN, Amsterdam, July 11, 2002.

*Collective Leadership of the NSCN is the distinctive feature of the NSCN. In all matters of policies and programmes, collective decision of the Central Committee is necessary. The Organisation, Government and Army are all controlled by them. Collective Leadership is applied to both, at the Centre and at the Regional levels, so as to make their governing and functioning more democratic. It also seeks to avoid any credulous error of the leaders.

12

The Conceits of Peace

Civil Societies and Naga's Peace Process

Soihiamlung Dangmei

Introduction

The discourse on civil society in North-East India mostly trail from the expedition of strengthening ethnic group interests. This is largely because the state had maintained firm control over politics, economy and society, leaving little space for democracy and market economy. The idea of democracy in the region is also limited, in the sense it is often relegated in electoral politics. Democracy must be based on autonomous and voluntary institutions and associations, so that, it would bring individuals into social and political participation who would act as social fortifications for guarding human rights and the rule of law. In the Western world, the emergence of market economy had considerably depoliticized bureaucratic structures and its institutions. The neo-liberal economic policies further added a congenial atmosphere for the smooth functioning of civil society. The region of North-East India, being a bureaucratic controlled economy leaves little space for public participation in social, political and economic activities. Besides, the multiple existence of various ethnic groups in the region further aggravated a situation where the concern of civil society is formulated based on ethnic interests. Therefore, the use of the term 'civil society' in the sense of the European/ Western tradition becomes problematic.

The classical usage of the term 'civil society' is often identified with the State. The modern idea of civil society emerged in the Scottish and Continental Enlightenment of the eighteenth century. In the wake of the Industrial Revolution, thinkers of the Scottish Enlightenment, such as

David Hume, Adam Ferguson and Adam Smith developed the influential theory of political economy in which the processes of economy are governed by laws of their own and must be kept free from the control of the state. This new thinking reflected changing economic realities: the rise of private property, market competition, and the bourgeoisie. Modern society, for Hegel, consists of three separate domains: family, civil society and state. Hegel was the first thinker to clearly define the term civil society. Civil society in the Hegelian sense is the sphere of pursuit of private or sectional interests in an open market. It is based on the principle of unrestrained individual egoism. In the Marxist literature, state is neither independent of nor neutral towards civil society but deeply embedded in civil society. In the twentieth century, Gramsci enriched the concept of civil society retaining Marx's idea of class war. In Gramsci's formulation, the dominance of the ruling classes is not maintained solely on the basis of their control of the coercive apparatus of the state, but also by acquiring dominant intellectual and moral leadership in civil society.

The use of the term 'civil society' in this study is based in the broad sense that includes organizations and associations that exist outside of the state. It refers to a set of institutions and associations which are public, voluntary, and independent from authority. The traditional forms of association such as tribes, ethnic groups and kinship are also accommodated as they have come to occupy a central position in the use of the term 'civil society'. In some sense, ethnic based civil society organizations are not voluntaristic but constraining and compulsory social associations which imposed hierarchical and binding authority on individuals. For an instance, frequent economic blockades in Manipur suggest that there exist a strong ethnic based civil society organizations and a weak state. The individuals in this case have no freedom in the association or organization. Therefore, civil society organizations are considered as hot-blooded association of social groupings, which are based on ethnic interest or on religious mobilization by conceiving the idea that they are assimilated coercively. However, the ethnic based civil society organizations maintained a condition of civility, the acceptance of differences and commitment to peaceful procedures for managing conflict.

The Post-colonial State and Civil Society

The ability of civil society to prevent the state from exercising absolute control is an essential condition. In North-East India, the state does not favour the expansion of civil societies because the interaction between state and civil society often results in a compromise at the cost of the ruling elite. The interaction of the state with civil society in fact is necessary for the smooth functioning of the democratic system. However, the state often tries to charge the leaders of civil societies identifying and branding them as anti-social. This results violent activities of civil societies in response to the authoritarian nature of the state.

The subordination of the individual to the ethnic group is also a common feature in North-East India. This is hindering in the democratic experiment and particularly in evolving a genuine civil society in the sense of the Western tradition. In the Western liberal democracy, individual identity forms the citizens of the state. Therefore, associational life based on common interest is formed and in fact it reinforced the smooth working of democracy. The issue at state is that in North-East India, the ethnic based civil society organizations are not entirely free from their group loyalties and identities. Civil society organizations are plausibly incommensurable in the sense that some of them are either deeply embedded in the state while others are antagonistic towards the state. These two extreme positions held by most of the civil society organizations in the region aggravated the division. For an instance, the United Committee, Manipur declared the 18th June Uprising as integrity day of Manipur and the state officially observed on behalf of the government. But the United Naga Council objected to the idea of Manipur integrity day and opposed the State government for declaring the uprising as integrity day. The idea of individuals as citizens and members of a political community, and partners in governance with the State became a distant reality.

The Naga Peace Process

In spite of the peace initiative and progress made in the last fifteen years between the Government of India and the Nationalist Socialist Council of Nagalim NSCN (IM), the fragility of the peace process continue to be tested at all levels and demands immense wisdom and integrity from both the parties. The Naga civil society and traditional organisations supporting the peace process have continued to seek opportunities and initiatives to strengthen political negotiations for a democratic and honourable settlement. Apart from the Naga civil societies, the inclusion of a non-governmental organisation like Kreddha from the Netherlands and with the personality like Yash Ghai, an eminent international constitutional experts, and Anthony Reagan Constitutional lawyer from Australia in the present peace process bring more impetus for peace building and conflict prevention. However, the involvement of civil society remains *ad hoc*, a reflection of the culture of secrecy in an underground organisation and the historical experience of inter-tribal feuds and betrayal. Besides, although the Government of India and the NSCN (IM) rhetorically affirm the value of independent observers to monitor the ceasefire, there has been no progress in integrating civil society into the monitoring mechanism. This chapter is an attempt to critically investigate and analyse the role of civil societies in the present peace process between the Government of India and the NSCN(IM).

The signing of the cease-fire agreement between the Isaak-Muivah faction of the Nationalist Socialist Council of Nagalim (NSCN-IM) and the Government of India in July, 1997 promised to establish peace initiative to find honourable and lasting solution to the protracted politico-military conflict in North-East India. The terms of the agreement are: (a) the talks will be unconditional; (b) the talks will be at the highest level, i.e. at the prime ministerial level; and (c) the talks will be in the third country. Many peace talks were held at different countries, namely, Amsterdam, Switzerland, Tokyo, Paris, and Bangkok. After many rounds of talks, at the prompt invitation of the Government of India, the collective leadership of the NSCN has visited India for series of talks. In more than 15 years of cease fire, roughly 60 rounds of talks were held at different cities of the world and in India. Besides, the Naga civil society and traditional organisations supporting the peace process have continued to seek opportunities and initiatives to strengthen political negotiations for a democratic and honourable settlement. The NSCN(IM) has also taken initiatives to hold consultations with Naga civil society representatives including all the Naga tribal councils and churches. The NSCN collective leadership, as a matter of policy, stated that it will, in all stages of political negotiations, consult and seek the participation of the Naga people for better understanding and transparency. Apart from the Naga civil societies, the inclusion of a non-governmental organisation like Kreddha from the Netherlands and with the personality like Yash Ghai, an eminent international constitutional experts, and Anthony Reagan Constitutional lawyer from Australia in the present peace process between the government of India and the NSCN(IM) is considered as positive step for peace building and conflict prevention. However, no substantive resolution has been made, other than harbouring over the proposal of the NSCN collective leadership for "Special Federal Relations" between India and Nagalim (Shimray 2007: 125-126).

Civil Society and the Naga Peace Process

For the most part, civil society organisations draw their legitimacy from the traditional democratic structures of authority in Naga society. With the emergence of a broad based peace platform, the social organisations have acquired greater legitimacy and strength (Manchanda 2005: 10). Stating that they are responsible to the people, the NSCN collective leadership reaffirmed that no agreement would be entered into without the fullest understanding and consent of the Naga people. The NSCN further committed itself to any solution based on the history and rights of the Nagas, and promised to act in the interest of the people without sacrificing the rights that are most precious to the Nagas. In the consultations with the NSCN, the Naga civil society has extended its full support to the ongoing peace process between the government of India and the NSCN. The NSCN in return has made a clarion call to all Nagas, irrespective of their past and standing, to participate in the peace process. The consultations are an ongoing process to deepen the understanding between the NSCN and Naga civil society and to ensure that the NSCN embodies the aspirations and rights of the Nagas.

In this unwanted fiasco of the protracted conflict, the Naga civil societies took several important initiatives to strengthen the peace process by engaging with the Government of India, various Naga nationalists' groups, the India's civil societies, other communities in the North-East who shares close geographical boundaries with the Nagas. Even before the peace process began, apex body of the Naga organisations like Naga Hoho has been expressing their wish for third party intervention that the conflict be solved through peaceful negotiation. The third party mediation to the peace process was felt needed among the Nagas and international support groups to the longest known conflict in the region. It is believed that there would be more equilibrium in the negotiations and accountability on both the parties. However, this suggestion was ruled out by the Government of India as it was apprehended that such intervention from another nations or agencies will only internationalise Naga political issue and, likely at the cost of the Government of India to forgo the Nagas.

Nonetheless, the NSCN and the Indian government agreed the involvement of certain non-governmental agencies that have engaged with conflict resolution in other parts of the world. A non-governmental organisation like Kreddha from the Netherlands and with the personality like Yash Ghai, an eminent international constitutional experts, and Anthony Reagan Constitutional lawyer from Australia, has been engaging with the peace talks. "Ghai is the world's foremost expert on constitutional law and that is why his facilitation assumes importance. He is believed to be discussing the limits of flexibility of the Constitution of India and whether sub-national constitutions could be accommodated within it. The question of multiplicity of constitutions has become a thorny issue as the NSCN (I-M) has proposed negotiating a federal relationship with India" (*The Telegraph*: 20/05/2006).

To salvage the peace process, both the Government of India and the NSCN formally agreed Michael C. van Walt van Praag, the executive president of the international NGO Kreddha, to act as a third-party mediator during the talk in Bangkok on 16-17 December, 2005. Kraibo Chawang, Deputy Kilonser (Minister) confirmed that Praag would be the "pointsman" in the peace process (*The Telegraph*: Kolkota, December 24, 2005). Praag, a former General Secretary of Unrepresented Nations People's Organisation (UNPO), has been mediating unofficially in the peace process since 2001 and visited Nagaland in 2002 and 2004. It was in 2001 that Praag first got involved and saved the peace process from being derailed. "Again, it was the Government of India that sent him to the NSCN to convince to come to India", as according to an NSCN functionary (*ibid*).

Kreddha, an International Peace Council for States, Peoples and Minorities is dedicated to the prevention and resolution of violent conflicts between populations, groups and states. It believes that development of meaningful dialogue between governments and population groups aspiring to a large degree of self-rule is essential in efforts to end violent conflicts between them. Kreddha is administered by the council of nine eminent conflict-resolution experts. It has offices in the Hague, the Netherlands and the US. Its council members include former Rajya Sabha member Nirmala Deshpande and Nobel Laureates Mairead Corrigan Maguire and Jose Ramos Horta (*ibid*). Apart from him, many renowned international constitutional experts such as, Yash Ghai, and Anthony Reagan are lending their hands of support to both the NSCN and the government of India in their search for a concrete political solution.

The NSCN leadership has also been taking great responsibility of the people by approaching different international organisations and personalities. In the midst of the peace process the NSCN leadership has attended an international conference organised by the Parliamentarian for National Self-Determination (PNSD) in the British Parliament, Westminster, in UK on May 11, 2006 to appeal the international community to intervene into the conflict for early solution. The Naga leaders particularly appealed the British Government and the people to intervene as it has some responsibility as a colonial power. Naga Support Group (UK) was set up on May 13, 2006 to mobilise international favour to the Nagas aspiration. Earlier, the NSCN has set-up Naga-American Council in USA in 2003 with Grace Lyu Collins as the Honourary Ambassador of the Nagas.

In the peace process the NSCN has proposed a "Special Federal Relationship" between India and Nagalim (*BBC World Hard Talk India*, 2005). Some of the main points of the proposed relationship are joint-defense, external affairs, communications, monetary policies, recognition of the national identity of the Nagas, integration of the Naga areas. Joint-defense simply means the joint-defense of Nagalim by both the nations while in the external affairs, the government of India will have primary responsibility, but when it comes to the matters which affect the Nagas, then the Nagas will represent themselves. Similarly, there will be joint-exercise in the areas of communications and monetary policies. The relationship should effectuate in such a manner in which it recognise and respect the national identity of the Naga people.

In the present peace talks, both the parties are studying each other's Constitution to foster a "framework for relationship" which was proposed by Kreddha on 28-31 July, 2006 in Bangkok (*North-East Sun*, 2006). During this talk the Indian Government and the NSCN have officially agreed to study each other's Constitution. It may be noted that the political solution is envisaged to be incorporated in these two Constitutions. The NSCN has been reiterating its stance that solution within the Constitution of India or within the Union of India is not acceptable to the Nagas. It is imperative that both the parties respect each other's concerns such as the security of India is not threatened while at the same the historical and political rights of the Nagas are not undermined. This peace process is one of the finest moments in the history of the Government of India and the Nagas to find a mutually acceptable solution through peaceful means. It is imperative at this juncture that the conflicting parties demonstrate political will with utmost sincerity and honesty.

The Naga Hoho, while vehemently supporting the peaceful political negotiations between the Government of India and NSCN, also took initiatives to bring unity in Naga society and urge the warring groups among the Nagas to shun violence and unify for the greater interest of the

Nagas (*The Telegraph*, 1999). The rivalry between the NSCN and Khaplang group, and also with other Naga political organisations like Naga National Council (NNC) has left Naga society divided and inimically put to danger the lives of the innocent peoples.

Historically, there have been differences between various Naga socio-religious and political organisations. But, traditionally as it was made a distinct categorisation of powers between the religious and the socio-political authorities as it is in the Western modulation. Naga Hoho, as an apex traditional Naga civil society, which is in fact the custodians of the Nagas territory and guardians of the custom and traditions, reposed its primeval responsibility to the affairs of the Nagas. Therefore, they took the necessary steps and urged the conflicting groups of Nagas to bury the hatchet, and take this political negotiation as an opportunity to open-up their rigid political positions and seek forgiveness from misgiving and feuds. They strongly believed that unified Naga political front will not only strengthened the Nagas' position during the peace process, but also help the Government of India to lessen its burden.

In the peace process, members of Naga Hoho went to meet NSCN leaders all the way in Bangkok and holds substantive discussions. Some prominent Naga leaders felt that a piecemeal solution would not bring lasting peace and all the sections of the Nagas should be taken into confidence to find out a permanent solution (*The Asian Tribune*, 1999). Initially, the efforts by the Naga civil societies were received with positive response from Naga nationalists, and they were urged to hold ceasefire among the factions in the same way as it has done with the Government of India. After which, the warring factions formally declared ceasefire between them in 1997 during the celebration of 125 years of Christianity in Nagaland (*The Asian Tribune*, 1997). It was for the first time in 50 years the tensions deescalated for sometimes.

The fratricidal killings, and rampant violence created in the Naga areas among the Nagas and, the occupations of the India's military forces has made to witness the most outrageous human rights violations in the regions. For which, the Naga People's Movement for Human Rights (NPMHR) established in the year 1978, has played the major role among Civil Societies demanding for human rights in Naga society as well as in the region of North-East India. NPMHR, a beacon of human rights protection, among other things, took up various efforts to resolve conflicts in the regions. With a farsighted endeavour to find solution to the human rights violations in the region, the NPMHR, after interacting and having dialogue with other civil societies in India, have build up comprehensive understanding on various issues pertaining to Nagas with the people of India. During the peace process NPMHR took the initiatives to have people to people dialogue with the Indian masses. Since India's independence or even before that there has been virtually not much interaction between the Nagas and the people of other parts of India; which is responsible for creating a lot of confusions and misconception about the Naga political movement and the mindset of the Indian people. And India's media, by highlighting only the violence and negative aspects of Nagas is also responsible for most of the misconceptions generated in other parts of India about the Nagas. Accepting this unfortunate reality as a fact and a challenge, the NPMHR along with various other Naga civil societies and India's civil societies took up the 'journey of conscience to New Delhi' on 29 January, 2000 to "express their goodwill for a people-to-people dialogue" (NPMHR 2000). This journey was taken at the backdrop of signing the ceasefire agreement between the government of India and the NSCN (IM) in 1997.

Postscripts of Peace

Besides, international non-governmental organisations, Naga Hoho and NPHMR, many of the civil societies, particularly of the Nagas like, Naga Students' Federation, Naga Mother's Association, All Naga Students Association Manipur, and United Naga Council Manipur played significant role in the peace negotiations through various level of participation. Amidst rampant accusations, mistrust, and misunderstandings created in the course of the time, civil societies, bearing the voices of the mostly unheard played significant role in the peace negotiation indispensably. In order to overcome the stalemate and to encourage creative thinking at the negotiating table, civil societies are unavoidably a prime factors in creating democratic space and an environment for a congenial atmosphere.

Different Naga organisations continue to engage with the Government of India from different standpoint. Notably, the collective leadership of the NSCN has been actively engaged not only with the Government of India but with the Naga people too. To find the democratic consensus of the Naga people through various different civil societies, Hohos, and organisations, were rallied upon into a different consultations and meetings. However, owing to the relentless enmity among the nationalists, it has become the niche of problems.

Conclusion

The Indian political leaders in Parliament and Government representatives have intricacy considering the benefit of cooperation with various international and Naga civil society organisations in the peace process. Apparently, the involvement of civil society remains *ad hoc*, a reflection of the culture of secrecy in an underground organisation and the historical experience of inter-tribal feuds and betrayal. Although the Government of India and the NSCN (IM) rhetorically affirm the value of independent observers to monitor the ceasefire, there has been no progress in integrating civil society into the monitoring mechanism. Moreover, representatives of the institutions of the Indian state-civil and military have appeared more reluctant to democratise the peace process, which is perceived as the realm of parties to the conflict only. Besides, there is a need for civil society in addressing the issues and sensitise through people to people dialogue at the grassroot level. The intervention of civil society only at the negotiating table reflects the obscurity of civil societies in its function and approach.

References

1. Ao, A. Lanunungsang, (2002), *From Phizo to Muivah: The Naga National Question in North-East India*, New Delhi: Mittal Publications.
2. Baruah, Sanjib, (2005), *Durable Disorder, Understanding the Politics of North-East India,* New Delhi: Oxford University Press.
3. Bhushan, Bharat, "Constitution Expert in Naga Talk", *The Telegraph,* 20/05/2006.
4. Dholabhai, Nishit, 'Dutchman Steps in to Salvage Talks', *The Telegraph,* Kolkota, December 24, 2005.
5. Fischer, Martina, *Civil Society in Conflict Transformation: Ambivalence, Potentials and Challenges*, available at http://www.berghof-handbook.net.
6. Interview with Th. Muivah by Karan Thapar in "BBC World Hard Talk India" on April 29, 2005.
7. Iralu, Kaka D., (2009), *The Naga Saga,* Kohima, Nagaland: Author.
8. Manchanda, Rita, (2005), *Naga Women Making a Difference: Peace Building in North-Eastern India*, Waging Peace Policy Commission.
9. *North-East Sun*, August 15, 2006.
10. *NPMHR Press Release,* New Delhi, 31.01.2000.
11. Nuh, V.K. (1986), *Nagaland Church and Politics,* Kohima: Published by the Author.
12. Paul, Van Tongeren, ed. (1998), Prevention *and Management of Violent*

Conflicts. An International Directory, Utrecht: European Platform for Conflict Transformation.

13. Shimray, U.A. (2007), *Naga Population and Integration Movement,* New Delhi: Mittal Publications.
14. Singh, Chandrika, (2004) *Naga Politics*, New Delhi: Mittal Publications.
15. *The Asian Age,* New Delhi, 19.05.1997.
16. *Ibid.*, 27.11.1997.
17. *The Assam Tribune,* Guwahati, 01.06.1999.
18. *The Telegraph,* Calcutta, 19.05.1999.
19. Vashum, R. (2000), *Naga's Rights to Self-Determination—An Anthropological-Historical Perspective*, New Delhi: Mittal Publications.
20. Yonuo, Asoso, (1974), *The Rising Nagas: A Historical and Political Study,* Delhi: Vikas Publishing House.

13
International Criminal Court and North-East India

Sapam Dilipkumar

Introduction

Maintenance of international peace and security, by ensuring justice on the basis of the principle of rule of law, is the contemporary challenges of modern international law. International law can exercise its jurisdiction on the individuals if their activities are concern of international community and of mankind. It is proven by a lot of judgements passed by the international military Tribunals created by allied power as well as International criminal tribunals established by the UN Security Council. The establishment of the UN, after the end of the Second World War to save the succeeding generations from the scourge of war by maintaining international peace and security has accelerated the development of international law especially international criminal jurisprudence. Chapter VI and VII the Charter of the United Nations mandates the Security Council to maintain international peace and security. It is also the responsibility of all members of the UN including India to cooperate the Security Council in the maintenance of peace and security. The North-East India has been a conflict zone for more than half a century because of insurgency, ethnic conflict, internal displacement, illegal migration, among others. The conflict may also disturb the peace and security of the neighbouring countries.

Historical Background

After the end of the Second World War, the Allied power set-up international military tribunal in Nuremberg, Germany to prosecute and punish Nazi war criminals of Germany and the International Military Tribunal for the Far East, in Tokyo, Japan to try and punish Far Eastern war criminals charged for committing crimes against peace and, crime against humanity. The tribunals are now regarded as a milestone toward the establishment of a permanent international court, and an important precedent for dealing with instances of genocide and crimes against humanity. Important findings of the Nuremberg trial were incorporated in the United Nations Genocide Convention, 1948, Universal Declaration of Human Rights, 1948, and the Geneva Conventions 1949.

It seems that non-international armed conflict causes more injury than international armed conflict in the recent past. Ethnic cleansing in Rwanda and former Yugoslavia were the case in the point. The situation threatened international peace and security and was a major concern of international community. The UN Security Council established the International Criminal Tribunal for Rwanda for prosecuting persons responsible for genocide and other serious violations of International Humanitarian Law in Rwanda and Rwandan citizens responsible for genocide and other such violations in neighbouring States, and also set up International criminal tribunal for former Yugoslavia for the purpose of prosecuting persons responsible for serious violation of international humanitarian law in former Yugoslavia. The tribunals have narrow down the gap between the international armed conflict and non-international armed conflict. The two tribunals observed that systematic and widespread rape constitutes war crime and crime against humanity.

International Criminal Court

The International Criminal Court (ICC) is the culmination of more than five century old human effort to evolve a system of international criminal justice in the world. The establishment of the ICTY and ICTR paves the way for installation of the ICC, under the Rome Statue 1998. The creation of the ICC may be considered as genuine revolution in the system of modern international law because; it constitutes a qualitatively new step in the development of international criminal justice.

The jurisdiction of the ICC, as stated in article 5 of the Rome Statute, is limited to the most serious crimes concern to the international community as a whole. The ICC has jurisdiction in accordance with this statute with respect to the following crimes: (a) the crime of genocide, (b) crime against humanity, (c) war crimes, and (d) the crime of aggression.

The definition of the crime of aggression has also been adopted by the Review Conference on the 11 June, 2010. The ICC Statute's definition of crimes against humanity is groundbreaking as it omits a nexus to armed conflict, thus clarifying that crimes against humanity may be committed in peacetime as well as in the war. The jurisdiction of the ICC is not only based on the principle of nationality of the suspect, but also on that of territoriality. This principle implies that the ICC possess jurisdiction whenever crimes have been committed on the territory of a State party, irrespective of the citizenship of the suspect—which is the main reason why the United States rejects the authority of the court. The argument that article 12(2) transgress the treaty law that it should be binding only to contracting parties has overlooked the recent developments in international criminal law, *jus cogens*, international human rights laws, and the justification behind the making of ICTY and ICTR statutes based on termination of impunity.

The ICC may exercise its jurisdiction if a crime situation has been referred to the prosecutor by a state party or the UN Security Council or if the prosecutor has initiated an investigation of such a crime. The statute provides that it shall apply equally to all persons without any distinction based on official capacity. Official capacity as a Head of State or Government, a member of a Government or Parliament, an elected representative or a government official shall in no case exempt a person from criminal responsibility under this statute, nor shall it, in and of itself, constitute a ground for reduction of sentence. The article 27 excludes any form of immunity. Article 28 especially deals with the responsibility of military commanders. The court has no jurisdiction over any person under the age of 18 years at the time of the alleged commission of a crime.

The first page of the ICC trial has open after the arrest of first ICC subject Thomas Lubanga Dyilo, founder of the Union of Congolese Patriots (UPC) and the Patriotic Force Libration of Congo (FPLC), former Commander in-chief of FPLC and president of the UPC in 2006. The trial has been started from 26th January, 2009 after the confirmation of charges levelled against him. The Trial Chamber I convicted Thomas Lubanga Dyilo of committing, as co-perpetrator, war crimes consisting of enlisting and conscripting of children under the age of 15 years into FPLC and using them to participate actively in hostilities in the context of an armed conflict not of an international character. The trial chamber sentenced him to a period of 14 years imprisonment on 10 July, 2012. Thomas Lubanga Dyliyo appealed against the judgement to the Appeal Chamber of the ICC.

The ICC has started functioning and exercised jurisdiction, considered admissibility matters quite successfully. This hard won human institution to terminate impunity, fix individual criminal responsibility, promote international due process of law, rule of law and international criminal justice system has come to stay However, India has not signed and ratified the Rome statue, 1998 even though she has participated in the Rome Diplomatic Conference which adopts the statue. Indian delegates expressed that the issue of nuclear weapon, weapon of mass destruction and terrorism should be incorporated in the statue, but the family of nations found uncomfortable with the lone voice as an act of insincerity and dubious intensions. The neighbouring states of India—Nepal, Pakistan and Bangladesh have signed the statue expressing their willingness to be the party to the statue.

Issues of North-East

The North-East India has been a theater of conflict for the more than half a century because of insurgency. The people of this region have also been victims of the conflict for the many years without having no way out from the situation. It seems that state has adopted only coercive measures for solving the problem of insurgency rather than finding out a peaceful means to solution of the problem from the beginning. Despite of acknowledging the fact that political solution would be the real solution of the problem of the North-East, the intention of the government to used armed forces to the fullest extent necessary is reflected in the secret letter of the first Prime Minister of the country to the Chief Minister of Assam on the 13th May, 1956. What was secret had been open on the floor of Parliament in two years by passing. The Armed Forces Special Powers Act, 1958 in the Parliament. The Act has been opposed by the people of Manipur even in the debate for passing the Act. The minority MPs' of the small state could not convinced and the Act was hurriedly passed in the Parliament. Since then, the Act has been imposed in the state. The Act not only provides extra power to the armed forces of the union government, but also gives immunity to them from prosecution. The Act excludes the scope of judicial review which is the sin qua non of the principle of rule of law. However, the Supreme Court upheld the constitutional validity of the Act in 1997.

Civil society coalition on human rights in Manipur and UN estimates that a total of 124 women and children were killed and a total of 24 women including at least 5 girl child were raped by the armed forces in the State of Manipur from the year 1974 to 2013. The State government took action against the perpetrators of crime by initiating criminal proceeding only for the name sake. Such indifferent attitude of the State in initialing criminal proceedings against them seems to encourage the armed forces to commit more inhuman crimes under the cover of the Armed Forces Special Powers Act, 1958 with immunity and impunity

The movement for repealing the draconian law has been intensified after the arrest, detention, torture, custodial rape and killing of Th. Monorama by the security forces in 2004 in the State of Manipur. The Central Government constituted Jeevan Reddy Committee to look into the loophole of the Act and the Committee has recommended to repeal the Act. However, Central Government is still silent on the recommendation of the Committee for nearly a decade. The Human Rights Committee, the Committee on Elimination of Discrimination against Women also have recommended to the government to repeal the Act as it is incompatible with the universally accepted human rights standard. The Prime Minister of India, in many occasion assured to the people of North-East that the Act will be repealed. However, the government never took up any visible action to this effect till date. The Defence Ministry and top army officials keep on justifying the imposition of the Act in the region on the ground of suppressing insurgency. The government has also turned its deaf ear to the legitimate demand of Irom Sharmila, who has been fasting for nearly one and half decades, to repeal the Act. The attitude of the government indicates that the Act could not be repealed until and unless the insurgents of the North-East have been wiped out completely. In such situation, there is the need for world judicial body which could exercise its jurisdiction over the State actors and non-State actors and fix criminal responsibility for their inhuman and intolerable acts committed during conflict.

Conclusion

Justice has been considered as an indispensible intrinsic value of every society from time immemorial. It is one of the most important conditions for maintaining peace and security both at the national and international level. History proves that peace and security of the world is mainly threatened by the individuals by way of flagrant violation of international law particularly international humanitarian laws. The establishment and the judgment of Nuremberg and Tokyo Military Tribunal by the Allied power really marked a legal evolution and led the foundation for evolving international criminal law relating fixing individual criminal responsibility. The ICTY and ICTR made an international benchmark not only relating to ethnic cleansing and intra-tribal genocide but also narrow down the gap between international and non-international armed conflict. The establishment of the ICC is the culmination in the involution of International Criminal Jurisprudence. The Court was mainly established for achieving justice for all and to deter future war criminal by ending impunity. India, as a keen contender for the permanent member of the UN Security Council, ought to honour the authority of the court by the shining and ratifying the Rome statute. Such bold steps would help in bringing peace in the Region of North-East India.

14
Polemic on Peace, Negative or Positive in Manipur

Dhanabir Laishram

Many writers have written a good number of books on problems of the North-East and its armed conflict rather than resolution of conflict. One who wrote lamentable deficiencies that this region has not overcome? If discontent and conflict ferments and keeps on in these areas, how can a country claim to be progressive, to be at the high table of international politics and economics? It is entirely in confusion because of that I am inevitable to penetrate; and bring notable research as said—action research, which bring descriptive and analytical type of research matching with participatory one. I am entirely involved. I am entirely interested in the outcome conflict must pave the way to resolution of that conflict because changing new dimension of trance-border insurgency and new changing political equation of Burma give more interesting to study based on logical query with observation and interpretations of it.

For bringing peace, setting goals and top down peace building of Government could be shorted out yet. Simply presenting as dialogue is needed and warned them come out to mainstream is just like inviting reaction from them. Though some of insurgencies in NE are in the peace process demanding with special federal relationship, major armed opposition groups in Manipur denied peace talk. So, this chapter is mainly emphasis to the study of Manipur, its problem and response of the people towards peace and development. There is also, in some key circles, a realization that the past negligence committed by Government of India need to be erased and tried to give up using carrot and stick measures to wipe out political violence of this region. Nevertheless, the three stages given by the GoI, i.e. entering in to ceasefire, political negotiations and economic development in the states are not bad.

People of Manipur are also opening their eyes and to see the very positive beginnings when ULFA's leaders have willingness for unconditional peace talk with the Government of India. Now Rajkhowa, the chairman of the banned organization is allowed to hold public meeting and cadres of the outfit are allowed to roam freely. The organization could ply its convoys with its flags flying. That means they are underway of peace process in between the Cadres of ULFA and the Government of India. A few days later, Sanayaima, the chairman of UNLF, he was arrested by the Security forces of India in Bangladesh, was in the Guwahaty NIA's special court and stated that Plebiscite is only the option of him and his organization. Some of the Manipuri people including women shouted the slogan that Plebiscite is the demand of us. It clearly indicates that both the insurgencies as well as people of the two states are antagonized as far as their views on peace process are concerned. Yet that is the vexed problem of Manipuris. Then what is the next? The answer of this question is the core issue of this chapter.

Most of the organizations are in favour of the proposition that there is no peace where there is no development. So, All Manipur United Clubs Organisation (AMUCO) launched the campaign for unity, development and peace. The campaign was supported maximum numbers of District's united clubs. Yangso So Koireng, the former president of AMUCO told me that, "we have need unity of hill-valley first. It could be brought by the process of unity criticism unity. Then discontenmemts of both the people of hill valley regarding the development that the Government turns off for a quite long time, would be sorted out and pursue to the government to take necessary action for that. After that peace will be followed. Otherwise, how one could expect common political aspiration of the region which is the basic foundation of peace building."

But Government and most of their agents would prefer to appeal that there is no chance of development if there is no peace. Hence, peace should be imposed first. Again many of us comment a simultaneous existence of both; there is no question of first or later. The argument may be correct to some extent. But the people's apprehension is that even in this armed struggle, the ranking in corruption of North-East, Assam and Manipur become first and second (latest report of the National Crime Record Bureau 2011). So Jinine Laishram, human rights activist, rightly observed that "the government ignores the universal interpretation of peace that involves human rights. The peace in Manipur has been of negative implication, as the active militarization, factional violence, ethnic enmity, and the lasting talk not the lasting peace is on the scene." He further mentioned that "I do not rule out the partial correctness in the above debate. What I am attempting to suggest is, justice is the foundation of peace and development; in the absence of justice there is no chance of valid and viable peace and development" (*Which first—Peace or Development? Justice First! The Sangai Express*, 20 April, 2011)

Prof. Arambam Lokendra also subscribes his views that the gap between expectations of peace and what is delivered, the kind of 'Justice Gap' that has occurred needs to be filled. Further he observed that attempts by policy makers for peace not to be negotiation-centric at the expense of developing practices and frameworks for understanding how to create and sustain collaborative, non-violent processes of structural change had been formulated and disseminated widely in the academic institutions as well. Otherwise, how to understand region or community specific conflict situations and help assuage the impact of both direct violence and structural violence on society. Understanding the dynamics of conflict or violence, for ultimate establishment of lasting peace and durable orders, and contribution to development assistance has necessitated the inter-disciplinary approaches.

The debate over whom or how one should bring peace gets the more stimulating in a conflict situation, such in Manipur. The question is, should "Peace" have a normative definition and be treated as political space earmarked between the State and non-State actors. If that is only to stop the war without occupying the middle space by providing social, economic and political justice, robotically question should also be associated, peace for whom and for what.

Objective

Manipur is now on the frying pan. Armed conflict situation in other states of North-East India except Manipur are in the peace process including Assam. Manipur is the only State in which some major revolutionary groups are in favour of war over peace. Keeping in view these ideas the following objectives of the present chapter are spelt out.

1. To evaluate the nature and extent of negative peace and unmeaningful development in association with social security.
2. To highlight how the political violence turned as trance border insurgency and possibility of proxy war.
3. To focus the causes for the persistence of social exclusion in Manipur.

4. To asses how the voice of the people on plebiscite as their political aspiration in the democratic space.
5. To analyse the dissent views in the democratic space and government's peace initiatives.
6. To examine is there any possibility of holding dialogue for solving the vexed problem with ensuring economic development.

The polemic on peace and development in Manipur becomes so familiar today. It always associates with the issue of national security. But one notable thing is that it could not be served by projection of distorted perception of peace and development. Basically, if there is social security, political and economic security of individual why do we need to talk about national security because individuals are the units of the State and States are the units of the nation. Why do we impute emergence of dissent groups. Disagreement, on the ground of principle, is a healthy process of development. However, if the objective of dissent is positive, it encourages the individuals and the institutions to take positive step to drive home the authority for correction of omission and commission. In fact, they do not make denial of positive contention. Even we have to arraign destruction though they have total indifferent from positive contention. By keeping these views in our minds, it is better to see the correct perception of security, peace and development in the positive way and how it could be put into practice because like some European governments, India seems to place strong emphasis on development and poverty reduction programmes in order to counteract crises. Besides, the Government of India (GoI) has mainly acted on the need to contain potential spill-over of insecurity and unstable structures, by means of forceful intervention.

Peace and Violence

In a simple meaning peace means absence of "non-peace" otherwise a lot of terminology like respite from war, quite from suits and disorders, rest from any commotion, freedom from terror, silence, suppressions of thoughts etc. are coming up. In the traditional assumption peace as the counterpart to the state of war and hence peace is defined as "absence of war". According to Linus Pauling, the editor-in-chief of *World Encyclopaedia of Peace* (1986), "As history progress, peaks of joys and troughs of pain are experienced by the human beings populating the system, peace studies are usually concerned more with the avoidance of the latter, than with obtaining the former". Peace is thus largely identified as a lack of conflict of any serious kind. More often the term "peace-making" is associated with conflict resolution without the use of violence.

That's why could we study peace without reading of political violence of particular place. The major debate has been whether to define peace simply as the absence of war often called 'negative peace' or whether the concept encompasses both the absence of war and the presence of social and economic justice, often called positive peace. Those who argue that peace should be defined narrowly, hold that broadening the concept reduces its clarity. Those who favour the broader conception, argue that the violent, life-threatening characteristics of various forms of systematic repression and underdevelopment approach or exceed that of overt warfare. The two individual researchers most often associated with the poles of this debate are Johan Galtung of Norway who is credited with inventing the term 'positive peace' in the mid-1960s and Kenneth Boulding of the US whose "twelve friendly quarrels" with Galtung include this one. In practice, however, there is more consensus than this conceptual rift would seem to suggest. Few scholars would contest the argument that there is a relationship between the absence of war and the presence of other social values such as justice and freedom. According to Karl Deutsch, a security community is one in which there are "dependable expectations of peaceful change" for the foreseeable future.

Peace and Development

The twin basic national problems in connection with North-East states are survival and transformation or to put it in conventional language, peace and development. They are in extricably interlinked and the future hinges on their healthy growth. But it is not possible without thorough planning and permanent observation of the centre. It also could not be treated only as an economic factor when we discuss the problems of North-East states. It is easy to point out a number of societal problems which would remain, or even get worse, if the engine of growth got started again. The most important of these are:

1. Marginalization
2. The Social Crisis
3. Legitimization Crisis.

The term 'marginalization' means the transfer of people to the fringes of society. They loose their function in the system and become superfluous. They also feel unwanted and, as a consequence, loose their self-respect. Unemployment is only one form of marginalization part of the youth are marginalized; they are the ones who are simply stored in colleges because they have no place in the labour market. Old people are retired on pensions even though they would like to continue to lead an active life. Over and above the people of North-East are confronting the problem of migration. The people of this region are very much worry for their future. In short there is no future for them.

Manipur offers a vast storehouse of an ancient civilization disintegrating and bursting at the seams through the phenomenal occurrence of both 'epistemic' and political violence. The nature of violence one experiences today is felt in the interstices of family, or societal relations, rupturing all inherited values of grace and wisdom of the past. The tension in the social world is manifest in the language one speaks, that a simple phrase which was harmless in the past now takes a sinister form, with strong under-currents of suspicious, doubt and mistrust. Cultural transformation in the social reproduction of daily lives had taken an obsessive, contentless, exhibitory character, which the parasitic middle class turn into a status and power seeking rite. Joint families have broken apart, heralding the individualistic, nuclearised family values, and it has repercussions in family relationships. Inside the body polity, the development of class, groups or ethnicity and their conflictual setting of targets and goals for group aspirations have undermined past relationships of trust, goodwill and ethnic pluralism. An environment of hatred, animosity and rivalry has aroused passions, and an uneasy balance in ethnic relations pervade in the newly developing economic townships and trading centres. Expression of doubts and discontents are rather rapidly exteriorisd through physical harm and inter-personal relationships in the midst of conflict are based on an uneasy equilibrium of mutual advantage, rather than as a revered balance in the practice of respect or trust. Pursuit of knowledge in the educational institutions is not free from the imposition of received experiences as dominant norms, and free mental development of the young are constrained. Subjection of the mind is prevalent in the institutions of higher learning, offices, social organizations even families, and there is structural violence in all forms of relationships, in social universes and in the construction of values. All these are manifestations of the tension filled life world of the Manipuris created by the processes of development and conflict (Loken. A).

Moreover, there is internal contradiction of established major religions groups like Hinduism and revivalists of indigenous culture and religion of this region. The present generation is really in struggle to pass out from the frozen layers of forced assimilation, which was taken place in the past. Besides, in every houses husband and wife are at stake to defend challenges of immature feminist movement, its framework planted from Western countries. It is completely doggerel but effulgent among them. In short, one could see both macro- and micro-level internal contradiction in the region; it is also more and more voluminous day by day. Maximum number of population both men and women have not permanent and stable economic status.

Furthermore talented young people are compelled to move to the industrial growth pools of outside the region even in abroad because of completely cut off industrial map in North-East states. Thus, they lost contact with their parents, relatives, former friends and neighbours. So, such condition upturns their social environment to a critical social relationship. People are transformed into passive, isolated consumers of private goods and public services. They can't do much by themselves, and so a number of social problems arise. Isolated people can't take care of themselves of they get sick; they are apt to seek consolation in alcohol and drugs. Another gloomy picture of the youth of this region are becoming the youths who are counting the days for death, because of having HIV positive and consequently of living with AIDS. They are the victims of counter-revolutionary movement. Both the Centre and the State governments look like to give syringes in their hands in order to carry off guns from their hands. These big burdens are on the heads of the all elders of family members of this region.

The problem I have called the legitimization crisis, what we call 'development' lacks a firm legitimation basis. We have lost our belief in the myths that one gave meaning and value to the great industrial project. The legitimation crisis has many components. There is a crisis of confidence; the loyalty of the citizens to the political system is decreasing. There is also a crisis of motivation; quite a few people have lost all desire to perform the alienating role of production and consumption that are required if they are in a technological society.

Mistrust in government is only one indicator of a general decline of confidence in authority figures. In 1970, for instance 25 per cent of the people of North-East agreed that one cannot trust the government to do what is right. Forty one years later 75 per cent endorsed the same statement. There is much talk about contempt for politicians but the crisis of confidence also hits company managers, union bosses, government officials, scientific experts and religious heads. The only elite without growing faults in the eyes of the people is the teaching profession of higher educational institutions. They never demand money when their students *pur sue* them to take more classes. They seem to understand, they are paid for the service of the students. Except them both temporary and permanent executives are demanding money for discharging their concerned duties in the offices. In other words, maximum of them are more and more degraded.

Another indicator of decreasing trust is the absence of political will and economic power. So, maximum electorates are not party oriented and have not been party loyalty. More and more voters have lost faith in the ability of their party and its leaders to solve the political problems. Hence, they are now searching for alternatives. Even in some states of the region there is government without opposition in spite of having both other national and regional political parties.

Models of Development

It is well known that North-East states have lagged far behind in development despite its vast potentials, the untapped hydropower (not mega dam), mineral resources, virgin forests, sturdy people and water resources of the region could change the face of the region. Lack of development has brought about a sense of neglect and frustration among the people. Young people are feeling alienated and getting unrest. For them, development means to meet the needs of the future generation without jeopardizing the needs of the future generation. So, they asked so often that development for whom. It should be development of all not for a particular handful of people.

In the development process, there is the tendency of depending upon money power rather than on real economic growth. Plethora of money is spent in the North-East States without corresponding fundamental change in productive structure. In the North-East States, being in special category, Central Government fund flows, not always in proportion. This has resulted in demoralizing the administration and the people. Money allocated for social welfare activities, partly goes to the poor but largely to the privileged and few. Social values of dedication and commitment to the society have largely been eroded and are replaced by greed and personal aggrandizement. The socializing virtues of tribal society is yielding place to individual and self-seeking opportunism. Being in special category, almost the entire expenditure of these states is run by the Central government. One result is that the people do not have to bear the corresponding cost of the benefit they are enjoying. State governments, on the other hand, have very limited financial strength. State revenues being very low, the State government expenditure, mainly on administrative purpose, is met by central fund. The easy money thus glowing in the State has also made the State administrative sector almost parasitic and inefficient.

A long-term strategy of development of the region would be meaningless unless this region prepared itself for such economic integration with the neighbouring economies. Its internal preparedness is crucial for benefits from mutual trade and travels. In the beginning, it has been pointed out that the whole understanding of the North-East's resource complex is misplaced that needs reassessment. Without such a review, it may not be feasible to make important strategic internal changes. What construes the natural resources of the region? It has land, both fertile valleys and hills and forest tracts of immense beauty. It has water both, flowing-plenty of it, and the potential hydro-power resources. It has people with their variegated culture, skills and generally a highly literate pool of manpower that is little used because of the lack of employment opportunities. It has the forests and the biological (and genetic) resource pool. The resource complex, therefore, is not the dead minerals, but a living pool of resources. Its development strategic must therefore, be based on this *living complex* of resources, not necessarily industrialization understood in the common parlance. It is not meant here that the other industries like oil and petrol-chemical or coal or limestone based industries are to be discouraged. It is more in changing the emphasis on the direction of development (Mohapatra AC).

But the tragic part of development scenario in the North-East is that the recommendations and observations of various commissions and studies have not been implemented. Complaints about the miss-use of funds and rampant corruption abound. Funds received by the states under the Prime Minister's package for numerous schemes and projects, for many other regular schemes and programmes, specially for rural development, and that received under the annual plans, are not properly utilized. Often, there is fund diversion. As often reported in the media, "bureaucrats, politicians, bank managers, contractors and their cohorts siphon-off major portions of funds, consequently leaving very little—and at times nothing for the poor. As a result of the diverted funds, there is exponential increase in the construction and luxury business, particularly in the urban areas."

It would need a new blue print. Therefore, it's better to see suggestions given by Mohapatra, AC, Professor of Geography, NEHU.

1. A strategic shift in emphasis is agriculture (crop farming) in the valleys from monsoon based practices (which may continue) to irrigation based farming during the off season. This region has one of the least irrigated areas of the country, since the traditional monsoon farming was considered adequate—irrigation was not promoted. From the farmer's point of view, monsoon not only provides water for the rice paddies, it also brings in the floods and the concomitant risks on investment. Flood protection thought is necessary; it neither can be effectively controlled in the same manner as in other areas of the country, nor is desirable due to the sheer volume of discharge from the region. An effective alternative appears if the dry-season farming. This of course, needs substantial public investment in irrigation. Agriculture can than yield a livelihood and may absorb a good proportion of the idle manpower. The region is currently food deficit. If farming practices, crop calendar are changed enabled by irrigation, in a decade's time the region can turn the corner and become food surplus. But it may not gain comparative advantage *vis-à-vis* other grain farming areas of the country due to high transportation cost. This is when opening in links with neighbouring region of the South-east Asia will come handy. However, rice will not enjoy a comparative advantage in those regions that already are surplus (Thailand and Myanmar) and are technologically superior and more efficient. A change in product mix will be necessary. Trade and travel will bring in demonstration effect on the farming practices, since the agro-climatic conditions of North-East is much closer to the South-east Asia than mainland India and thus, farming practices and technologies of that region will be more effective in North-East than the current practices promoted.
2. In the hills, however, the strategy need not be grain farming, but a complex of silviculture, horticulture and animal husbandry, which whenever initiated have yielded excellent results.
3. There must be accentuated research and development of plant genetic resources of the region and promotion of economic species at the field level. This also needs appropriated documentation and potential of genetic resources.
4. The region also needs re-working of its manpower development from general education to professional and vocational

programmes and skill upgradation programme including farmers training for the suggested package strategy. Though a good literacy situation is an adequate starting point, it may not be enough without appropriate filtering of skills right down to the grass root level.

5. The region ought to promote its natural and cultural heritage as a marketable product. This again requires more investment in tourism development and skill upgradations in tourist services. The region can also promote its traditional products like cottage textiles with their wonderful designs and motifs as exportable commodities. Specialised designing training centres will be essentials. Though this is being done to some extent now, it is not enough and more specialized inputs and governmental support may be necessary.
6. There would also be the need for considering and giving more emphasis to the informal sector for the economic development of the region. It was experimented in Nordic countries and got benefit of informal economy.

Whenever, we are in the discourse on development in case of North-East India, we have got various paradigms of development in the interaction in between people and government. They are Imperialism as development, anti-imperialism as development, anti-centrism-*cum*-separatism as development, national integration as development, nationalist *versus* cultural development paradigm, development *versus* sustainable development. All these inputs of development should be chanalised in the dialectics of State and civil society. After that we will get the real output. It could also be in the process of feedback loof if the environment defies them. As reaction, if the government understands that development in the real sense one will have to either deconstruction or negate the civil society oriented development paradigm, who could not see his future. So, AC Mohapatra rightly remarks that "the choice is to be with the people—whether a more liberal, integrative outlook on development or an inward looking perspective that may keep the region in the morass of backwardness, poverty and unemployment. If an inward looking autarchy like China could break open in nineties and becomes a super power in no time, why the North-East cannot become prosperous? It has the means—it needs the will." Moreover, an integrated action is needed in five areas where there is core competence. Agriculture and food processing, education/healthcare, information and communication technology, reliable and quality electric power, surface transport and infrastructure for all over the country besides self-reliance in critical technology, are essential for our food, economic and national security.

Lastly, now our discourse on peace is also paradox. Mention has been made in the sense that before 1980 there was full of peace in North-East India, but not develop. Even today, Arunachal Pradesh is land of peace and harmony, but not develop in comparison with other states of North-East. So, it is not true to say that development should be there if there is peace. From the people's view, the states of North-East India are in the process of development after arms struggle have been launched. Peoples also want to bring solution by political dialogue not by military means. People of North-East have been witnessing the existence of deadly conflict. It is designed as organized violence that kills large numbers of individuals. It includes war between states and war or genocide within states. But in using this shorthand, most thoughtful proponents of this objective do not seek peace at any price. 'Preservation of conflict' includes non-states, and often unacknowledged, measures of 'justice' and 'freedom'. Consider China's programme that is successfully 'preventing deadly conflict' in Tibet today. It succeeds by effectively suppressing basic rights of the Tibetan population. Nowhere does Tibet appear as successful cases of preventing deadly conflict nor should it.

The tension between 'order' on the one hand, and 'freedom' and 'justice' on the other, is one of the oldest themes in political theory. It is said that "we seek not peace at the expense of fundamental freedom". That is the same case that the people of North-East want to have fundamental freedom for not questioning right to life so often. Moreover, they want to have real test of rule of law.

Peace Process in the North-East India

The following pattern emerges from governmental initiatives for peace in the North-East India.

- Unconditional denial of the demand for complete sovereignty or the right to self-determination.
- Using developmental initiatives for particular schemes to create the context of peace has been a constant theme in the centre's policy on conflict resolution in the North-East. Since 1996, Billions of rupees have been announced as special packages for North-East.

- Poor implementation of each and every government programme, including the special package continues to create beneficiaries of conflict.
- Surrender of a section of militants and another section continuing to fight.
- Breaking of existing states and reorganization.

From the governmental initiatives for peace in the North-East States, we come to understand that government is using developmental initiatives to create the context of peace as constant theme and even for negotiating with underground organizations; there is possibility of altering the existing boundary of states. That means the gun fighting in between underground militants and security forces will be stopped, but it invites to fight among the various communities. Can we accept it as the constructive peace process? In case of development by pouring huge amount of money as economic package, could it be meaningful of development of all. It should be for a few groups, they are ministers, their relatives and dear ones and bureaucrats. So, the question will remain in the minds of the people forever, 'Development for Whom'?

Statement of the Problem

Thus, the distorted concept of peace and development manifests itself in the following forms:

- denial of meaningful independence with fundamental freedom;
- denial of dissent in the democratic space;
- every area of activity in the State, including the find art of statecraft, one overwhelming question remains the common denominator—the law and order situation.
- Denial of constitutional and human rights.
- Emerging of negative peace with development for a handful of people;
- Imposition of security without positive value-loaded—there is not at least some degree of value consensus among the actors;
- Lack of social security makes emergence of social exclusion; and
- There is Legitimisation crisis, which leads crisis of confidence, loyalty of citizen to political system, crisis of motivation.

Tripura as Model State to Overcome Insurgency in North-East

Some states of North-East are facing the vexed problems of political violence, but Tripura seems to overcome it. The pertinent question is that how did it so. Whether the same method could be applied in Manipur? That is also questionable because the ruling elites of Manipur didn't have a well-crafted, multi-dimensional strategy, a positive mindset, resolute will, the right vision and direction, sagacious, honest and credible leadership, sincerity of intent, creative responses to the challenge, even socio-economic-infrastructure dispensation to all sections of society. So, to study Tripura's experience will be helpful in this work in order to find out how to bring peace in North-East.

The evolution of insurgency in Tripura can be traced to the formalization of the Tripura Upajati Juba Samity (TUJS) in 1971, followed by the Tripura National Volunteers (TNV) in 1981. The National Liberation Front of Tripura (NLFT) was formed on March 2, 1989 and its armed wing, the National Holy Army and All Tripura Tiger Force (ATTF), in July 1990, queering the pitch. The two outfits came up with a secessionist agenda, disputed the merger of the kingdom of Tripura with the Indian Union, demanded sovereignty for Tripura, deportation of "illegal migrants," the implementation of the Tripura merger agreement and the restoration of land to the tribal people under the Tripura Land Reform Act, 1960. Between 1990 and 1995, the insurgency remained low-key. But it grew in extent and magnitude between 1996 and 2004—and then started melting. How such high voltage insurgency could be defused.

High voltage insurgency and chain of violence disrupted civic life and communications, and led to the closure of many educational and financial institutions, threatening the authority of the State. D.N. Sahaya, he was Governor of Tripura from June 2003 to October 2009, observed that "the state took on the problems in a strategic and resolute manner under the sagacious and visionary leadership of Chief Minister Manik Sarkar." He further stated that "it formulated a multi-dimensional and fine-tuned construct to respond creatively to the situation. The control mechanism was subsumed in counter—insurgency operations intent on swift area-domination and ascendancy, as well as psychological operations and confidence building measures. An accelerated development thrust, management of the media, civic action programmes of the security forces, and the political process were additional factors" (D.N. Sahaya, *How Tripura Overcame Insurgency*, *The Hindu*, September 19, 2011, p. 6).

In Tripura, counter insurgency operations (C.I. Ops), a potent instrument in any fight against insurgency, formed the core of the interventions. These were not set as exclusive, hawkish, one-dimensional combat in the nature of conflict-management. The combat was invested with a broader meaning and constructive contents in the nature of a productive conflict-resolution aimed at defusing insurgency (Sahaya 2011).

Some of the measures taken by the Tripura Government are given below:

1. The counter-insurgency operations, intensive, extensive and covert as they were, did not take the Army on board—as had happened in other insurgency-bound states. Only the Central Paramilitary Forces and State police forces were drafted. Special Police Officers (tribals included) were inducted and channeled into the operations. This proved to be valuable in terms of gathering intelligence and keeping a tab on the activities and movements of the insurgents, collaborators and harbourers. The Central and State security forces were forged into a synergetic, coordinated and cohesive mode to derive optimal gains. Their conduct was under close observation at the highest level (including at the level of the Governor and the Chief Minister), in order to check personnel from going berserk and being ruthless, trigger-happy, oppressive and violative of human rights.
2. There were no complaints of human rights violation, except one or two and that too minor, came up in the course of operations. No antipathy against the security forces or the establishment surrounded the minds of citizens.
3. Psychological operations were forged to work on the minds of the target group—for all conflicts, big or small, begin in the human mind. Brainstorming sessions centred on unwinding the deeds, misdeeds and subversive designs of insurgency and to unmask its hypocritical conduct. This strategy was carried through the media, both print and electronic, art groups, intellectuals, and interactive seminars and discussions. Confidence-building exercises and healing touches encompassed special recruitment to the security forces and other government services, especially in the insurgency-bound pockets.
4. The provision of jobs to tribals in particular, and to the family

members of victims, attractive rehabilitation packages comprising monetary benefits, and vocational training to induce insurgents to return to the mainstream and earn a peaceful living and decent livelihood, were other features. There was a good response to this. It brought back a number of them, including an entire group of the NLFT-NB in 2006 along with a cache of arms before the Governor.

5. As the security forces achieved success in area-domination, no time was lost in implementing governance and developmental interventions swiftly and vigorously. The government reached out to the tribal people with the delivery of basic services such as health care, rural connectivity, drinking water supply, employment generation and income growth. Socio-economic advancement and a change in the quality of life were ushered in. The impressive gains from development were perceptible to the people in general and the tribal community in particular. They discovered a connection with the mainstream and the state. The outcomes were active community participation in the development process and in the fight against insurgency, the militants' return to the mainstream and consequential retreat from insurgency.
6. Micro-democratic institutions such as autonomous development councils, *gram panchayats* and village councils were strengthened, revitalized and legitimized. They turned vibrant and actively functional as local governance modules. This brought all the communities, notably the tribals in particular, into the development stream, bringing about substantial empowerment and a sense of fulfillment.
7. The security forces presented a human face, a pro-citizen, people-friendly, development-oriented face of the State, and earned the trust, admiration and gratitude of the people. Civic action programmes proved to be of tremendous significance in clearing doubts and apprehensions about the intentions of the security forces and the State. This brought fort community participation in the moves against insurgency.

In this experience, the response of the Manipur insurgency is that theirs is not related with the question of development and good governance. Their demand is related with forcibly annexation of Manipur to India without consent of the existing Assembly of that time and plebiscite. The best example is Junagarh in 1947. Junagarh had given acceptance of instrument of accession with Pakistan. But India sent army to Junagarh then plebiscite was held three times. Finally, people of Junagarh had given more votes to integrate India. So, it is quit evidence that the political solution of Manipur is neither development nor good governance, which is the question of self-determination of the masses of Manipur through plebiscite. Such stand of armed opposition groups could not be bargained by the development and good governance of existing government.

In the light of the above theoretical perspective of peace and development, in this research work an attempt has been made to examine as to how conflict transformation and peace building will be brought. For a meaningful transformation of conflicts, it is necessary to identify and consolidate support structures that tend to strengthen peace. Positive opportunities can be improved through the awareness of mutual dependence on one another. Changing psychological dimensions of adversarial relationship supported by the opportunities to understand different views is undoubtedly an inevitable part of the movement toward conflict de-escalation. Moreover, efforts to end hostile, competitive and coercive processes would be fruitless if one party's domination continues to be allowed. Newly forged relationship has to be supported by structural transformation of social conditions.

In a transformative framework, identity and power relations continue to be re-negotiated in an on going process of resolving conflict. Dynamics of conflict are not likely to be transformed toward resolution by an attempt to protect existing interests. Re-establishing a *status quo* would not dramatically change conflict relations. In transformative perspectives, roles and relationships have to be redesigned in the process of re-structuring the patterns of transactions and interactions.

Resolving conflict in transformative perspectives has to be geared toward helping the underprivileged break out of the discriminatory social roles assigned to them within the *status quo*. The existence of injustice in asymmetric conflict structures requires strategies to deal with power imbalanced situations. Social change for promoting justice, by which conditions for decent human life can be established, is the most appropriate means for peace building. Thus, peace building is largely equated with the construction of a new social environment that advances a sense of confidence and improves conditions of life. Leaving an abusive and dependent relationship intact is incompatible with peace building. Conflict transformation can underscore the goal of peace building through empowering a marginalized population exposed to extreme vulnerability in such a way to achieve self-sufficiency and well-being. The successful outcome of conflict transformation therefore, contributes to eliminating structural violence. This research is enough to increase and disseminate knowledge on these issues.

References

A.C. Mohapatra, Development and Underdevelopment of the North-East Region: Search for a paradigm, in Eds, Bimal, J. Deb, *Development Priorirties in North-East India*, Concept Publishing Company, New Delhi, 2002.

Action for Conflict Transformation a global initiative from the grassroots, 2003.

AMCTA, *Manipur: Fact File*, Imphal, 2001.

Andrew Robinson, *The Rhizomes of Manipur*. Seminar Paper, Institute of Asia Pacific Studies: University of Nottingham, 2005.

Centre for Organization Research and Education (CORE), "The Manipur Nation: A Position" in Laifungbam, Debabrata, Roy., Immanuel, Zarzosang, Varte. *Contour of Conflict. Pathway of Peace*, Guwahati: ICTCP-North-East Zone 2007.

CORE, Manipur: A Report on Impunity of Human Rights Violations under the AFSPA 1958, Amended-1972. Submitted to the Special Rapporteur on the Human Rights and Fundamental Freedoms of Indigenous People, 2002.

Dhanabir L., *Gandhian Means to End Ethnic Hatred*, in the Stitch, Akanksha Publishing House, 2009.

Dhanabir L., *Resolution of Armed-Conflict in Manipur: An Alternative Perspective, Eastern Quaterly*, Vol. 4, Issue 1, April-June 2007, MRF, Delhi.

Dhanabir L. *The Middle Space*, Akanksha Publishing House, New Delhi, 2011.

Duursman Jorris, *Fragmentation and the International Relations of Micro States*, Cambridge: Cambridge University Press 1996.

Hakan Wiberg, *Peace and Development Concepts of Security: A Logical and Analytical Framework*, in eds., Narinda Siopment, Lancer Press, Delhi, 1988, p. 33.

Holsti, K.J., *War, the State, and the State of War*, Cambridge University Press, 1996.

J.J. Roy Burman, Contour of Naga Upsurge, *Asia Europe Journal*, 6, 1, 2008.

K. Das, *Stilwill's Folly*, The Sentinel, Guwahati, Assam, November 10, 2002.

Karen Parker, "Understanding Self-Determination: The Basics", Paper presented to first *International Conference on the Right to Self-determination*, United Nation, August, 2000.

Kunal Chattopadhyay, Aninda Banerjee, Saurobbijoy Sarkar. *The Permanent Revolution and Results and Prospects—Leon Trotsky*, New Delhi: Aakar Books, 2005.

Myanmar Snubs India, Frees Ultras, The Hindustan Times, March 17, 2002.

N. Sanajaoba, *Manipur Past and Present*, Vol. 1, History, Policy and Law, New Delhi: Mittal Publication, 1988.

Naorem Sanajaoba, Armed Forces Special Power Act, 1958—a Law for extrajudicial execution in perpetuity. Paper at AASU Apunba Lup, One Day Convention, Guwahati, 2006.

Naorem Sanajaoba, *Manipur Past and Present Volume III, Manipuri Nagas & Kuki-Chins, New* Delhi: Mittal Publications, 1995.

Pages of People's Voice, Vol. 4 number 2, April-June 2004, Published by ROE Units & CSD.

Rajkumar Maipaksana, "Constitutional Development in a Nut Shell" *in Annexation of Manipur 1949, Imphal*: Peoples Democratic Movement, 1995.

Richard A. Falk, *Human Rights Horizons: The Pursuit of Justice in a Globalizing World*, London: Routledge, 2000.

R.K. Nimai, Ways and Means for Economic Development in Manipur, paper presented in the Seminar on *Development and Peace,* organized by Edirors' Forum, Manipur, at State Guest House, Imphal on 28-29 October, 2004.

Robertson, David, *A Dictionary of Modern Defence and Strategy.* Europa Publication, London, 1987.

S. Bhubol, "Governance Deviate Peace-Path-Now Ripe for Resolution", *The Orient Vision*, 6: 1 and 2 (2009).

Sajal Nag, *Contesting Marginality: Ethnicity, Insurgency and Subnationalism in North-East India*, New Delhi: Manohar Publications, 2002.

Sanjib Baruah, *Durable Disorder: Understanding the Politics of North-East India,* New Delhi: Oxford University Press, 2005.

Shibadas Bhattacharjee, *China, Myanmar and Issues of the North-East,* The Sentinel, Guwahati, Assam, May 20, 2010.

Shibadas Bhattacharjee, *Don't Expected Much from Myanmar*, The Sentinel, April 8, 2010.

Shoma Chaudhury, "Life in a Shadow Land". *Tehelka Magazine*, 6, August 15, 2009.

Shukhdeba S. Hanjabam, "The Meitei Upsurge in Manipur", *Asia-Europe Journal*, 6, 1, 2008.

Smoker, Paul, Ruth Davies and Barbara Munske (eds.), *A Reader in Peace Studies*. Oxford, Progamon Press, 1990.

Sobhapati Samon, "Talks only on the issue of sovereignty of Manipur", *North-East Sun,* May 31, 2009.

Soyam Lokendrajit Singh, *Why AFSPA should be Repealed*. Imphal: Manipur University Students Union, Manipur University, 2004.

Stiglitz Joseph, *Globalisation and Its Discontents*, New York, Allen Lane. 2002.

The Hindu, National English Daily, Madras.

The Hueiyen Lanpao. Popular English Daily, Imphal.

The Imphal Free Press. Popular English Daily, Imphal.

The Sangai Express, Popular English Daily, Imphal.

The Sentinel, National English Daily, Shillong.

The Seven Sisters Post, National English Daily, Shillong.

Tulasi R., *Integrating Peacebuilding into Development Work: The Vital Role of Influencing,* Applied Conflict Transformation Studies, January, 2008.

United Committee Manipur, *Influx of Migrants into Manipur: A Threat to the Indigenous Ethnic People*, Imphal, 2005.

15

SoO and Resolving Hydra-Headed Chikim Insurgencies in Manipur

Aheibam Koireng Singh

Prelude: SoO in Undercover Overture

"*I am totally blind in this matter and more so on the conditions maintained between the concerned underground group and the army*".[1]

The above citation was from the statement by Shri Okram Ibobi, the Manipur Chief Minister (CM) on 15 July, 2006 while clarifying that the State government was unaware and yet to receive any formal intimation from the Central government as regards the ceasefire was concerned. It mirrors the murky manner with which Suspension of Operation (SoO) began as the State government was being sidelined and not taken into confidence though law and order is a state subject. It was the army which initiated the move of suspending the operation against the 'Chin Kuki Mizo (CHIKIM)' armed outfits. Previously Ceasefire under SoO was between the Indian army and central paramilitary forces and some armed groups belonging to CHIKIM communities. The Ministry of Defence in a press release dated October 7, 2005, disclosed that eight 'Kuki' and one 'Zomi' militant group in Manipur had entered into an informal 'ceasefire' with the Union Government. 'Cessation of operations' agreements was concluded with these groups with effect from 01 August, 2005.[2] The Manipur government demanded details on the SoOs signed with the eight Kuki-Zomi rebel groups by the army and made it clear that those agreements would be summarily rejected if it involved state's territorial issues.[3] The Manipur CM stated that the ceasefire maintained between the "Indian security forces and some Non-Naga insurgents" was not acceptable as it lacks the consent of the State government. Further he stated that the State government would form modalities and concrete ground rules for holding dialogues with insurgents groups operating in the State.[4] The Intelligence Bureau (IB) is also understood to have been upset with the army's ceasefire agreement with the Kuki groups. By signing the agreement, the IB felt, the army had given marginal Kuki groups a more exalted status.[5]

Pursuit for State Recognition

Zomi Council in the early part of March, 2006 called on the CM and reiterated the demand to initiate talk with non-Naga tribal underground groups operating in the State. It issued a statement that CM showed his willingness to hold talk with non-Naga tribal underground groups operating in the State.[6] Ahead of the Ninth Manipur Assembly Election, 2007, a meeting of the Strategy and Operational Group (SOG) presided by the Chief Secretary, attended by Director General of Police (DGP) and top ranking officials from the Home Department, State police, Army, Assam Rifles (AR), Central Reserved Police Force (CRPF) and intelligence agencies was held on 19 September to discuss the overall security scenario. The officials present at the meeting while expressing strong apprehension of the CHIKIM armed outfits which have struck a truce pact with the Central Security force might try to intervene in the election, asked the army to see what best could be done.[7] In this connection a faction of the Kuki National Front (KNF) had issued a threat that "if the ruling State government did not apply the SoO (Ceasefire) pact in the State between Kuki revolutionaries with Centre there shall be no room for Congress (I) in the forthcoming state election in the Kuki dominated hills in the state". The outfit spelled out that it would ban any Congress (I) workers, candidate and campaign in the Kuki dominated areas.[8] It can also be cited that the Kuki Liberation Army (KLA)/Kuki Liberation Organisation (KLO) in its press release on 7 January, 2007 had stated that despite entering into SoO with the Indian army and the Central security forces, the congress led State government refused to recognize and endorse the SoO agreement even after repeated approaches from the organisation. KLO also alleged the State government for not taking any initiative of approaching the centre to start a peace talk. On these grounds, the KLO had imposed ban on the candidates of the ruling alliances who were contesting the elections.[9] The outfit also carried out bomb attacks at the residence of Minister, Ph. Parijat and the President of Manipur Pradesh Congress Committee (MPCC), Mr Gaikhangam. The CHIKIM armed outfits which entered into the said informal ceasefire include Kuki National Organisation (KNO)/Kuki National Army (KNA), Zomi Revolutionary Army (ZRA)/Zomi Reunification Organisation (ZRO), KLA/KLO, Kuki Revolutionary Army (KRA), Kuki National Front—Zogam (KNF-Z), Kuki National Front- Military Council (KNF-MC), etc.

SoO with KNO, UPF and the State and the Union Government

The SoO between the conglomerate groups of CHIKIM outfits namely, the United Peoples' Front (UPF), and the KNO, State Government and the Central Government was signed at Delhi on 22 August, 2008. The State Cabinet presided over by the Chief Minister gave its approval to the said SoO agreement signed within the framework of Constitution of India after the State Government rejected demand of the Kuki outfits for Kuki homeland or Zalengam to ensure the territorial integrity of Manipur.[10]

While the KNO represents 11 groups, the UPF represents eight outfits. After a series of turns and negotiations and brain storming sessions, the ground rules for the suspension of operations between the Government and Kuki armed groups were signed on 22 August, 2008. In it, Joint Secretary in the Union Government in charge of North-East, Mr. Navin Verma appended his signature on behalf of the Government of India (GoI) while the State government of Manipur was represented by Principal Secretary (Home). Eight members each from the UPF and the KNO also signed the SoO. The signatories from the KNO are its vice President Mr. Lanminthang Vaiphei, Defence Secretary, Mr. T.S. Haokip, Cabinet member, T.S. German Kuki, and another member, Mr. Joshua Kuki signed on behalf of the KNO. While its General Secretary, Mr. S.T. Thangboi Kipgen, members Mr. Calvin H., Mr. T.L. Jacob Thadou and T.L. Hangshing signed on behalf of the UPF.

Profile of the CHIKIM Ethnic Outfit Under SoO

> KNO comprises of 11 different CHIKIM armed ethnic outfit. They are Kuki National Army (KNA), Kuki National Front-Military Council (KNF-MC), Kuki National Front-Zogam (KNF-Z), United Socialist Revolutionary Army (USRA), Zou Defence Volunteer-KNO (ZDV-KNO), United Komrem Revolutionary Army (UKRA), Zomi Revolutionary Force (ZRF), Hmar National Army (HNA), Kuki Revolutionary Army (Unification), Kuki Liberation Army (KLA-KNO) and United All Kuki Liberation Army.[11] While the UPF represents eight outfits which

include Kuki Revolutionary Army (KRA), Kuki National Front-P (KNF-P), United Kuki Liberation Front (UKLF), Zomi Revolutionary Army (ZRA), Hmar Peoples' Conference/ Democratic (HPC-D), Kuki Liberation Army (KLA/KLO), Kuki National Front-S (KNF-S), etc.[12]

The main objectives of the KNO/KNA is to bring together all the Kuki-inhabited areas separated by artificial boundary created in 1935, specifically in the Kabaw valley of Myanmar and the Kuki inhabited areas in the hill districts of Manipur under one administrative unit called 'Zalengam' (Land of freedom). In case of the eventuality of such integration not materializing, the KNA aims at the creation of two Kuki States: one within Burma, i.e. 'Eastern Zalengam' and the other within India, 'Western Zalengam'. The KNA has an estimated strength of 600 cadres armed with an array of weapons like AK-Series, G-series, M-series and 60mm mortar.[13] Zou Defence Volunteer (ZDV) was said to be formed in 1997 however, its existence came to be known in 2003. ZDV strives for maintaining their intermediary "Zou" identity without aligning to either the "Zomi" or the "Kuki". KNF was founded on 18 May, 1988 with the objective of the demand for Kukiland which consisted of the districts of Churachandpur, Chandel, parts of Tamenglong and parts of Senapati.[14] Another objective of the KNF was to defend the Kukis from the atrocities and brutalities of the "anti-national Naga activists". KNF split in 1995, with one unit identifying itself as the "presidential faction" and the other as the "military council". The former again split into Samuel faction (KNF-S) and Zougam faction (KNF-Z). The total cadre strength of the outfit (inclusive of all factions) is estimated to be between 400 and 500.[15] United Komrem Revolutionary Army (UKRA) was formed on 23 October, 2004 to protect the interests of the Komrem community.[16]

KRA was formed in December, 2000 by a group of disgruntled cadres of the KNF-MC faction with purported objective of securing a "separate State" for the Kuki tribe within the Indian Union. In Assam, where the outfit operates in the Karbi Anglong district, KRA aims at the establishment of a "Kuki National Council", an autonomous administrative council for the Kuki tribes. It has approximate cadre strength of 250. National Socialist Council of Nagaland-Isak-Muivah (NSCN-IM) was instrumental in training and arming the KRA cadres.[17] KLA was formally re-established in 1993 with the sole objective of safeguarding the political interest of the Kukis and their inhabited areas which purportedly claimed to have inherited from the Kuki ancestors.[18] Hmar People's Convention-

Democratic (HPC-D) is an offshoot of the HPC, which came into existence in 1986, as a political party spearheading a movement for self-government in the north and North-East of Mizoram. The Mizo Peace Accord of 1986, failed to address their demand of a 'Greater Mizoram' integrating all areas inhabited by Hmars in Mizoram, Assam and Manipur under a single administrative unit. Since April 1987, the HPC waged an armed struggle for autonomy. However in 1992, HPC representatives and the Government of Mizoram mutually agreed signed a Memorandum of Settlement (MoS) at the Mizoram capital Aizawl on July 27, 1994, for establishing the 'Sinlung Development Council' and subsequently, 308 HPC militants surrendered along with their arms. HPC-D was formed by a section of the HPC cadres who were dissatisfied with the implementation process MoS. The purported objective of the outfit over the years has changed from an autonomous district covering the north and north-east Mizoram to an independent Hmar State (Hmar ram) consisting of the Hmar inhabited areas of Mizoram, Manipur and Assam. The cadre strength of the outfit is estimated to be between 100 and 150.[19]

ZRA was formed in 1997 as an armed wing of ZRO which was formed in 1993. The purported objective of the ZRO/ZRA is to protect the interests of the Paite community from the "onslaught of any community or group". It further attempts "to bring all the Zomi people, divided by artificial State boundaries in various countries, specifically in Myanmar (Chin State), India (Manipur and Mizoram) and Bangladesh (Chittagong Hills Tracts), together under one administrative unit, a 'Zogam', which means 'land of the Zomi' under the Indian Union".[20] ZRF was formed by a group of Paites defected from ZRA. USRA was formed by Vaiphei cadres who defected from ZRA to uphold the dignity and identity of the Vaipheis. United Kuki Liberation Front (UKLF) was formed on March 29, 2000 with the purported objective of upholding the interests of the Kuki community and forming a separate Kuki state called 'Kukiland'.

Cadres and Designated Camps of the Chikim Ethnic Outfit under SoO

In the later part of December, 2008, after the completion of four rounds of meetings on the SoO between the CHIKIM ethnic outfits led by UPF and the KNO, the JMG of the government finalized the process for issue of Identity Cards to around 1745 cadres out of a total of 2519. At a meeting held on 19 December, 2008 a list of 500 cadres of KRA, 377 cadres of KNF-P, 419 cadres of UKLF, 111 cadres of KLA, 717 cadres of ZRA,

250 cadres of KNF-S, 110 cadres of HPC and 45 cadres of ZDV have been proposed by the Kuki groups for official recognition. 23 numbers of designated camps operating under different Kuki militant groups have also been proposed for official identification. The camps include the areas of Angkhuino, Vangai Ridge, Parvachon under Parbung police station in Churachandpur district and Tipaimukh areas operated by HPC(D), Nathanjang Chongkhonjou under Thanlon police station jointly operated by KNF(S), KNF(P) and ZDV, Chelap in Chandel district operated by UKLF, N Phaisat under Henglep sub-division operated by KNF(S), T. Gamnom and L. Songphel areas under Saikul sub-division operated by KRA, Salam Patong under Andro operated by the KRA, Songtal in Thanlon sub-division operated by ZRA, Leijangphai under Tipaimukh operated by UKLF, G. Tonjang in Churachandpur operated by KRA, Thinkeu in Henglep operated by ZRA, Ngaijang Aimol in Tengnoupal sub-division operated by KRA, S. Lengthengnom in Chakpikarong sub-division operated by KNF, Moulphai/T. Hangnom at Sajik Tampak operated by UKLF, Vaitonphai in Kangpokpi and Sehjang/Gomnom in Sapermeina operated by KNF(P), T. Khanjang/Thinghat in Singhat operated by ZRA, G. Tanjang/Tuining areas in Singhat operated by ZRA, Maphou dam operated by KRA and Samusong area in Saikul jointly operated by KLA/KRA. Designated camps at Angkhuino under Parbung Police Station operated by HPC-D, Nanthanjang/Chokhonjou under Thanlon Police Station jointly operated by KNF-S, KNF-P, Chelap in Chandel district operated by UKLF and Samusong area under Saikul sub-division operated jointly by KLA and KRA had been recognised as official designated camps and six designated camps including Moulvaiphei and Nathajang in Sadar Hills, Parvachom, N. Phaisat and Leijangphsi in Churachandpur and Vangai Range in Tamenglong were proposed for official recognition as designated camps. The said meeting between the JMG and the KNO and UPF was attended by the State Principal Secretary Home; Binoyranjan Jha, Deputy Director of Subsidiary Intelligence Bureau (SIB); Colonel Sanjay Gupta of GS (HQ) Inspector General Assam Rifles (IGAR)-South; Mr. Rakesh Dhakarwal, Commandant, Central Reserved Police Force; Lieutenant Colonel D. Mishra, GSD (Int), 57 Mountain Divison; KMS Rao, Assistant Director, SIB; Major S. Jung, HQIGAR (S) and seven other representatives from the KNO and UPF.[21]

SoO Ground Rules

With the signing of the tripartite agreement, SoO came into force initially for a period of one year with the provision that it could be extendable on the basis of mutual agreement and understanding. The KNO spokesman, Dr. Seilen Haokip took SoO as a pre-requisite to political dialogue's commencement.[22] While voicing on behalf of the KNO he stated that the tripartite agreement was a structural necessity. He exemplify by stating that the Joint Monitoring Group comprising representatives from GoI, KNO and the Government of Manipur will be dealing with issues related to the field or the ground rules. JMG are going to be responsible for monitoring the activities of KNO's cadres and the security forces. JMG is an administrative body, which will take decisions pertaining to the camps and ground issues; it is not going to be responsible for making political decisions. However, this was not KNO's preferred model. Instead KNO would want GoI to engage in dialogue with them and referred to the Manipur state government any relevant issue as and when necessary. A Joint Monitoring Group headed by Principal Secretary (Home), Mr. D.S. Poonia with a representative each from the UPF and the KNO had also been formed. Issuing of identity cards to all the cadres of the two groups by the government, payment of Rs. 2000 to each cadre monthly for maintenance as well as identifying and building the designated camps. The cadres will not be allowed to move out of the designated camps with arms and all the designated camps will be located at a good distance from the national highways as well as international boundaries, and strict adherence to the rules so laid down are some significant points of the ground rules. As per the agreement, the enforcement of the ground rules would be the responsibility of the State government with the help and assistance of the Central Police organizations, Assam Rifles and Army deployed in the State of Manipur.[23]

When the SoO agreement was due to expire on 23 August, 2009, the Peoples' Consultative Committee for Peace (PCCP) while calling upon the parties involved to respect the terms of the SoO appealed to the authorities concerned to have it extended for another term.[24] SoO was extended for a year with effect from 22 August 2009 with the condition that SoO will continue to be defined by the earlier "Ground Rules". The agreed "Ground Rules" demands all the parties to stick to the conditions that admit them into the SoO group. Exercising any sort of military might, particularly by the armed groups, is bound to be seen as violation of the contract that they have mutually entered into. On the part of the armed groups, it appears that none would immediately choose to stand in the way of the peace process in their quest to walk the talk towards securing "political solution". In this connection the KNO spokesman stated that the main purpose of SoO was to engage in political dialogue to find a political settlement for the Kukis within the Constitution of India. "Extension of SoO signals a positive stand on the part of all the parties concerned", he further said. He also averred that inclusion of 'territorial integrity' in the ground rules could not prevent the KNO from raising their political demand when the talks started. Calvin H. member of the UPF also asserted that "despite the stand of the Government of Manipur" for territorial integrity, "there is no binding clause in the constitution that says the boundary of the state cannot be changed".[25] UPF's convenor of the Joint Monitoring Group (JMG) TL Jacob Thadou stated that the armed groups are adhering to the agreed conditions of the "Ground Rules" in good spirit. He said that the armed groups have been pragmatically engaged in a learning process that requires them to make peace, build confidence and resolve differences. Further he said, the preparations, thus far, have been held in a positive atmosphere with certain progress, though without definitive agreements for the political talks. Commander of 59 Mountain Brigade, Brigadier Anil Chauhan stated on 27 November, 2009 that the tripartite Suspension of Operation (SoO) pact signed between the Central Government, the State Government and Kuki militant groups were still in transitory phase and no political dialogue has been initiated as yet.[26]

Violation of Ceasefire Ground Rules

The CHIKIM ethnic armed outfits despite being in SoO with the State and the Union Government continued to engage in extortion, fratricidal turf wars and internecine factional clashes, kidnapping for ransom, intimidating the civilians, interference in developmental programmes, and influencing the outcome of the Autonomous District Council (ADC) election 2010 results through sheer coercion. An amount of Rs. 21,48,095 was released for the purpose of payment of compensations to the land owners affected by the land acquisition for the construction of the ICP at Moreh. From the compensation amount, KNA/KNO maintaining cease fire trust under SoO imposed diktat that they will cut 57 per cent of the compensation amount received by the land owners. Out of the compensation amounts KNA/KNO had collected Rs. 17,76,000.[27] In this connection the Integrated Check Post-Joint Action Committee (ICP-JAC) had earlier on 04 April, 2010 demanded the Chandel district administration that distribution/payment of compensation should be delayed until the KNA was permanently driven out from 'Moreh'[28] and Chandel District.

The KLA on 17 November, 2009 while declaring its decision to no longer go along with the KNO/KNA alleged the later of repeatedly violating the ceasefire ground rules in the name of KLA in the form of levying taxes, extortion, kidnapping, etc. to blacklist the KLA.[29]

On April, 2010, there were reports of villagers of Bungbal Khullen, Seichang and Suongthel areas in Senapati District fleeing their respective villages following continued clashes between suspected rival Kuki militants under SoO. A particular outfit under SoO had on 27 May, 2010 spelled out that contractors who have violated the outfit's instruction of seeking prior permission would not be entertained for undertaking works under the Pradhan Mantri Gram Sadak Yojana. The same outfit abducted the chief of Kom village, Thayong in the Senapati district and imposed a fine of Rs. 100000 for not attending a meeting of village chiefs of the area and eventually released on payment of Rs. 80,000. KLA despite in a SoO agreement locked up the Imphal-Guwahati passenger bus from outside at a place near Dimapur and set it on fire with 32 passengers still inside on October 2008 because of the bus owner's failure to pay their "tax" demand. It resulted in the death of two passengers.[30] On 2 June, 2008, the United Committee Manipur in a memorandum submitted to Manipur Governor Dr. Shivendra Singh Sidhu blamed the Suspension of Operation (SoO) agreement signed with the Kuki militant outfits for the rising crime and unchecked violence in some parts of the State. It stated that due to the improper implementation of the truce details there were unrestricted and open extortions being carried out along with abductions for ransom which had become routine further adding that the Imphal-Moreh Sumo service was suspended due to monetary demands imposed by the KNA on the transporters. Cadres of the CHIKIM armed outfit under SoO was found in the fraudulent withdrawal of Rs. 4.54 Crores of public fund in between 03-14 October 2010 from the Churachandpur branch of United Bank of India.[31] KNA allegedly intimidated the voters belonging to Kom community in Sagang and Tuibuong areas in Churachandpur District and at Moreh area in Chandel District and disrobe them of their right to vote in the Autonomous District Council (ADC) held in May, 2010.

Conclusion

It would be pertinent to recall the incidents occurred in Moreh in the early part of June, 2007 that KNA after pumping bullet to six mason workers left their bodies considering all to be lifeless corpse as obvious revenge for killing five Kukis by the UNLF whom they alleged as KNA cadres. One of them was later found alive to tell the stories of the cruel incident. By that time KNA was already in SoO with the Indian army. During those days of heightening tension and anxious moments, Meiteis in Moreh fled to Myanmar as they did not feel secure with the Indian army and security personnels deployed there. When the Additional Deputy Commissioner of Moreh along with Sub-Divisional Police Officer (SDPO) met their Myanmarese counterpart to take back those who took refuge at Myanmar following the eruption of imbroglio, the Myanmarese officials, while contending that the situation continued to be volatile and still not calmed down refused to oblige with the Additional Deputy Commissioner of Moreh and SDPO at the first instant. Some among those that fled to Myanmar expressed that they fled to Myanmar side of the border sensing the futility and consequent risk of their lives because of the perceived inaction of the Indian Armed Forces (IAF) as the KNA by that time was already in SoO with the IAF without any definite ground-rules. Just in the aftermath of that violence, the proscribed United National Liberation Front issued a hand out alleging the KNA of driving a wedge of ethnic hatred to create hostility among the co-existing communities in connivance with the security personnel, further adding that the passivity of the Assam Rifles (AR) by remaining as mere spectators even when five Meitei civilians were killed clearly illustrates their nexus. The upshot of recalling this episodic event is that those CHIKIM outfits under SoO shall not be engaged either as guides or in any other form in counter-insurgency operations. Why? Such engagement would escalate hostilities among armed outfits cutting across community lines. As past experience of the Moreh June, 2007 episodic event stands vivid that rivalries between the armed outfits often have a trickledown effect among the people whom they claimed to represent.

The State and the Central Government shall ensure that those CHIKIM outfits under SoO did not inconvenience the civilians. The KNO as well as the UPF took SoO as a significant step in the right direction and a prerequisite to the commencement of political dialogue. Though different warring groups and factions have come under SoO, there is little evidence that their hostilities have ceased. JMGs should motivate the armed groups under SoO to initiate confidence building measures among the warring factions and groups to sort out their differences without resorting to violence. Notwithstanding the lapses in enforcing the SoO ground rules, Autonomous District Council elections in the year 2010 was held and conducted with relative ease in the areas where the CHIKIM outfits under SoO are operating in comparison with the areas where the NSCN-Muivah led Nagas reigned supreme. While engaging in SoO Grassroots democracy should be strengthened and the strong presence State administration should be made felt which otherwise have for so long remained as ungovernable grey areas because of difficult geographical terrains and thriving CHIKIM insurgency. Since, SoO is the first ever peace initiative involving the State government, it should pave way for substantive dialogue towards durable solution of the hydra-headed CHIKIM insurgencies. Successful resolution of the CHIKIM insurgent problems through SoO would invite the willingness of other armed outfits which are still eluding the offer for peace talks.

Notes and References

1. CM unaware of another Ceasefire with UG group, *Imphal Free Press,* Popular English Daily, Imphal, 15 July, 2006.
2. Insurgency and Peace Efforts in Manipur, *G:/CDPS, Manipur Insurgency.htm,* assessed on 21 June, 2010.
3. *Imphal Free Press,* Popular English Daily, Imphal, 28 August, 2005
4. Indian Army-UG Ceasefire without State Government's consent, *Imphal Free Press,* Popular English Daily, Imphal, 25 February, 2006.
5. Datta, Saikat, Manipur CM Gave Rs 1.5 Crore to Separatists *The Outlook,* 12 December, 2005.
6. Zomi Council, *The Imphal Free Press*, Popular English Daily, Imphal, 4 March, 2006.
7. SOG reviews security ahead of polls, The *Sangai Express*, Popular English Daily, Imphal, 20 September, 2006.
8. KNF to ban Congress, *Imphal Free Press,* Popular English Daily, Imphal, 12 August, 2006.
9. KLA na Congress ta athingba thamkhre, tr., KLA bans Congress, *Poknafam,* Vernacular Manipuri Daily, 8 January, 2007. KLO again reiterated its reasons for the banning at a press conference on 6 February, 2007 held in connection with the pulling up of a Vaiphei community leader, President of the Vaiphei People's Council, Eastern Block (VPC, EB) for issuing a statement to the media declaring support of (VPC, EB) to sitting Saikul Assembly Constituency MLA.
10. Cabinet nod to SoO deal, The *Sangai Express*, Popular English Daily, 24 August, 2008.
11. State Government authorizes Principal Secretary to sign SoO agreement with Kuki militants, The *Imphal Free Press,* Popular English Daily, Imphal, 4 August, 2008.

12. SoO with Kuki groups, The *Imphal Free Press,* Popular English Daily, Imphal, 6 September, 2008.
13. Kuki National Army, *www.satp.com*, assessed on 26 June, 2010.
14. Aide-Memoir to the Prime Minister of India Shri Atal Behari Vajpayee for Immediate Creation of Kukiland, submitted by Kuki National Front on 8 April, 1998. Cited in Koireng Singh, Aheibam, Ethnicity and Inter-Community Conflicts, N. Delhi: Akanksha Publishing House, 2008, p. 99.
15. Kuki National Front, *www.satp.org*, assessed on 26 June, 2010.
16. Manipur Outfit rears head, *The Telegraph*, National English Daily, Calcutta, 26 October, 2006.
17. CDPS Militant Groups Profile, *file:///G:/CDPS,%20Manipur%20 Insurgency.htm*, assessed on 20 June, 2010.
18. KLA celebrates anniversary, *The Imphal Free Press,* Popular English Daily, Imphal, 18 December, 2007.
19. Hmar People's Democracy, *www.satp.org*, assessed on 26 June, 2010.
20. Zomi Revolutionary Army, *www.satp.org*, assessed on 26 June, 2010.
21. 1745 Kuki undergrounds to be given I-cards, 23 camps proposed for official recognition, *The Imphal Free Press,* Popular English Daily, 22 December, 2008.
22. Kuki solution should be within Constitution of India, *North-East Sun*, October 15, 2008.
23. SoO signed enforced, *The Imphal Free Press,* Popular English Daily, Imphal, 23 August, 2008.
24. PCCP calls for SoO extension for another term, *The Imphal Free Press,* Popular English Daily, Imphal, August 3, 2009.
25. KNO, UPF and the SoO: Long Walk to Talk, *www. Kanglaonline.com,* assessed on 29 June, 2010.
26. He stated it while speaking at the inaugural function of the administrative block of a designated camp built for KNF at Saparmeina. SoO in transitory phase, *The Sangai Express*, Popular English Daily, Imphal, 27 November, 2009.
27. Court orders government to.recover money cut by UGs under SoO, *Hueiyen Lanpao*, Popular English Daily, Imphal, 1 May, 2010.
28. Moreh is a border town of Manipur in the Indo-Myanmar territory of Manipur known for the illegal resources borne out of illegal trade.
29. KLA leaves KNO, joins UPF, *The Imphal Free Press*, Popular English Daily, Imphal, Wednesday, 18 November, 2009.
30. Inter-state bus services suspended over burning down of state bus in Assam; Two charred to death inside locked bus, *The Imphal Free Press*, Popular English Daily, Imphal, 25 October, 2008.
31. SoO group found to be behind UBI bank fraud case: 57 Mt Di, *The Imphal Free Press*, Popular English Daily, Tuesday, 03 November, 2009.

16
Suspension of Operation (SoO)
Prospects and Challenges

Sonthanghaokip

The States of North-East India witnesses a mushrooming growth of insurgency movements, for this a number of factors may be held responsible. Some groups call for a separate state, others for regional autonomy while some extreme groups demand complete secession from India. The North-East India consists of 7 States—Assam, Arunachal Pradesh, Manipur, Mizoram, Meghalaya, Nagaland and Tripura (also known as *the seven sisters*). Tensions exist between these states and the Central Government as well as amongst the tribal people, who are natives of these states, and migrant peoples from other parts of India. Regional tensions have eased off as of late, with Indian and State governments' concerted effort to raise the living standards of the people in these regions. However, militancy still exists within the region. At present insurgent activity is still prevalent in the States of Assam, Manipur, Nagaland, Meghalaya, and Tripura. While in Mizoram insurgency problem has come down steadily, with the signing of the Shillong Accord in the eighties.

The main focus in this chapter is envisioned to highlight the armed insurgency movement *vis-à-vis* the Kukis of Manipur and how and why they have entered into the path of peace process. To understand better the armed movement of the Kukis of Manipur, it is felt imperative to look into the genesis of Kuki political movements from its initial phases.

Genesis of Kuki Political Movement

Even before India's independence, the Kuki National Assembly (KNA) which was formed in 1946, started putting strong pressure for a satisfactory solution concerning land alienation problem of the Kukis, abolition of the forced labour system and the grant of equal rights with the plainsmen, the hill representatives in the Assembly (Manipur) be nominated by the hill people etc.[1] After India's independence the Kuki National Assembly (KNA) demanded a separate state for the Kukis within India. In this regard the Kuki National Assembly submitted several memoranda to the Central Government, but yielded no response. In pursuance of their demand, the Kuki National Assembly sent a Memorandum to the First Prime Minister of Free India, Pandit Jawaharlal Nehru, on 24/03/1960 that reads:

> "The only solution for the Kuki problem is the Kuki state, where the Kukis will have their own government to take care of their needs within the Union of India. A separate state for the Kukis with Manipur as the bastion will also give them the full opportunity to attain full growth. The Kuki state, as demanded, will enable collection of the Kuki minorities elsewhere together in a place where their lives and properties can be secure and their due share of development ensured".[2]

Though the Kuki National Assembly was not in a position to fulfill the dreams of the Kukis in materializing a homeland, nevertheless it became a harbinger of Kuki political Movements in the subsequent years. The history of Kuki Political Movement may be classified into two phases:

(a) KNA Period, 1946-1980's. (b) Post-KNA Period, from 1980's onwards. The former may be compared as the Moderate Phase of the India National Congress (INC) and the latter as that of the Extremist era. During the former period, the Kuki national leaders have firm belief and sincerity on the part of the Government of Free India; relying on peaceful methods - memorandums, petitions and other peaceful mechanisms so that their plights are look into. The unresponsive attitude of the then government and the futility of adopting a peaceful mechanism, constrained the younger generation to take up arms to achieve their long unfulfilled demands by violent means. The year from 1980's onwards witnessed the mushrooming growth of numerous Kuki insurgent groups, fighting for amicable solution to the Kuki problems which have long been ignored.[3]

Formation of Kuki Armed Movements, 1980's

The Kukis were in dilemma in the post-independence era, as their future status as a nation was at stake, coupled with the merger of Manipur to the

Indian Union in 1949. The states in independent India are organized on ethno-linguistic lines giving due recognition to their ethnic identities, languages and culture. However, the Kukis argue that this right to govern their affairs within their traditional territory has been denied to them, while it has long been granted to other major ethnic entities in the North-East India. The demands of the Kukis for the creation of a 'Kuki State' within the framework of Constitution of India, in the 1960's nor the creation of Kuki dominated Sadar Hills into a full-fledged district in the 1970s and 1980s through a peaceful means have not been acknowledged both by the Manipur and Central governments.[4] All these dissatisfactions, unresponsive attitude on the part of the government of India may have resulted in the escalating growth of various Kuki UG groups in the hills of Manipur in late eighties.

Unification of different Kuki Armed Groups

The first platform created to bring unity among different Kuki armed groups was the formation of the Indigenous Peoples' Revolutionary Alliance (IPRA), under the initiative of KNO on May 27, 2000. The IPRA comprised of the ZRA (Zomi Revolutionary Army), Kuki National Army (KNA), Kuki National Front, Military Council (KNF-MC), Kuki National Front-President, (KNF-P), and Hmar People's Convention-Democratic (HPC-D). The objective of IPRA as stated by its leaders was to live together as an indigenous people without disturbing each other, although its main objective was to stop the infiltration of valley-based militants into their territory.[5] It however, lasted only for a few years. In 2002, the Kuki National Council (KNC) was formed as an umbrella organisation of the Kuki Revolutionary Army (KRA), Kuki National Front-Samuel (KNF-S) and United Kuki Liberation Front (UKLF). In 2006, KNF-P, KLA, HPC-D, KNF-S, ZRA, and UKLF formed the United Peoples' Front (UPF) as a common platform at Aizawl to fulfil the ethnic aspirations of the Kuki people. During those days, the UPF comprises of Zomi Revolutionary Army (ZRA), KukiNational Front-Samuel (KNF-S), Kuki National Front-President (KNF-P), United Kuki Liberation Front (UKLF), Hmar Peoples' Convention-Democratic (HPC-D), and Kuki Liberation Army (KLA).

The KNO's second attempt in bringing the various Kuki militant groups under its umbrella began in 2005, when KNF-MC and KNF-Zogam (KNF-Z) became its armed wings besides the KNA. In 2008, eleven armed groups became constituent armed wings of the Kuki National Organisation

(KNO). The armed wings of the KNO were Kuki National Army (KNA), Kuki National Front-Military Council (KNF-MC), Kuki National Front-Zogam (KNF-Z), United Socialist Revolutionary Army (USRA), Hmar National Army (HNA), Zomi Revolutionary Front (ZRF), United Komrem Revolutionary Army (UKRA), United Minorities Liberation Army (UMLA), Zou Defence Volunteers (ZDV), Kuki Liberation Army (KLA), and Pakan Reunification Army (PRA).[6]

The regrouping of Kuki armed groups under two umbrellas—KNO and UPF, which initially was largely based on threat perception of one group by another, is a significant development in the history of Kuki armed movement. With this, one main obstacle for forging unity has been resolved, as they have slowly stopped training their guns on each other. The leaders of Kuki armed groups seem to realise that the ideology of land and ethnic nationality is paramount over other issues. This stand categorically rejected motivations of clannishness in support of a clear sense of ethnic nationalism to unify the people under a common and historical identity.

SUSPENSION OF OPERATION (SoO)

The advent of the Suspension of Operation between the Kuki armed groups and both the governments at the centre and the State indeed was a boon to the Kuki ethnic population, which marked the dawn of a new environment. With the signing of the SoO Pact, the days of fratricidal killings, communal tensions, factional executions, extortions, threatening lives of common man has become the story of the past! Thanks to SoO !

The suspension of operation Agreement was signed between the Indian Army and Kuki armed groups in August 1, 2005. On August 22, 2008, the Kuki National Organisation (KNO) and the United Peoples' Front (UPF) formally entered into tripartite Agreement with the Central and Manipur State governments and signed the SoO to create conducive atmosphere for political dialogue. The suspension of operations agreement was signed on August 22 by D.S. Poonia, principal secretary (Home) of Manipur and Navin Verma, joint secretary (north-east) of the Union Home Ministry on behalf of Manipur and the Central governments respectively. Eight members each from the Kuki National Organisation and the United People's Front also signed the agreement on behalf of different Kuki militant outfits, the sources said. KNO and UPF represented eleven and eight Kuki militant outfits respectively. KNO vice president Lalminthang Vaiphei and UPF general secretary S.T. Thangboi Kipgen were also among the signatories from the side of the militants, the sources added.[7] This was indeed a positive measure at working out a tangible solution through peaceful means. In fact, this has been the desire and aspirations of the Kukis since the commencement of their movements in the post-Independence era.

However, at this stage, the relevant question is, would this be more effective than other ceasefire agreements that the Government of India has signed with other armed groups in North-East India? Will this serve to help the armed groups to reinforce their writ more openly and in a more brutal manner? Will it give the security forces the opportunity to divide the Kuki armed groups by playing off the weaker groups against the bigger ones and clandestinely instigating them to fight? The biggest challenge, however, is whether the signing of 'Suspension of Operation' (SoO) would lead to political dialogue to address and resolve the political problems of the Kuki people. The apprehension of the Kuki people is that it would not usher in a peaceful solution. Such SoO or ceasefires, as seen in other parts of the region, have made little difference in terms of de-escalation of violence or stepping up of the process of political settlement. Although the SoO was supposed to be a transitory step towards final conflict resolution, it is on the threshold of becoming an end in itself providing some sort of legitimacy to the Kuki armed groups to carry on with their agenda. The State and the Central Governments are more interested in using the Kuki armed groups to win elections rather than having dialogues.[8]

The Kuki revolutionary groups on their part vehemently asserted that the 'Kuki Nation' which has a distinct ethnic and socio-cultural identity has every right to self-determination, and that would be possible only when political autonomy (Self-governance) is granted to them within the purview of the Indian Constitution. The fulfilment of their aspirations is based on, "Article 244 and 244(A) and Schedule I to IV of the Constitution of India "....the tribals of the North-Eastern India may or shall have a separate administrative units for their own...", and thus, the question is, "Why not Kukiland for the Kukis"?[9]

Nevertheless, the Suspension of Operation has opened up a new chapter in the annals of Kuki history. Emulating, John F. Kennedy's, "Let us never negotiate out of fear. Let us never fear to negotiate". The Kuki armed groups have signed the Suspension of Operation with the Central and the State Governments. According to the spokesperson of the KNO, Dr. Seilen Haokip, "The purpose of signing the Suspension of Operation with Central and State governments is to hold a tripartite dialogue for a viable political settlement for the Kuki people within the Constitution of India".[10]

Conclusion

The signing of the SoO Pact and the impact thus felt has been a remarkable step forward in restoring peace and tranquillity in the region, but the pertinent question is—will the SoO be able to bring a viable and permanent peace?

Before the signing of the Pact the two Kuki UG groups hardly met and talk, as doubts and apprehensions are looming large, where one cannot trust the other. But with the signing of the SoO pact, the two groups could now meet and talk, which is hoped to boost each other's trust. Though the two groups may have got different ideologies and programmes of their own, the signing of this pact greatly acted as a catalyst for confident building measures in as far as the two UG groups are concerned. In the efforts of bringing normalcy in the region, the initiatives undertaken by the District administration receives much applauds from the civil populace of the region, whereby a joint football matches christened as '*integrity Leaders' Meet*' is being convened annually with the active involvement of members of the KNO and UPF, besides other members from various District Philanthropic organisations, Social and Student bodies etc. from which 'understandings and trust' through sports is achieved. Peace and tranquillity has finally returned to this region, but the big question now is—How long this peaceful atmosphere last?

The much-talk about the move of the Government of India (GoI) in assigning an Interlocutor in the person of P.C. Haldal, a retired Director of the Intelligence Bureau (IB) for holding political talks with the Kuki UG groups evoked a sense of nearing a peaceful conclusion to the Kuki political issue. But it has been a wait-wait situation, for nothing concrete happens till date. The lackadaisical attitude and red-tapping strategy being practised by the Government of India may definitely jeopardise the hopes of a peaceful solution. It is feared that such indifference attitude adopted by the government may derail the peace pact, signed more than seven years back, which was earnestly signed with a firm belief to resolve the vex Kuki issue.

To accelerate the proposed political dialogue, the KSDC[11] (Kuki State Demand Committee, which has its genesis in the 1960s, and was revived in 2010) started resorting to *bandhs* and strikes of various magnitudes in the recent years, urging the Governments at the Centre and in the State to speed-up the dialogue process. Mention may be made of the recent ASEAN Car Rally.[12] The Ministry of Home Affairs (MHA), fearing the declaration of the KSDC to sabotage the maiden Car Rally, issued an assurance letter to the KSDC, urging to withdraw the strikes forthwith, with a promised that soon after the end of the ensuing Winter Parliament Session, Political dialogue would be initiated. But nothing happens till date. What a sarcastic promise!!

A complicated situation has arisen now, as one of the two Kuki UG groups have declared to take up arms and go back to jungle, if political dialogue is not initiated forthwith, thereby declined to sign any SoO extension deals anymore in the near future. It is a well-known fact that under the SoO Deal, the UG cadres are constrained to adhere to SoO Ground rules—do's and don'ts's. But with the break-down of the SoO Pact, the days of chaos and turmoil, factional killings, extortions, kidnappings, communal tensions, fear psychosis may once again reign back, thereby rendering the hard-earned peace and tranquillity brought about by it go in vain. Who is to blame for this?

Forget about holding political dialogue, the SoO groups are not content with the apathy of the Governments shown towards their welfare. The tall and high-sounding promises made are hardly fulfilled. As a result of all this, some of Kuki UG groups prefer to walk out of the SoO Pact. The delaying mechanism employed by the government will only invite more problems in the near future. A meagre of just Rs. 3000 stipend a month is promised for each cadre as a part of the Centre's surrender-*cum*-rehabilitation package, cadres are getting restless and dissatisfied for its irregularity and red-tapism, sadly unlucky ones were kept in complete illusion about the stipends being provided. The government's promise of providing vocational training has also not been implemented. Besides the danger of so-called 'peace process' getting derailed, the other concern is the presence of so many armed groups in the area. Like all groups on ceasefire, they too violate ground rules with impunity and allegedly indulge in regular extortion which they call 'donation'. The KNO Spokesman Dr. Seilen Haokip admits that extortion is a reality, but they are dependent on raising funds when they can neither leave the designated camps to earn money nor is the government following up with its promise of talks. "When you talk about our extortion maybe five hundred rupees here or Rs. 50,000 there and that is for our sustenance because we are not getting our due," he says. "If the government is not sincere and if suspension of operation doesn't mean dialogue, the inevitably at hand is, we have to resort to other means. These guns are not for decoration, they cost a lot of money and it's an investment because it appears that memorandums and all efforts to this date have no bearings on the government," he said.[13] Hundreds of UG groups across the North-Eastern region are ready to give up arms but the government's so-called 'peace process' appears to be just a euphemism for appeasement rather than a clearly laid out policy for peace to integrate them to the mainstream and fulfil their demands. The sluggish mentality of the government (in its dealing mechanism with SoO Signatories) may deter other UG groups operating in the state to enter into any SoO Pact or ceasefire agreement in future.

To sustain peace in the region, both the Governments at the Centre and in the State should give up delaying tactics, hitherto being practiced, so, that the hard-earned peace is not distorted in the mid-way to logical conclusion.

Notes and References

1. *Resolution of the Kuki National Assembly*, Working Committee, Imphal, on 16th May, 1947.
2. *Memorandum of the Kuki National Assembly* to the First Prime Minister of Free India, Jawaharlal Nehru, on 24/03/1960, as per Resolution adopted in its General Meeting held at Thingkangphai, Churachandpur, Manipur, from 19th to 22nd, January, 1960.
3. Haokip, Sonthang, "The Kuki National Assembly: Historicity and Evolution" in the *Journal, Alternative Perspectives*, Volume VI, Issue II, July-Sept., 2011, p. 48.
4. Haokip, T.T., "Kuki armed Movements", in the Sadar Hills, *District Level Kut Souvenir*, 2010, p. 5.
5. *Ibid.*, T.T., 2010, p. 8.
6. *Ibid.*, T.T., 2010, pp. 8-9.
7. Cabinet nod to SoO deal, in *The Sangai Express*, Popular English Daily, Imphal, 23 September, 2008.
8. *Ibid.*, Haokip, T.T., 2010, 10.
9. Quoted from Kipgen, Nehlun, Founder President, Kuki National Front (KNF), in *The Shillong Times*, Popular English Daily, Shillong, 1 October, 1993.
10. NDTV interviewed KNO Spokesman Dr. Seilen Haokip, 08 December, 2012, 11:57, Ist.
11. In pursuance of the long unfulfilled dreams of having a State for the Kuki people, a Committee christened as the Kuki State Demand Committee (KSDC), was formed in recent years that seeks a political solution for the

Kuki people within the Constitution of India, i.e. the attainment of Kuki Statehood. The KSDC following the footprints of the erstwhile Kuki National Assembly (KNA) Leaders pressurises the Government of India (GoI) so that the latter give a favourable response to the demands made by the Kukis in the sixties, for the establishment of a Kuki State. The KSDC has already sent a number of representations to the Government of India in this regard.

12. *The Sangai Express*, Popular English Daily, Imphal, 15 December, 2012
13. NDTV interviewed KNO Spokesman, Dr. Seilen Haokip, 08 December, 2012, 11:57, IST).

17

Dimensional Peace in Manipur

EIMI (Chikimz) Experience

Priyadarshni M. Gangte

> Peace cannot be kept by force. It can only be achieved by understanding.
>
> —***Albert Einstein***

Introduction

Peace means freedom from the cessation of war, i.e. peace with honour and it is at any price.[1] As a comprehensive enterprise, it requires a transformation in our thinking of sense of valued wills, resources and solidarity of all. Thus, it is a way of life in which one experiences inner equality, harmonious relationship and interconnectedness with the world.[2] Peace is always, associated with clarity and inner stillness that often give rise to playfulness and inspired activity, so, it comes from non-resistance and acceptance of what is it is not necessarily a state of passivity, rather it gives rise is choices that are free from automatic resistance, thus, it is the real sense a state of being.[3]

Manipur is a home of different ethnic groups and everybody are having their own political and socio-economic agenda. This politically motivated ideological difference among the indigenous people of different communities in the State is contrary to national interest often posed a great threat to maintain internal security and peace in its course of sustaining peaceful co-existence over the years.[4] The idea of Manipur or composite nationalism is lacking among the groups has always made peace elusive to each others in the forefront due to sell, centric interest thereby completely undermining the common issues.

In this prevailing situation, the Chin-Kuki-Mizo-Zomi (CHIKIMZ) or the better appellation would be the Eimi, despite a number of efforts being made by larger group of the community common goal perhaps is parable castle in the air. It is widely believed that the existence of ideological difference among the Eimi (Chikinmz) communities or Ethnic group may be discussed as follows.

Nomenclature Issue

The term "Kuki" being at the moment gradually disowned by most of the ethnic groups hitherto been known as such.[5] As we all know that nationalism is an expression of a feeling of political sentiment with strong bond of origin to which each community or ethnic group (clan) forms part of a state-nation. And each of such group has its entity based on ethnic ties as are inalienably consanguineous in relationship through mythical or legendary ancestor[6] such ethnicities are essentially built on genealogical tree, each member of which is believed related to one another. Thus, several ethnic groups whose culture, tradition, customs, language, forms of government, method of cultivation, etc. which had mistakable ethos that established their being one and same stock of people their distinctive entities different from each other, such as Naga, Kuki, Meiteis, Chin, Mizo, Zomi, etc.[7]

Kuki Nationalism as a blanket acceptance witnessed a bitter experience which led to disunity among the communities with the exception of the Thadou Kuki speaking group since the late 1952 till date. These ethnic groups have coined their own nomenclature rather than the term "Kuki" to be maintained as generic term for them. However, they are yet to build up a consensus over the issue remains still unresolved. In fact, this is the main hindrance to the process of prevailing peace among these ethnic groups. Hence, peace is still remained as elusive irrespective of their ages bond of belonging to same blood brothers.

Emergence of Different Ideologues and Principles

Eimis/CHIKIMZ have been swaged apart by political ideologies of their own of differences in socio-economic and political issues including that of Kuki-Thadou controversies and *vice-versa.* With the emergence of new ideological and principle attached to these ethnic groups under their own political and socio-economic agendas[8] have conversely posed a great impediment in the way resolving various outstanding issues within these Eimis (CHIKIMZ) ethnic groups in finding a space to bring them together in a one platform.

(a) Unification of Kuki Armed Groups

According to Haokip, the first platform to bring the unity of Kuki armed groups was the Indigenous People's Revolutionary Alliance (IPRA) with the initiative of KNO on May 27, 2000. IPRA comprised of the ZRA (Zomi Revolutionary Army), Kuki National Army (KNA), Kuki National Front, Military Council (KNI-MC), Kuki National Front, President (KNF-P) and Hmar People's Council, Democratic (HPC-D). The objective of IPRA, as stated by its leaders was to live together as an indigenous people without disturbing each other, although a main objective was to stop the infiltration of valley based militants into their territory[9]. It however, lasted only for a few years. In 2002, the Kuki National Council (KNC) was formed as an umbrella organization comprising the Kuki Revolutionary Army (KRA), Kuki National Front, Samuel (KNF-S) and United Kuki Liberation Front (UKLF).[10] In 2006, KNF(P), KLA, HPC-D, KNF(S), ZRA and UKLF formed the United Peoples' Front (UPF) as a common platform at Aizawl to fulfil the ethnic aspirations of the Kuki-Chins. At present, the UPF comprises of Zomi Revolutionary Army, Kuki National Front(S), Kuki National Front (P), United Kuki Liberation Front, Kuki Revolutionary Army, Hmar People's Convention(S) and Kuki Liberation Army.[11] Apart from this, recently, we have noticed the increase of armed groups, they are KNA(L), Kuki National Liberation Front (KNLF) and KNF(N) where I and N stand for India and Nehlun.

KNO's second attempt in bringing the various Kuki militant groups under its umbrella began in 2005, when KNF (MC) and KNF(Z) became its armed wings besides the KNA.[12] In 2008, eleven armed groups become constituent armed wing of the KNO. The armed wings of KNO are Kuki National Army, Kuki National Front (Military Council), Kuki National Front (Zogam), United Socialist Revolutionary Army, Hmar National Army, Zomi Revolutionary Front, United Komrem Revolutionary Army, United Minorities Liberation Front, Zou Defence Volunteer and Pakan Re-unification Army.[13]

Further, he has maintained that the United People's Froint, another Kuki umbrella organization was formed in August, 2006, at Aizawl in Mizoram under the aegis of Zoramthanga, the then Chief Minister of the State.[14] UPF's founding constituents are Kuki National Front (P), Zomi Re-unification Organisation, Kuki National Front (S), Hmar People's Convention (D), and United Kuki Liberation Front. In a press release (15 August, 2006), UPF declared its objective as "to fight for a separate political administration for our people in the present state of Manipur."

The regrouping of Kuki armed groups under KNO and UPF, which initially was largely based on threat perception of one group by another, is a significant development in the history of Kuki armed movement.[15] With this, one main obstacle for forging unity has been resolved, as they have slowly stopped training their guns on each other. The leaders of Kuki armed groups seem to realize that the ideology of land and ethnic nationality is paramount over local issues. This stand categorically rejected motivations of clannishness in support of a clear sense of ethnic nationalism to unify the people under a common and historical identity.[16]

(b) Ideology

The political objectives of both KNO and UPF are identical in terms of the people represented and their territory. The only difference between the two is that KNO demands statehood (one in India and another in Burma). The UPF demands on administrative unit in India within existing Manipur.[17] The UPF and KNO share the ideology of unifying the Kukis by adopting an inclusive Kuki Identity base on its pre-British status and principles of federalism to ensure equal status of all constituents.[18] Both the KNO and UPF argue that Kuki Identity has existed in the pre-British period reigning sovereign over their land, arbitrarily divided by the British in the twentieth century. The Kukis fought against the British from 1917-1919 to protect their territory and again in 1943-1945 to regain their territory from the British.[19]

(c) Suspension of Operation

The peace pace Suspension of Operations (SoO) was signed between the Indian Army and Kuki armed groups since August 1, 2005. On August 22, 2008, the Kuki National Organisation (KNO) and the United Peoples' Front (UPF) formally entered into tripartite agreement with the Central and Manipur State Governments and signed SoO to create in atmosphere conducive for political dialogue.[20]

In this regard, Haokip is of the opinion in raising several questions, that, the relevant question is would this be more effective than other ceasefire agreements that the Government of India has signed with other armed groups in North-East India?[21] Will SoO serve to help the armed groups to reinforce their writ more openly and in a more brutal manner? Will it give the Security Forces the opportunity to divide the Kuki armed groups by playing off the weaker groups against the bigger ones and clandestinely instigating them to fight? The biggest challenge, however, is whether the signing of SoO would lead to political dialogue to address the political problems of the Kukis to lead to its logical conclusion.[22] It is fair to state that from the time SoO was signed unprecedented peace has prevailed in the Kuki hills. However, the apprehension of the Kuki people is that it would not usher in lasting peaceful political solution to the aspirations of the Kukis.[23] Such SoO or ceasefires, as seen in other parts of the region have made little difference in terms of the de-escalation of violence or stepping up of the process of political settlement. Although, SoO was supposed to be a transitory step towards final conflict resolution, it is on the threshold of becoming an end in itself providing some sort of legitimacy to the Kuki armed groups to carry on with their own agenda. The Manipur state and Central Governments are more interested in using the Kuki armed groups to win elections rather than engage in political dialogue.[24]

Emergence of Zo Re-unification Organisation (ZORO) as Common Nomenclature

As the Eimis (CHIKIMZ) have begun to realize the fact of their origin and therefore, the birth of the idea of the so called re-unification[25] among themselves. To materialize this novel concept of aspirations the people seemingly appear to accept the term Zo as a common nomenclature. However, to properly achieve this objective is a different question.[26] In this regard, Sing Khao Khai[27] has stated that Kuki Chin people bear different names, almost all of which were obviously given by their neighbours with reference to how they say and knew them in an abusive or degrading sense. In fact, these names are derogatoring terms. As an impact of British rule, on their politics was tremendous on the negative side, they were divided up all the Zo inhabited areas under different rulers and reduced them to status not deserving to be reckoned with. On the positive side, they established law and order which provide the Zo people an opportunity to consolidate themselves in their respective areas and to interact with each other more widely under a settled administration.[28] As a result, Zo integration process look place and the First World Zomi Convention on Re-Unification, the most emotional Zo gathering so far was held at Champahai from May 19-21, 1988[29] was a living example—a historic event for these groups of ethnic communities.

KNO and Zo Re-unification Organisation (ZORO)

Despite eight years of SoO (since 2005), during peace has reigned in the Kuki hills, the desired atmosphere conductive to engage in a tripartite political dialogue, consistent apathy towards Kukis demonstrated by the State and Central Governments have made KNO realize that as a minority tribal people there is no future in India, as well as in Myanmar (Burma) and Bangladesh, the three countries, the British divided our people and territories.[30]

Therefore, with a view to strengthen unity of Kukis in present day Manipur. KNO projected to the UPF its willingness to name Zogam as our future self-administered land because it embodies and represent the Zo ethnic people known as Kuki, Chin and Mizo.[31] This holistic KNO ideology for consolidation of Zo people converged with the main objective of Zo Re-unification Organisation with its headquarters at Aizawl in Mizoram.[32] As a measure of solidarity and common purpose, several conferences followed in 2013 in which members of ZoRO and KNO jointly participated to further the cause of re-unification of Zo people.[33] The first such conference was held on 14 March at Young Paite Association Hall, Hengtam Lamka, Churachandpur and on 24 October, with the theme, 'SALVATION FOR THE ZO PEOPLE', Zo-Renification Organisation (ZoRO) Conference-*cum*-Celebration of the 68th United Nations Day was held at Galngam Lentol, Moreh, ZALE'N-GAM.[34] Today, support for ZoRO has been further extended with the Kachin people joining the movement. The Kachins have expressed affinity with Kuki, whom they regard as their elder brother separated from them in the course of journey eons ago.[35]

If the much about talked and momentum gained, i.e. ZoRO blanket accepted as natural gift to these ethnic groups as a factor for re-unification of all factors, it would be the only viable option for those groups opposing the term 'Chin', 'Kuki', 'Mizo' and 'Zomi' to accept the same as the common/generic term as consensus one.

Suggestion for Re-unification of Eimi (CHIKIMZ)

The process of re-unification of Eimis (CHIKIMZ) communities will not take place until the common nomenclature issue is amicably resolved as it holds the key to one political stand point of all factions. In order to accomplish, it would be desirable to take a decision collectively through consensus by all the tribe leaders of Eimi (CHIKIMZ) communities including the leaders of KNO and UPF should take a proactive role on resolving this core issue through understanding and negotiations.

Conclusion

As briefly highlighted in the above paragraphs it is difficult to make an assessment about dimensional peace in its true sense among the Eimi (CHIKIMZ) communities as each of them have been influenced by their own ideological difference which is thc ground realities but without comprising their political goal for the nationalism of them.

Notes and References

1. J.B. Sykes (ed), *The Concise Oxford Dictionary of Current English*, (7th Edition), Oxford University Press, 1987, p. 753.
2. Dr. L. Leiren's Article, *Peace Education in the 21st Century*, Imphal, Free Press, 1st September, 2006.
3. Wikipedia, *Vision of Humanity org/21st Centuray Peace*- 01/02/2010 (8.41 pm)
4. Shokholon Touthang, 44 yrs, Chief of Berea, Churachandpur District, Manipur interviewed on 08/03/2014.
5. T.S. Gangte, *Chin-Kuki-Mizo Nationalism—an old wine in a new bottle* - Unpublished paper.
6. *Ibid.*
7. *Ibid.*
8. Shokholun, *Ibid.*
9. T.T. Haokip, *Kuki Armed Opposition Movement* in S. George Guite. (ed.), Souvenir of the ZoRO Conference 2013, ZORO, Northern Zone, 2013, p. 46.
10. *Ibid.*
11. *Ibid.*
12. *Ibid.*
13. *Ibid.*
14. *Ibid.*
15. *Ibid.*
16. *Ibid.*
17. *Ibid.*
18. *Ibid*, p. 48.
19. *Ibid.*
20. *Ibid.*
21. *Ibid.*
22. *Ibid.*

23. *Ibid.*
24. *Ibid.*
25. According to S. George Guite, Editor of Souvenir ZORO Conference 2013 who is also the Information & Publicity Secretary of ZORO, Northern Zone, the Chin-Lushai conference held at Fkort William, Calcutta on 29th January, 1892 is the first attempt to re-unify the Zo ethnic people. Read a memorandum submitted to the then Secretary General of United Nations, Dr. Boutros Ghali on May 20, 1995. Earlier, the same leaders also submitted a Memorandum to President Bill Clinton of the United States of Americ on May 20, 1993 in an attempt to materialize the idea of Re-unification amongst the Zo ethnic group, the First World Zo Convention was held on May 19-21, 1988. In this convention, Zo was adopted as a common nomenclature for the divided ethnic origin. Information provided on 27/04/2014 at my residence.
26. Sangkima, *Essays on the History of the Mizos*, Spectrum Publications, Guwahati, Delhi, 2004, p. 39.
27. Sing Khau Khai, *Zo People and their Culture,* Khampu Hatzaw, New Lamka, 1995, p. 24.
28. L. Keivom, *Zo Re-unification Process* in P.M. Gangte (ed.) *Why Must We Be Mizo?* Spectrum Publications, Guwahati, Delhi, 2006, p. 146.
29. *Ibid.*
30. T.T. Haokip, *Ibid.*, p. 49.
31. *Ibid.*
32. *Ibid.*
33. *Ibid.*
34. *Ibid.*, p. 50.
35. *Ibid.*

18
Perspectives on Conflict Resolution in Manipur

Shukhdeba Sharma Hanjabam

Introduction

The erstwhile Asiatic sovereign kingdom of Manipur was colonised by the British in 1891. After British suzerainty lapsed on midnight 14 August, 1947, Manipur promulgated the Manipur State Constitution Act, 1947 on 26 September, 1947. With the holding of the elections based on universal adult franchise in June, 1948, the Maharaja inaugurated the first Assembly Session (read Parliament) on 18 October, 1948. This sort of a democratic and independent Manipur came to an end once it was forcefully merged with the Indian Union. The State Assembly with 53 (fifty-three) seats, which enjoyed the mandate of the people and which was in place before the instance of merger, was dissolved and the Asiatic Kingdom was degraded to the status of a Part C State. The weakness of the Agreement lies in the fact that the people of Manipur did not give consent in any form to the Merger Agreement. In fact consent of the people was not sought at all on the issue. Therefore, in the view of the armed opposition groups, the Manipur Merger Agreement of 1949 does not have any legality or constitutional validity. Moreover, the "National Convention on Manipur Merger Issue" held at Imphal on 28-29 October, 1993, passed a resolution stating that the Agreement signed by and between the Maharaja of Manipur and the representatives of the Dominion of India on the 21 September, 1949 does not have any legal and constitutional validity.

The contentious merger was resisted through an armed movement led by the legendary leader Hijam Irabot. His idea of an independent

Manipur was endorsed by the people of Manipur at a public meeting held on 3 August, 1949. Hijam Irabot passed away on 26 September, 1951, and subsequently the armed movement was suppressed. However, his legacy continued. Within a short span of time the Manipur National Union proclaimed Manipur's independence in 1953. It was followed by the Meitei State Committee taking to armed struggle in 1960. The United National Liberation Front (UNLF) was formed in 1964 with the stated objective of restoring the sovereign independent status of Manipur. On account of differences among the leadership of the UNLF on the question of launching armed struggle, Oinam Sudhir broke away to form the Revolutionary Government of Manipur (RGM) in 1968 with its headquarters at Sylhet in the erstwhile East Pakistan (now Bangladesh). In the late 70s, the PLA emerged in 1978.

Armed Conflict in Manipur: Points of Divergence

The difference of position of the State and non-State on the root cause of armed conflict in Manipur has been the major contention in the process of conflict resolution in Manipur. The official or statist views, the views of the non-State armed opposition group as well as the position of the people are discussed in this section.

The Official Position

The Ministry of Home Affairs, Government of India notifies the reasons for banning the armed opposition groups (namely PLA/RPF, UNLF, PREPAK, KYKL, KCP and MPLF) in Manipur as follows:

(i) openly declared their objectives as the formation of an independent Manipur by secession of Manipur State from India;
(ii) been employing and engaging in armed means to achieve their aforesaid objectives;
(iii) been attacking the security forces, the police, government employee ad law- abiding citizens in Manipur;
(iv) been indulging in acts of intimidation, extortion and looting of civilian population for collection of funds for their organization;
(v) been making efforts to established contacts with sources aboard for influencing public opinion and for securing their assistance by ways of arms and training for the purpose of achieving their secessionist objectives; and

(vi) been maintaining camps in neighbouring countries for the purpose of sanctuary, training and clandestine procurement of arms and ammunition.[1]

However, the Indian State on the root cause of armed conflict in Manipur still maintains that it is a "law and order" problem arising out of frustration of the "unemployed" and "misguided" youths in an underdeveloped and backward state. The reasons given are simply beyond the boundary of law and order problem. Justice Reddy[2-3] while reviewing the infamous AFSPA under the directives of the GoI observed that the duty and power of the 'union' under Article 355 to act on its own to protect the state from internal disturbances without their consent comes into play only in case of "*internal disturbance*", i.e., '*domestic chaos*' or '*internal commotion*'. Considering these facts, the report of the Justice Reedy stated that the problem in Manipur is not merely that of a '*law and order*' but an '*internal disturbance*' which required invoking Article 355 of the Constitution of India. It further admits that it has become a symbol of oppression, an object of hate and an instrument of discrimination and highhandedness. The committee recommends the repeal of the Act altogether. Similarly, the ORDER (dated 06/09/2012) of the Court of the Special Judge, National Investigation Agency (NIA) Assam Guwahati regarding the trail of R.K. Meghen (Sanayaima) and other 25 members of the United National Liberation Front, (UNLF) Manipur have formed the opinion that, the accused person did the illegal act to achieve the goal of independent Manipur by Illegal means. To cite the Order

> *... These incriminating circumstances formed a chains of events, that is to say, collection of money by extortion and under threat, purchase of arms and ammunition, armed training of its cadre, formation of armed wing of the organization, ready to challenge Indian Security Forces etc. forms opinion that the accused person did the illegal acts to achieve the goal of independent Manipur by illegal means...*[4]

Internationally, Begum Khaleda Zia of Bangladesh National Party had acknowledged the armed struggle of Manipur as a liberation struggle in the Bangladesh Parliament.[5]

Hidden War

Officially, the State has been claiming that the issue in Manipur is a law and order problem however, unofficially it has been dealing with the issue as that of a hidden war or internal disturbance which has been substantiated in this chapter. For instance, in the process (including covertly) of suppressing the movement, it has militarized the state. The draconian Armed AFSPA 1958 and other security centric legislations[6] such as the Unlawful Activities (Prevention) Act, 1967 (UAPA), the Prevention of Seditious Meetings Act 1911, the Official Secrets Act 1923, the Maintenance of Public Order Act 1947, the Punjab Security of the State Act 1953, the National Security Act, 1980 (NSA), the Prevention of Terrorism Act, 2002 (POTA), the Code of Criminal Procedures (Manipur Amendment) Act 1983, and the National Investigation Agency Act 2008 (NIA) was imposed to support the military engagement. CNN-IBN—a national based media house in 2007 after visiting the general headquarter of some of the militant groups reported for the first time since the beginning of the armed conflict as *"Hidden War*[7]". Similarly, Manipur is reported by the Peace and Conflict report 2008 published by the University of Maryland[8] as one of the ongoing armed self-determination movement in the world.

Among the security legislations, AFSPA is the most draconian which has been condemned by almost all the human rights groups in India and aboard including the United Nations. The AFSPA provides immunity to the State actors and they cannot be tried in civilian court of justice. AFSPA is presented as an instrument '*in aid of civil power*' (Section 3 of the Act) to '*suppress*', '*armed revolt*' or '*armed insurgency*' in the North-East. And it was supposed to be a '*temporary measure*'. But over four decades of its existence has shown up all the stated claims ('*in aid of civil power*', '*suppression*' *of* '*armed revolt*' or '*armed insurgency*' and '*temporary measure*') as false. The Act is an act of legitimizing the involvement of the military in the domestic space, and that it does not supplement, but supplant the '*civil power*'. More than being cases of '*human rights abuses*', those '*excesses*' for which no accountability can be fixed on anybody are reminders of the militarism that has subverted the democratic institutions and ethos in the North-East.[9]

By year 2012, an unofficial report puts that there are more than 60,000 security personnel deployed in Manipur.[10] As an analyst at the Institute of Defence and Strategic Analysis, New Delhi asserts, "The overt presence of the armed wing of a democratic state like India, i.e. its army has fostered the idea of a militarised India amongst the population".[11]

Table 18.1: Paramilitary forces operating in Manipur, 2008

1. Under 57th Mountain Division (Headquarters: Leimakhong)	
A. 59th Mountain brigade (Churachanpur)	19 Rajput Regiment and 9 Raj Rifles
B. 73 Mountain Brigade (Bishnupur)	11 Garhwal Rifles, 5/8 Gorkha Rifles, 12 Grenadiers, 10 Assam Rifles (AR)
C. 44 Mountain Brigade (Chakpikarong)	7 Sikh Light Infantry, 27 Madraj Regiment, 9 Rajput Regiment
D. 26 Sector Assam Rifles (AR) (Chandel)	16 AR, 36AR, 37 AR, 24 AR, 18 AR, 33 AR
E. 57 Mountain Artillery	9 Para Regiment, 26 AR Medium Regiment
2. Under Inspector General Assam Rifles-South (Headquarters: Mantripukhri)	
A. 9 Sector AR (Mantriprukhri, Imphal)	4 AR- (at Mantripukhri), 34 AR- (at Thoubal), 32 AR (at Keithenmanbi), 22 Maratha Light Infantry (at Tulihal)
B. 10 Sector AR (Ukhrul)	1 AR, 12 AR, 19 AR
C. 27 Sector AR (Lairouching)	14 AR (at Leirouching), 15 AR (at Mao), 35 AR (at Tamenglong), 38 AR (at Noneh), 2 Independent Operations (Leimakhong), Special Force-Para Troopers
3. Central Reserved Police Force (CRPF)	10 Battalions under one inspector general
4. Boarder Security Forces	About two battalions
5. Manipur State Police	10 battalions (including Indian Reserved Battalion) and Special Manipur State Force, Commandos deployed mainly in the valley

Source: *Justice First,* Vol. I, No. 1, December 08-March 09, 2009.

Counter-Insurgency Operations

As early as 1955, Jawaharlal Nehru ordered "the Indian army to conduct a counter insurgency campaign against the rebel Naga tribesmen in North-East India, a campaign that has since haunted the region".[12] Since then, the use of army and paramilitary forces in the North-East for counter insurgency operations has become a regular feature. Today, counter insurgency operations are carried out, in most cases as a joint operation between the Central and State forces or separately as the situation demands. One of the cardinal principles of counter insurgency operations is the unity of command. At the operational level it means integrated civil-military operations under one military commander appointed by the civil government. The concept of unified command in counter insurgency-operations was first experimented in Kashmir. In Assam a three-tier system was evolved; at the top was the Strategic Planning Group (ostensibly under the Chief Secretary) to lay down the policy; the second tier, the operation group, was headed by GOC 4 Corps, the senior military commander in Assam. It was here that key operational decisions were taken; the third tier was headed by the District Collector supported by the Battalion Commander and the Superintendent of Police of the area. The strategic group at the top had GOC 4 Corps, State DGP and IGP of BSF and CRPF as members. GOC 4 Corps attended the meeting whenever the Chief Minister chaired it. In the case of Manipur, the insistence on the part of the State Government to make the DGP of the State head of the unified headquarters resulted in the Army keeping out of it.

Military operations are a regular feature in Manipur. With the improving relationship between India and Myanmar, in numerous instances, joint operations are conducted to flush out armed opposition camps in the Indo-Myanmar border areas. Moreover, combing operations, either to nab a suspect or as a deterrent measure, are undertaken from time to time at any specific area, and comprises of cordoning off a specific location, use of a mask informer (locally known as Zorro) to identify an armed rebel, house searches, etc. Table 18.2 gives a select list of major military operations in Manipur. These operations are known and remembered for the gross violations of human rights.

Position of the Armed Opposition Groups

The armed opposition groups maintain that Manipur was an ancient Asiatic Kingdom with a written Constitution and maintained political relationship with the British as well as other neighbouring kingdoms. The Kingdom of Manipur had been ruled by 76 indigenous kings from A.D. 33 to 1955 and was governed based on the written constitution *"Loyumba Shinyen* since 1110 A.D. issued by King Loiyumba. Oinam Bogeshwar, the renowned Meitei scholar observed that there was a centralized constitutional government since A.D. 429. All the events in Manipur are recorded in the Kingdom Chronicle "Cheitharol Kumpaba" which is available in the Royal Palace of Manipur, Local custodians as well as the Indian Library Office London and archives around the world especially in United Kingdom. Manipur was recognized by foreign nations, especially by the Shan with the 1470 Agreement between the King Kiyamba of Manipur and Khekhomba of Pong in upper Burma. It was

Table 18.2: Select list of Military Operations in Manipur[13]

Sl. No.	*Name of Operation*	*Year**	*Objective*	*Area of Operation*	*Security Forces Involved*
1.	Blue Bird	July-October, 1988	To recover arms and ammunition taken away by Naga underground group	Surrounding thirty villages of Oinam Village, Senapati District	Assam Rifle
2.	Sunny Vale	August, 1993	To flush our armed rebels from the valley districts of Manipur	Greater Imphal Valley	Assam Rifles, Manipur Rifles & Manipur Police
3.	Loktak	10-16 March, 1999	To flush out rebels from Loktak area. Thanga and Karang are considered to be stronghold of underground armed rebels.	Thanga and Karang islands, Loktak Lake, Bishnupur District	Indian Army, CRPF & Manipur Police
4.	Stinger	3-5 October, 2005	To flush out rebels from Loktak area. Thanga and Karang are considered to be stronghold of underground armed rebels. After the Operation Indian Army set up a permanent Camp	Thanga and Karang islands, Loktak Lake, Bishnupur District	73 Mountain Brigade under the aegis of 57 Mountain Division based at Leimakhong Army base, Manipur
5.	Torrnado	October, 2005	To flush out militants from the Barak circle, Jiribam	Barak Circle in Jiribam subdivision, Imphal East	Five battalions of security forces namely 9 Para Field regiment, 13 Dogra regiment, 53 engineering regiment, 26 Assam Rifles and 26 Rajput Rifles
6.	Dragnet	January, 2006	To clear the two remaining subdivisions in south Manipur from the stronghold of the armed rebels	Parbung and Thanlon sub-divisions along National Highyway 150, Churachandpur District	Troops of 57 Mountain Division under the aegis of 3 Corps
7.	Khengjoi (Somtal I)	December, 2006	To clear the area of UNLF presence	Somtal Area, Chandel District	Indian Army's 10 J&K Light Infantry Battalion

followed by the Anglo Manipur Friendship Treaty in 1762, Anglo-Manipuri Defense Protocol of 1763, Treaty of Yandaboo, 1826 between the British government and the Burmese government after the Burmese occupied Manipur (1819-1826 remembered as "Seven Year Devastation"). Britain and Manipur continued their friendship by mutually opening offices of political agents in each other's territory. In 1835, the British decided to retain a Political Agent in Manipur with a view to preserving friendly relations, and preventing border feuds and disturbance. The Political Agent acted like an ambassador in the country. Manipur also had its Political Agent in the British Territory in Lakhimpur (Cachar) as well as Calcutta. Moreover, the available maps beginning from 1500 AD by Henry Yule indicate an identifiable territory of Manipur.

But the ancient kingdom was annexed by India with the use of military power in 1949. V.P. Menon, the then Advisor to the Government of India during the integration drive of the Princely States with the Indian Union is often cited to justify the claim. He stated that, Manipur was "taken over" because of being a "border state" and "backward", and therefore, a "strategic necessity"[14] Thus, according to the armed opposition groups, the ongoing armed movement in Manipur is justified and taken as a movement for independence, restoration of lost sovereignty and self-determination movement or national liberation or de-colonialization movement, etc.

The position of the AOG is substantiated by the academics and others such as such as (i) Sanjib Baruah[15] writes that the Maharaja was virtually imprisoned in his residence in Shillong. His house was surrounded by soldiers and under the pressure of considerable misinformation, the Maharaja 'isolated from his advisors, council of ministers, and Manipuri public opinion' signed the merger agreement. When the ceremony which proclaimed an end to the ancient kingdom took place on 15 October 1949 in Imphal, the Indian army was in place to guard against possible trouble, (ii) Kunal Chattopadhyay[16] and others reiterate about the forced conquest of Manipur by the Indian government. The Kangla fort in Imphal, from where the kings of Manipur used to rule, was brought under military control in 1949 and retained till 2004. As a result of savage exploitation and decades of uneven development national liberation struggles have raised their heads. They are based on the struggles for self-determination. All shades of mainstream parties in India have flatly rejected the right of the people of Manipur to self-determination and (iii) Centre for Organization Research and Education[17]—an NGO with UN Consultative Status observed that, the Indian dominion being a member of the United Nation since

Table 18.3: Armed Opposition Groups and their Goals[18]

Organization	*Founder*	*Year of establishment*	*Goal*	*Comment*
United National Liberation Front (UNLF)	Arambam Samarendra	November 24, 1964	'Independence' and establish a socialist society; restoration of lost sovereignty	Took up arms only in the 1980s with the establishment of its military wing Manipur Peoples Army
'Government-in-exile' called Revolutionary Government of Manipur (RGM)	Oinam Sudhir Kumar	December, 1968	'Liberate' Manipur through an armed struggle	Breakaway group from UNLF. Most of its leaders were arrested during the Bangladesh liberation war in 1971. The movement gradually fizzled out with rest of the leaders accepting the amnesty offered by the then Chief Minister of the State, Mr RK Dorendro Singh.
People's Liberation Army (PLA)	N. Bisheswar Singh	September 25, 1978	'Independence' through armed struggle	N Bisheswar Singh was a member of RGM.
People's Revolutionary Party of Kangleipak (PREPAK)	RK Tulachandra Singh	1977	'Independence' through armed struggle	
Kangleipak Communist Party (KCP)	Yumlembam Ibohanbi Singh	1980	'Independence' through armed struggle	
Kanglei Yawol Kanna Lup (KYKL)	Achou Toijamba	January, 1994	Independence and to save the revolutionary movement in Manipur	Formed following merger of the Oken faction of the UNLF, the Meiraba faction of PREPAK and the Ibo Pishak faction of KCP
CORCOM[19]		July, 2011	United Front to bring unity among revolutionary groups to free Manipur from India's "colonial regime"	Comprise at least top two leaders from the seven underground groups.

1945 have failed to oblige to the United Nations Charter Article 2(4) which reads as "*All members shall refrain in their international relations from the threat or use of force against the territorial integrity or political independence of any state, or in any manner inconsistent with the purpose of the United Nations*", by committing aggression to Manipur and thereby breach of peace. Further, United Nations General Assembly (UNGA) Resolutions 2625 (XXV), 1970 and 2734 (1970) provides that no territorial acquisition resulting from the threat or use of force shall be recognized as legal. The national liberation movement is exercising its right to self-defense and self-preservation, without any prejudice to the genuine integrity of India. Following table shows the goals of the major armed opposition groups operating in Manipur.

RPF and its military wing PLA unilaterally signed Article 3 of the Fourth Geneva Convention in 1997 and also submitted a memorandum to the Secretary General United Nations and the Chairman of the Decolonisation Committee (Committee of 24) for De-Colonisation of Manipur from Indian Colonialism and Alien Racist Regime, enlisting Manipur in the list of the Non-Self-Governing-Territories of the United Nations and, restoration of independence and sovereignty of Manipur[20].

In July 2011, the Coordinating Committee (CoreCom) was formed to carry forward the national liberation movement in Manipur. RPF President, Irengbam Chaoren was appointed Convenor of CorCom. A Joint Press Statement was signed by seven top leaders of the militant groups, and indicated that the coordination committee would comprise at least top two leaders from the seven underground groups, and was intended to establish a United Front to bring unity among revolutionary groups to free Manipur from India's "colonial regime".[21]

Conflict Resolution Process

The armed conflict in Manipur has reached a stalemate situation with each side claiming to pursue their views without any compromise. However, in the last few decades, we have experiences the process of conflict resolution which is not yet very productive. This section will deal with the conflict resolution process of the State, non-State and the people.

State and Conflict Resolution

Although the Government had earlier given calls for peace talks including unilateral ceasefire particularly by Governor Ved Prakash Marwah and

Governor Oudh Narayan Shrivastava, the most serious one which received response from the armed opposition groups emanated from Governor of Manipur, S.S. Sidhu in 2005 and 2006. He appealed to the "insurgent" groups of the State to come forward for peace talks during the occasion of the Republic Day celebrations, no other follow up has been made. Instead, what is largely seen as a peace initiative from the Indian State such as Suspension of Operation (SoO) and ceasefire agreements without political dialogues are followed, but these are measures for containing insurgency.

Successive speeches by the governors of Manipur, since it became a full-fledged state in 1972, testify the Official/Statist position that what is happening in Manipur is a law and order problem. To corroborate the point, selective comments of successive governors of Manipur since 1972 are shown in the following table. As the table shows, most recurring words are "insurgents", "insurgency", "law and order", "extremist", etc. Key words are put within parentheses. After the 9/11 incident, there is change in the vocabulary of the State. From insurgents, the armed opposition groups came to be identified as terrorist groups, which threaten and destabilize the internal security of India.

Table 18.4: Official/Statist Position on the Armed Opposition Group[22]

Year	*Governor*	*Comment*
1972	Shri B.K. Nehru	"The economic growth of this young State may continue to be inhibited by violent underground groups and opposition, who have unwisely been misled into such activities".
1973	Shri B.K. Nehru	"Senseless insurgency" by a few who hold the welfare of the majority to ransom.
1975	Shri Lallan Prasad Singh	"Misguided insurgents" to return to the path of peace and tranquility.
1976	Shri Lallan Prasad Singh	Overall improvement in the "law and order" situation. The Government has used sparingly the provisions of MISA and COFEPOSA[23] and the orders of detention under these Acts have been reviewed periodically.
1978	Shri Lallan Prasad Singh	Despite isolated underground activities, the "law and order" situation generally remained satisfactory.

(*Contd.*)

Table 18.4 (*Contd.*)

Year	Governor	Comment
1979	Shri Lallan Prasad Singh	"Misguided elements". Some "extremists" who had gone to Tibet for training returned to Manipur. It is a cause of concern in the valley.
1980	Shri Lallan Prasad Singh	Experienced seriously disturbed conditions in the valley with various "extremist groups" indulging in a serious of violent activities.
1981	Shri Lallan Prasad Singh	It was difficult to tackle it with the normal law enforcing agencies. As a result, the entire State had to be declared as "Disturbed Area" from the month of September, 1980 and the Army called in to assist the civil administration in counter "insurgency" measures.
1982	Shri Sayed Muzafffar Husain Burney	"Some misguided youths continue to disturb the law and order situation.
1983	Shri Sayed Muzafffar Husain Burney	"The activities of the Meitei extremists which had been causing immense concern during the year 1981 have decreased now" Sustained its pressure on counter insurgency operations.
1984	Shri Sayed Muzafffar Husain Burney	"Restoring normal law and order situation in the State". "The activities of extremists in the valley which had been causing immense concern to my Government in the previous years have come down appreciably".
1985	General Kotikalapudi Venkata Krishna Rao	"Tangible improvement in the law and order situation". "A large number of extremists with arms and ammunition were arrested in counter insurgency operations, which has subdued the insurgent groups to a great extent and helped in restoring normalcy".
1986	General Kotikalapudi Venkata Krishna Rao	"The environment is also congenial for this surge because the law and order situation continues to be satisfactory. The activities of a section of insurgents in the hill districts and the attempts of some misguided elements to renew insurgency in the Valley areas were no doubt a cause for concern".
1987	General Kotikalapudi Venkata Krishna Rao	Contained the activities of the "extremists" operating in Valley areas/measures to contain NSCN activities effectively in the Hill Districts/re-vamping the State Police set-up.
1988	General Kotikalapudi	"I am happy to mention that, my Government

(*Contd.*)

Table 18.4 (*Contd.*)

Year	Governor	Comment
	Venkata Krishna Rao	has successfully contained the activities of insurgents, operating in Valley area, with the active support from Security Forces". "Misguided youth" who form a microscopic minority will realize follies of their illegal ways; refrain from violence and join National mainstream.
1989	General Kotikalapudi Venkata Krishna Rao	"Four major incidents of extremist activities leading to loss of lives", "active policy of rehabilitation of surrendered extremists".
1990	Shri Chintamani Panigrahi	The District Police succeeded in apprehending 93 active members/sympathizers of various extremist outfits during the year under review besides recovering 16 weapons of different categories.
1991	Shri Chintamani Panigrahi	"it is sad to note that some anti-social elements have been trying to disturb social harmony and to wean away our youth from the main stream".
1992	Shri Chintamani Panigrahi	Normal crimes were comparatively less, the State witnessed spurt on "insurgency" front/ appeal to the insurgents to come to the negotiating table through an apex forum for the talks with the Centre.
1993	Shri Chintamani Panigrahi	Believes in solving the problem of "insurgency" through peaceful negotiation and I have repeatedly appealed to the "insurgents" to come to the negotiating table. "The insurgents" instead of responding to the magnanimous gesture of the Government have embarked upon senseless killing of innocent public... "I appeal to all right thinking people of the State to extend their whole-hearted co-operation to the Government in meeting the challenge posed by subversive and anti-national forces which have eaten into the vitals of the economy and prosperity of the State and seriously impaired the quality of life of its people".
1994	Lt. Gen. (Retd.) V.K. Nayar	I am hopeful that our brothers and sisters who have been misled to become insurgents would also listen to the appeal of the Government, eschew the path of violence

(*Contd.*)

Table 18.4 (*Contd.*)

Year	*Governor*	*Comment*
		and come to the negotiating table for peaceful settlement.
1995	Oudh Narayan Shrivastava	To instill, in the common man, a sense of security by strengthening and modernizing the "law and order" machinery, protecting the territorial integrity of Manipur and the country, bringing the "misguided youths" back to the mainstreams/appeal to the "insurgents" to come forward, lay down arms, and share democratic approach to resolution of their problems".
1996	Oudh Narayan Shrivastava	Already aware of my Government's preparedness for peaceful dialogues as means for resolution of the problems of "insurgency" which has imperiled the State and impeded its development effort. I would sincerely reiterate my Government's appeal to the "misguided youth" to lay down arms and to join the national mainstream.
1997	Oudh Narayan Shrivastava	Adopted a two-pronged approach, i.e. peaceful resolution of the "law and order" problems caused by the "undergrounds" and instilling in the minds of the common man a sense of security by strengthening the "law and order" machinery. A National Highway Security Scheme has been formulated, for extensive patrolling.
1999	Oudh Narayan Shrivastava	Efforts to improve the general "law and order" including the "insurgency" problems/appeal to the "insurgents" to come forward to lay down arms and adopt democratic approach for resolution of their problems.
2000	Ved Prakash Marwah	Appeal to all sections of the society, especially the youths, to eschew violence. My Government has exhibited unflagging commitment to peaceful resolution of conflicts by following an open-door policy for dialogue with the insurgents. My Government is also actively pursuing liberalised policy of rehabilitation of "surrendered insurgents". I sincerely appeal to the youths, who are today following the path of violence, to come forward for meaningful dialogue.

(*Contd.*)

Table 18.4 (*Contd.*)

Year	Governor	Comment
2001	Ved Prakash Marwah	Initiative to declare a unilateral ceasefire against all "insurgent" groups and has appealed to them to come for talks for resolving their grievances. The ceasefire, which is effective for one month from 1st March, 2001, has been announced as a good will gesture towards the insurgent groups. ...My Government recognises that it will not be easy for the insurgent groups to respond immediately to the declaration of unilateral ceasefire and appeal for talks. It is, therefore, proposed to constitute a Contact Group comprising eminent persons from different walks of life to establish contact with the "insurgent groups" before formal talks can commence.
2002	Ved Prakash Marwah	I am sad to say that our people have suffered for too long. The canker of "insurgency" is eating into the very vitals of our society. There is almost no section of society which is left untouched by this malaise. I hope, and my optimism may not be misplaced, the various insurgent outfits will take cognizance of the suffering of our people and respond favourably to the appeal for a negotiated settlement.
2003	Ved Prakash Marwah	Manipur in particular, continues to be affected by violence perpetrated by various "insurgent" organisations operating in the region. Many of these insurgent organisations have their bases in the neighbouring countries adjoining India. The efforts made by the law enforcement agencies to curb the activities of the cadres owing allegiance to such organisations have proved inadequate.
2004	Arvind Dave	Manipur has been afflicted by "internal conflict" for the last many decades which not only caused loss of precious lives and property but also seriously hampered the process of socio-economic development. The state police, with the active assistance of the army and the central security forces deployed in the state, were able to contain the activities of various "insurgent groups"

(*Contd.*)

Table 18.4 (*Contd.*)

Year	Governor	Comment
		operating in the state to a large extent during the year. Central government should increase the strength of the Central Security Forces deployed in the state and to take expeditious steps for effective guarding of the porous Indo-Myanmar border.
2005	Shivinder Singh Sidhu	Despite the sincere efforts made by the State Police, Army and other Para-Military forces to curb the unlawful activities of the "insurgents", incidents of extortion, kidnapping for ransom, unauthorised collection of taxes etc. however still continue. My Government believes in solving the problem of insurgency through peaceful means. Hence, I appeal to the insurgents to come forward, lay down arms and adopt democratic.
2006	Shivinder Singh Sidhu	The severe financial crisis coupled with the "internal conflicts" faced by the State during the preceding years have remained a matter of serious concern of my Government ... I would like to reiterate that my Government believes in solving the problems of conflicts through peaceful means and once again appeal to the youth who have taken up arms against the Government to come forward, lay down arms and adopt democratic and peaceful means for resolution of the problems.
2007	Shivinder Singh Sidhu	"Security and law and order" issues have continued to pose a major challenge to the State Government and its development initiatives/the 3-tier Unified Command Structure, established to synergize counter insurgency operations of State and Central Government agencies, has worked cohesively and effectively. Counter-insurgency operations conducted and coordinated action taken through this mechanism has put the "insurgent" groups and the "unlawful" outfits under considerable pressure.
2008	Shivinder Singh Sidhu	My Government believes in resolving all the issue through peaceful means and I once

(*Contd.*)

Table 18.4 (*Contd.*)

Year	*Governor*	*Comment*
		again appeal to the youth who have taken up arms to come forward, lay down arms and adopt a democratic and peaceful means for resolution of the issues... I am happy that some militant groups have responded positively to the initiatives of the government for talks. ... During the year, 1296 "extremist" of different underground groups were arrested and 121 extremist were killed...
2009	Gurbachan Jagat	Concern that state continues to face the challenges of "insurgency and law and order" problem
2010	Gurbachan Jagat	Over 30 "underground" outfits Manipur continues to grapple with the problems of "insurgency" and this severely hamper the development and growth of the state/in the line of action, the police force has been strengthen
2011	Gurbachan Jagat	Highlighting the achievement of the state government with regard to signing of the Tripartite Agreement with KCP (MC)-Lallumba Group, the Governor pointed out that KCP (MC)-Lallumba Group is the first Valley-based "militant" group to enter into Agreement after the Suspension of Operation (SoO) Agreement with Kuki UG groups under KNO and UPF.
2012	Gurbachan Jagat	"improvement in the law and order situation in the hills following signing of agreement with Kuki militant outfits in 2009. "...the tripartite agreement with valley-based Kangleipak Communist Party (military council) Lallumba group was also renewed for another year to facilitate the rehabilitation of the cadres.

Source: Hanjabam and Thangjam (2013).

Armed Opposition Groups and Conflict Resolution

The Armed Opposition Groups have not initiated any peace proposal in the true sense of the words. However, UNLF had responded to the "invitation" by Shri Ved Prakash Marwah on 31 January, 2005. It put forward a four-point formula to resolve the armed conflict in Manipur[24]. The Four points are given below:

(a) A plebiscite under United Nations (UN) supervision to elicit the opinion of the people of the State on the core issue of restoration of Manipur's independence.
(b) Deployment of a UN peace-keeping force in Manipur to ensure the process is free and fair.
(c) Surrender of arms by the UNLF to the UN force, matched with the withdrawal of Indian troops.
(d) Handing over of political power by the UN in accordance with the results of the plebiscite.

It is worthwhile to recall that earlier, on 26 November, 2000, the UNLF Chairperson, R.K. Sanayaima *alias* Meghen, had put forward three conditions for talks with the Centre (Government of India). First, the Centre should include the agenda of sovereignty if it was truly serious about its offer of talks. Second, India must first demilitarise the region. And finally, a third country should monitor the talks. After UNLF's call, there was a mass movement for holding plebiscite in Manipur in two phases. However, it was suppressed by the Government.

The Governor renewed his appeal in his address to the August House on the opening day of the Budget Session of Manipur State Assembly on February 22, 2006.[25] However, the proposal was rejected by the armed opposition groups. For example, RPF and its armed wing PLA reaffirmed its stand not to have a political dialogue with the Indian Government except on the issue of independence and sovereignty of Manipur after their second congress (July 14 to December 4, 2008). Explaining India's notion of peace, Irengbam Chaoren asserted that peace talk from the Indian perspective meant making the armed cadres give up their arms, persuading the revolutionaries admit they are Indians and then resolving the issue under the Constitution of India.[26] He further observed that such an arrangement would not be able to provide scope for accommodating the independent and sovereign aspirations of the Manipuris. The statement while reasserting that peace talk could never substitute the armed struggle to attain the stated objective and goals, remarked that taking recourse to such a process would amount to cheating the people.

People and Conflict Resolution

UNLF's call for plebiscite was endorsed by the civil society bodies in

Manipur in the same year, i.e. 2005, as it may provided a solution to the ongoing armed conflict in Manipur. Numerous public meetings were held in different parts of Manipur. The first phase ended in 2006. The second phase was resumed after the arrest of RK Sanayaima on 29 September, 2010 in Bangladesh. Following Table 18.5 shows some of the meetings organized by different civil society bodies with regard to holding a plebiscite for conflict resolution in Manipur.

Table 18.5: Select list of Meetings for Conflict Resolution through Plebiscite

Date	*Place*	*Organiser*
First Phase		
13 October, 2005	Kondong Lairembi Ground, Moreh	Meitei Council, Moreh; Kha-Nongpok Apunba Nupi Lup and AMSU Chandel District
13 October, 2005	Khurai Lainingthou Puthiba Sanglen, Imphal East	Seven social organisations
1 November, 2005	Sangeet Natak Mandir, Nambol	UWDO, NLYSC, SLYCL, EDC and KAYAC
20 November, 2005	GM Hall	Manipur Intellectual Forum (MIF)
29 November, 2005	Conference Hall, Manipur University	UPF
30 January, 2006	Andro Kangjeibung Lampak	All Yairipok United Clubs' Organisation (AYUCO)
30 April, 2006	Community hall of Yaipharok marjing Village	All Manipur Progressive Farmers' Association and Yaipharok Maring Village Authority
8 June 2006	MDU hall	AMKIL, Nupi Samaj, All Manipur Tammi-Chingmi Apunba Nupi Lup, Thoubal District United Women's Development Organisation, Apunba Nupi Lup Bishnupur District, Thangmeiband Apunba Nupi Lup, Khwairamband Nupi Keithel Shemgat Shagatpa Marup and Imphal West Women Development Organisation
Second Phase		
5 December, 2010	Khabam Maning Leikai	Yaipha Sindam Naharol Club and the Social Reformation and Development Organization
17 January,	Koujengleima	Advance Women Society

(Contd.)

Date	Place	Organiser
2011	Community Hall, Sekmai, Imphal West	
29 January, 2011	Yairipok Leirongthel Community Hall, Thoubal district	Panthoibi Youth Club and Leirongthel Women Development Association
28 February, 2011	Mayang Langjing community hall	Mayanglangjing Semgat Sagat Lup inn association with Taning Development Club and Mayanglangjing Youth Library
1 March, 2011	Yairipok Khoirom Laimang, Thoubal district	Khoirom Nupi Lup, Yairipok Khoirom Makha Leikai
6 March, 2011	Saiton Keithel, Bishnupur district	
13 March, 2011	Pukhao Laipham Imphal East	Awang Lam Pukhao UMO Unit
15 March, 2011	Community hall of Iram Siphai	Laiphrakpam Samaj Thoudang Nupi Kanglup and Iram Siphai Mamang Leikai Nupi Kanglup
17 March, 2011	Keithelmanbi community hall	Keithelmanbi Bazar Board
25 March, 2011	Lamdong Leikai Yaipha Thourang Lup.	Bright Way Club and Nisha Bandh Nupi Marup
27 March, 2011	Kumbi Keithel, Bishnupur	All Kumbi Kendra Women Welfare Association
29 March, 2011	Kakmayai Community Hall	Eastern Youth Development Club and Mahila Mandal Kakmayai
31 March, 2011	Kangmong Langoljam Mayai Leikai Community Hall, Imphal West	Kangmong Langoljam Mayai Leikai Committee
2 April, 2011	Konthoujam Makha Leikai Pakhangba Community Hall	Konthoujam Makha Apunba Meira Paibi Lup
3 April, 2011	Ningthoukhong Kha Meitei Leikai Community Hall, Bishnupur district	Ningthoukhong Gopinath Meirapaibi Lup, Ningthoukhong Sport Club
5 April, 2011	Tangkham Awang Leikai Kalita Shanglen	All Manipur Kanba Ima Lup (AMKIL), Tangkham Awang Leikai Meira Paibi Lup
9 April, 2011	Ngairangbam UJB School	North Imphal Meira Paibi Apunba Nupi Lup

(*Contd.*)

Date	*Place*	*Organiser*
10 April, 2011	Naharup Mayai Leikai Thongkhong	Naharup Mayai Leikai Women Welfare Association and Naharup Awang Leikai Welfare Association
12 April, 2011	Huidrom Lairembi Lampak, Yurembam	Nongchup Imphal Meira paibi Apunba Lup (NIMPAL) and YAC, Yurembam
15 April, 2011	Khongnangpokpi Village, Senapati District	Khongnangpokpi Village Authority
19 April, 2011	Keirao Bitra Community Hall, Imphal East	Keirao Awang Leikai Nupi Semgat Sagatpa Lup
22 April, 2011	Phoijing Community Hall	Phoijing Awang Apunba Nupi Lup
24 April, 2011	Sekta Lainingthou Achangba Community Hall	Sekta Meita Paibi Lup
28 April, 2011	Hougrampat Mandab, Moirangkhunou	UMO Moirang Khunou Branch and Hougrampat Meirapaibi Apunba Lup
7 May, 2011	Gurumayum Mandab, Nachou	Nachou Sports Development Association
8 May, 2011	Ground of Keibul Lamjao Awang Club, Keibul Lamjao	Keibul Lamjao Youth Sporting and Cultural Association
9 May, 2011	Leishram Community Hall, Bishnupur	Loyalakpa Woman Organisation, Leishram
11 May, 2011	Khekman Community Hall, Thoubal	Khekman Lairembi Youth Association
13 May, 2011	Charangpat Mamang Leikai Community Hall, Charangpat	Charangpat Women Development Organisation, Super Sporting Association, Echam Khunou, Bhengi and Thokchom Nupi Lup
15 May, 2011	Kangchup Chiru Community Hall	Kangchup Chiru Women Development Society
18 May, 2011	Khundongbam Club Ground Kiyam Siphai	Kiyam Siphai Khundongbam Leikai Meira Paibi
21 May, 2011	Yaingangpokpi Community Hall, Yaingangpokpi	Yaingangpokpi Meira Paibi Apunba Lup, Yaingangpokpi Bazaar Development Committee, Youth United Club, Youth Progressive Club
23 May, 2011	Kiyam Wangmataba Community Hall, Thoubal	Thoubal Kiyam Wangmataba Meira Paibi Lup

Resolutions adopted in the public meetings had three major characteristics, which are summarized as given below:

1. Plebiscite should be conducted so that everyone can take active part. In other words Manipur people should participate in the plebiscite towards conflict resolution and usher in peace.
2. The criminal cases pending against persons involved in the liberation movement of Manipur should be handed over to Manipur Government.
3. United Nations in its official capacity must be the mediator of the plebiscite.

However, there was no positive response from the Government of India. Since, India considers the problem in Manipur to be an internal problem it is against the involvement of a third party, including the United Nations, to settle its internal affairs. In fact, the public meetings were considered to be seditious and many people were arrested under the National Security Act. On account of repressive police actions the movement for plebiscite came to an end by 2011.

Conclusion

Even after more than 60 years of armed conflict in Manipur, the Government and the armed opposition groups are moving in parallel directions in terms of defining the situation or identifying the root cause(s). The Government has not accepted the position of the armed opposition groups. Similarly, *in-spite* of engaging with international cooperation (military or otherwise), particularly with Myanmar, Bangladesh and Bhutan, to suppress the armed movement in the state, the government continues to claim that it is a law and order problem, and most recently, terrorism. There has been no meeting point for the conflict situation of Manipur. Reading from the governor speeches, it clearly indicates that the government does not have any policy or political will to address the situation. Any official documents that indicates the existence of Armed Conflict is out rightly rejected or concealed. For instance, the Justice Jeevan Reddy Report on AFSPA was concealed because the report indicates the situation of Manipur as "Internal Disturbance" which can be characterized as non-international armed conflict.

The people of the state have already indicated their willingness to resolve the conflict through democratic means. Unfortunately, the

Government has not responded to the people as well as non-state actors. Mere appeals for peace talks without any strategy from time to time along with military engagements cannot bring about any tangible solution or in addressing the problem. The government is simply managing the conflict but managing the conflict has the danger of not resolving it and this open up the possibility (in many cases certainly) that the conflict will come up again in the future[27]. Rajagopalan[28] after studying agreement, accords in the region since 1947 observed that it has barely shown any characteristics of processes that would lead to a lasting peace. Preaccords talks have not been inclusive; the provisions agreed upon with one groups frequently and patently conflict with the interest of others; and the accords either contains provisions to address core conflict issues n a manner that cannot be implemented or they do not deal with core issues at all. Finally, in six decades since Indian Independence, no responsive and accountable political infrastructure has been created either for conflict resolution or for governance itself.

The lack or absence of political will is another stumbling block in resolving the conflict in Manipur. The business of conflict seems to be benefitting the political class and other engaging in the conflict. Therefore, they don't want to resolve the conflict else four to five decades is a long time to come up with a policy or a strategy to address the issue.

Notes and References

1. *Notification,* Ministry of Home Affairs, Government of India, dated 13 November, 2013.
2. National Convention on Manipur Merger issue (1993), *Resolution of the National. National Convention on Manipur Merger Issue,* Imphal, Manipur.
3. Reddy J. (2005), *Report of the Committee to Review the Armed Force (Special Power) Act, 1958,* Ministry of Home affairs, (Officially not published) Government of India (Published by *The Hindu*).
4. ORDER, dated 06/09/2012 of the Spl. National Investigation Agency Case No. 01/2010.
5. Sobhapati Samon, "Talks only on the issue of sovereignty of Manipur", *North-East Sun,* 31 May 2009.
6. Civil Society Coalition on Human Rights in Manipur and the UN, 2011, *Status of Human Rights in Manipur—North-Eastern Region,* Submitted to the Office of the High Commissioner for Human Rights, 2nd Cycle Universal Periodic Review, Human Rights Council, United Nations, 28 November.
7. http://features.ibnlive.in.com/special/web2/indias-hidden-wars.html.

8. Quins, David. 'Self-Determination Movements and Their Outcomes' edited by Gurr, Ted, Robert; J. Joseph Hewitt; and Jonathan Wilkenfeld. *Peace and Conflict 2008*. Executive summary. CIDCM. University of Maryland, 2008.
9. Akoijam Bimol, and Tarunkumar Th. "Armed Forces (Special Powers) Act 1958: Disguised War & its Subversions". *Eastern Quarterly*. Volume 3, Issue I, April-June (2005).
10. Rupachandra, Yumnam, "UNLF owns up Manipur blast", Seven Sisters Post, Gauhaty, September 6, 2012, <http://sevensisterspost.com/unlf-owns-manipur-blast/>
11. Goswami, Namrata, "India's North-East 2020: Four Alternative Futures", *IDSA Occasional Paper, No. 13*, New Delhi: *Indian Defence and Strategic Analysis*, July 2010, p. 11.
12. Cohen, Stepen P. and Dasgupta, Sunil, *Arming without Aiming: India's Military Modernization,* New Delhi: Penguin/Viking, 2010, p. 4.
13. Hanjabam Shukhdeba Sharma, Thangjam Homen, Thakengchangbam Chaoba & Urikhimbam Nobokishore (2013), United Nations and Human Rights in Manipur, Forward Books, New Delhi.
14. Menon, V.P., *Integration of the Indian States.* Madras: Orient Longman, 1956.
15. Quoted in Baruah 2006, *Post Fronteirs Blues: Towards a New Policy Framework for North-East India*, Policy Studies no 33, East West Centre, Washington, pp. 15.
16. Kunal, Chattopadhyay., Aninda, Bannerjee., Saurobbijoy, Sarkar. *The Permanent Revolution & Results and Prospects- Leon Trotsky*. New Delhi, Aakar Books, 2005.
17. Centre for Organization Research and Education. The Manipur Nation: A Position' edited by Laifungbam, Debabrata, Roy., Immanuel, Zarzosang, Varte. *Contour of Conflict. Pathway of Peace.* Guwahati: ICTCP-North-East Zone, 2007.
18. Hanjabam Shukhdeba Sharma and Thangjam Homen (2013), Political will and Conflict Resolution in Manipur in L. Muhindro Singh (edt) *Conflict Transformation, Peace and Divide in India's North-East: The Context of Recent Trends*, Kamakhya Publishing House, Guwahati & SKWC Publication Cell, Nambol, Manipur.
19. Coordination Committee comprising of (UNLF, PLA, KYKL, KCP, PREPAK, PREPAK-Pro and United People's Party of Kangleipak.
20. Sanajaoba, Naorem, "*Armed Forces Special Power Act, 1958: A Law for Extrajudicial Execution in Perpetuity*", paper presented at the One Day Convention on the Armed Forces Special Power Act, 1958, jointly organized by the All Asom Students Union and Apunba Lup, Guwahati, 24 October, 2006.
21. "Manipur: An Ever-present Danger", *South Asia Intelligence Review/IBNS*, www.newkerala.com/news/newsplus/worldnews-74827.html

22. Hanjabam Shukhdeba Sharma and Thangjam Homen (2013), Political will and Conflict Resolution in Manipur in L Muhindro Singh (edt) *Conflict Transformation, Peace and Divide in India's North-East: The Context of Recent Trends*, Kamakhya Publishing House, Guwahati & SKWC Publication Cell, Nambol, Manipur.
23. MISA=Maintenance of Internal Security Act, 1971; COFEPOSA= The Conservation of Foreign Exchange and Prevention of Smuggling Activities Act, 1974.
24. ww.satp.org/satporgtp/countries/india/states/manipur/documents/papers/unlf2005.htm
25. "Manipur outfit spurns talks offer", *The Telegraph,* Guwahati, 27 February, 2006.
26. *Ibid.*
27. Kumarulzaman Askandar (ed), *Building Peace; Reflection from Southeast Asia*, Penang: Southeast Asian Conflict Studies Network.
28. Rajagopalan Swarna (2008), "*Peace Accords in North-East India: Journey over Milestones*", Policy Studies 46, East West Centre, Washington.

19

Constitutional Realism

A Peace Process in North-East India

N. Pramod

The constitutional law of India, consisting of both the written and unwritten rules, is a binding law of the land. The essence of justice, as outlined in the preamble to the Constitution, is primarily for the attainment of the common good for all the citizens of the country. The concept of fraternity, unity and integrity as mentioned in the preamble also need to be relooked and revisited in matching with the emerging dynamics and dimensions. Indeed this concept was the paramount in the mind of framers of constitution since the people of India had suffered a lot at the hands of colonial powers for a long period of time.

The constitutional realism basically aims to set up a just orderly society where the doctrine of rule of law, on which Indian legal system has been founded, reposes a mandatory obligation on the part of the state functionaries and also keeps them within the legitimate constitutional limit. Therefore, all the constitutional bodies not only obtain their respective authorities from the law of the land but they are also legally expected to follow and function according to it. In a parliamentary democracy like India, it is the constitutional propriety right as well as the prerogative function of the legislative to make and unmake laws; however, it does not mean that the legislative has the unlimited authority in discharging its function. As a matter of fact, every political institution including the judiciary shall be made accountable to the people, this is what the constitution and constitutionalism of India have mandated, on the other hand, a delegate cannot claim to be superior to his Principal. It is not that the democracy exists in the country simply, because, people are allowed to exercise their franchise once in five years to choose their respective government.

The Parliamentary democracy, as embodied in the constitution, shall only be meaningful if the citizens are given adequate opportunity to participate in the governance. A good governance, which is transparent and participatory, is per '*se sine quo non*' of every progressive democratic society. Interestingly, the actual working of constitutional governance in an effective way does not necessarily depend on the mere embodiment abstract safeguards of rights and freedoms of individuals. The constitutional experiences, shown for the last 64 years in India, indicate that such abstract declarations in the legal documents are of no meaning in reality unless there are well founded acceptable ways and means to exhibit them. In addition, India having a written constitution consisting of a bill of rights, it implies the limitations for all the powers of state functionaries even in the absence of article 13 of the constitution. So, the real issue is not the mere adoption of such declarations but it is, obviously the need of a competent, impartial and independent constitutional body which can uphold the constitutional governance inter alia the rule of law in the country.

The very concept of state and judicial institution are found intimately linked each other, as a result, individuals are made to realize the existence of state through the administration of justice, otherwise it could have been in a different way for the state even for its existence. It is the court which has a sacrosanct role to play not only for resolving inter se disputes but also to act as a competent constitutional balancing organ between and among the conflicting interests in the society. The constitutional court has also overcome those riders which were, primarily created by the law makers during the passage of time. In the past 1978, the judiciary has started resorting to the American due process of law with all its ramifications through the process of liberal interpretations of laws. Since, the court has opened a new dimension of justicing process through its judicial activism; it has given new hope to the millions of justice starved people. However, it does not mean that judiciary has become an unguided missile. In a way, such pro-active judicial approach has been increasingly signifying the constitutional objectives without allowing the country to face any massive constitutional change for the last six and half decades unlike the neighbouring countries. It is also worth mentioning that court does not act as a mere technocrat or an umpire but it has started acting as an efficient auditor of social, political, economic and culture, among others. On the top of it, people are convinced and understood that judges are the better promoters and protectors of their rights and freedoms than the legislatures and executives. In case judiciary does not step in where the legislature as well as the executive are found indifferent to the grievances of people, it would obviously circumscribe the people to find out the alternative option, such as, taking their grievances to street thereby indulging in the culture of agitation for which countless blames are made for the people by the people.

Issue in the NE India may be different forms and nature with different forms and nature with different backgrounds and reasons, however; one finds a common feature of such issue occurring in the region, that is why so called "Peace Process", initiated by the main stockholders could not either be proceeded or completed with any logical finding, despite having made various attempts in this regard. It is apparent that there may be many reasons for such failure, but it is also equally true that due to the absence of a competent and independent body, which can act effectively as a power centre of Parliamentary democracy, the peace process in the region would remain gloomy. Another reason is that every issue of any matter is seemed to be manifestly interwoven with such inherited doctrine of parliamentary democracy. In addition, there is an immense need of having a meaningful check on counter majoritarian rule as well. In a way, there are adequate numbers of constitutional functionaries assigned with the specific constitutional mandates to deal with any sort of issue occurring elsewhere in the country. However, one of the basic problems for finding such peace building process in the NE India could be the inactive attitude and conduct of the people, because it is the people who are legally allowed to activate the constitutional machineries. Apparently the constitution itself does not fail the system but the people, who enforce the constitution, have miserably failed it. As such, the people of this region have felt alienated from the mainland India in all respects having lost their faith and confident on the working of the constitutional system. Therefore, it is highly essential for both the stakeholders to believe and trust the culture of legalism for building an everlasting peace in the region.

20
Asoto: Settlement for Peace in the Mao Traditional Culture

Puni Losii Mao

Settlement for Peace (ASOTO)

'Asoto' is a very old traditional culture of the Mao for coming to terms and extending a network of goodwill and peace within and among the villagers. It even precedes the literate culture, as this has been in existence already before Mao people discover the art of writing. The effectiveness of Asoto and the obligations exacted by it from those who participate in it cannot be fathomed from the yard stick of 'Peace Treaty' as we know in today's parlance'. In Asoto as per its practiced principle, people from one village to another village, irrespective of whether enemy or friend were called to eat and dine together. If it was enemy or waging war between each other, they will make peace settlement between two villages and will not wage war anymore or not to have war between each other but can call peace settlement, that is, they will make friendship and will not quarrel for any reasons and will come to a mutual commitment to help each other in times of needs and adversities

Peace settlement can be done after the discussion with the villager's convenience or considering the benefit of the villages. Mutually agreeing to come to terms of the peace settlement may not be necessarily due to the sharing of delicious foods from each other but to come to realization that it is very meaningful and benefited to both the villages. They will debate the merits and demerits of the peace settlement with a particular village to make the settlement or not. The benefits of peace settlement are given as hereunder:

1. Before the advent of the British, the people of Mao were frequently in war between and among themselves. In the war if a particular village is defeated by another village, the defeated villagers will not take the food of the victorious village, due to the prevalence of the belief that, if in case, the food had been eaten on the way or in the journey unknowingly, he/she will be paralyzed due to his/her negligence. In order to avoid such inconveniences they will call the peace settlement, any difficulties will go away if the settlement is done.
2. In the earlier days, they live in one village, same origin with same parents. Due to un-avoidable circumstances they go in scattered and settle in different other places. They call for peace settlement in order to familiarize themselves by knowing each other with a purpose of with a purpose of circumventing and avoiding any unwanted actions in the future.
3. In the ancient times there are frequent waging wars to each other community, they need each other's help at the time of war, and peace settlement is very necessary during their period.
4. In forefathers' period peace settlement was made between them but after sometime their younger generations had forgotten the settlement, the present generation will then call for renew of the settlement with both the parties which will remember the earlier settlement promises.
5. In the settlement, all the males who can reach the opposite and adjacent village can go and make friendship. This will help to know each other's village quality and capability of each and every individual and all the villagers of the host people will come out and make people happy after knowing each other.

Contact for Peace Settlement

Starting of the villagers for the purpose of the peace settlement will have to approach to the opposite village after sending message to meet within a particular day by the village elders and some young intellectuals with the village elders to discuss about the peace settlement between the two villages. They will praise and respect each other expressing greetings with good words. On the day of making a peace settlement if a man dies in the village they will postpone or stop the settlement because in their time they were very superstitious or can fix another day. If they have decided to make a settlement between the two villages, elders of both the villages will bless each other that, before our settlement no one will die, no domestic animal will die, we two will consider as the sun and the moon.

After the agreement to have a peace settlement, the first host village will start to prepare meat, rice and all other necessities. All the youths will be busy cleaning the village and surroundings of the village thinking of the joy and happiness for the days to come on the settlement day. Broad minded and well wishers will prepare the arrangement, if the number of guests is more than the hosts it will be hosted with two three guests. If they hosted more than one village the people will respect them and take them as courageous man. Hosts of the settlement will send message to friends of other villages inviting them also to come and join the settlement, after receiving the invitation they will come along with presentation and enjoy together.

Preparation of Dresses

They will prepare their dresses before a couple of days ahead their wives will prepare their husband dresses in order not to face difficulty in arranging dresses. Both villagers will practice the voice of 'Movu' tune of happiness at the village ground. All male will dress in full traditional attire, if there is any incomplete dresses the villagers will inform to the people and will get ready for preparation of new dresses and do rehearsal at the village centre. Brave man will jump and pronounce that "I am the Oxen I will do whatever as I move on no one can block me on the day I move on" and will be shaking his head and jump over the ground. During this time villagers and women folks bursting to tears due to the recalling of the love and fond memories of the past.

Starting Day for Peace Settlement

On the day of starting to move out from the village, 'phehrimani' (local terms for genna) is observed, that is genna of free from any sickness. In the morning the village elders will come on the mount (tokhu) and shout as 'oh bless god, today our mother gave us a good day and we will move out' all are getting ready to move out from their own houses. After that all those who go for peace settlement will come out and will make rehearsal at the centre of the village. All the brave men in the war will put cock feathers on their head. All the males will start moving with their full attires by taking spears, guns, shields by the elders and all the youths will dressed up with full beauty and will go with 'oho- oho' tune of sound, the women folks and the remaining children will cry due to their love and remembrance of the past. During this day they go in line, no one is allowed to cross the line if anyone comes by crossing the line he can be killed at the spot, no one can claim that he is right! Women and children will not go for work in the paddy field and some brave men will be left as village guards for protection against any attacks by the enemies. All village males will go by putting their own war rank dress; no one will put their dresses without achieving their own titles. They will be entitled by the entitled seniors and the Village Chief.

Taking Luncheon for Peace Settlement

On the way to the opposite village, the guests-group will take their luncheon. While taking their luncheon, a leader will shout saying that "today our mother gave us a good day, no one will face any sickness and we will not get any accident, we will overcome from any difficulties". Everyone is strictly prohibited to violate the rules against the opposite sex. It is believed that if anyone who shared bed with the girl at the host village, the guest village generations will be lost or many great persons will die in the village.

Entering the Host Village

At the time of entering into the village, all the host villagers will be waiting at the mount by observing a genna. Guest villagers will first line up by the war head persons and secondly by the brave men of war title rankers, the middle by the common people and the last line by the war tails, they will come without breaking the line. One of the leaders will come and receive the guests outside the village gate along with a mug of water and two pieces of blemish iron pieces and will hand over to the hands of a leader of the guests group and will pronounce that, "We two villagers might have committed mistakes to each other in the past, but it will be left behind today onwards we will be like clear waters and like blemish iron". Guest leader also will pronounce as the host stated and will wash each other's hand and will proceed towards the village with the shouting of 'aho-aho' (movupfo).

Selection of Guests

After crossing the village gate and reaching the host's village they will shout with 'aho-aho' along with firing gun sound like the bursting of maize roasting in the pot, thundering storm and men will jump in the centre of the village. After their voice stopped, the host villagers will come and take their guests one by one and bring to their homes, they are allowed to take bath and change their dresses and will serve rice and meat, giving their rice beers and curry/chutney and will lead to the common gathering place.

Feast with the both Villagers

The host village will prepare rice beer according to their convenience, may be in one place or several places. They will take rice beer and enjoy happily with the new friends (hosts and guests), after enjoying with the villagers, late at night they are taken to host's residences.

Both Village Elders Meeting

On the next day or staying for the whole day, both the village elders will kill a dog and will eat together along with rice beer and discuss many good points/agreements that they will make promise between the two villages.

Points of Agreements

- "We might have committed wrongs and hunting head with each other in the past, maybe we should show the settlement to each other that such acts be left behind and shall never again be commited from today onwards, till the end of life. We will be friendly with each other so long as the sun and moon exists. If any of us face any problems, we will protect each other. In case of someone's property being snatched, we will support each other. Whosoever violated this agreement will die as many a times as the fur of the dog".
- The words of promise will be pronounced by the elders of the both parties afer killing a dog.

Competition of Games and Sports during Peace Settlement

On the day of staying for the whole day, games competition is held by the youths like taking short promises, Short Put, High jump, Long jump, wrestling, muscle hand punch, etc,. After that they will go to the gathering place where rice beer is well prepared. They will sing songs recalling the minds of each other. In the evening, they are led to the host's residence. After dinner, they are taken to good place for taking rest (sleep).

Day of Departure (Peace Settlement)

On the third day, all the guests will get ready to go back to their own village. At the time of leaving the guests, the host villagers will give a spear along with coins. At the time of giving spear and coins they will pronounce that, after taking this we will not break our promises, go home safely in the name of God. The guests will take the spear and coins pronouncing that "our promises will not break till the end of time" giving the best wishes to the host villagers with the blessings of God and then they will depart.

Taking Luncheon on the Way of Going Back Home

On the third day, on their way back to the village they will eat luncheon what the hosts had prepared at a suitable place. The sisters who married to other villages will come and request them to drink their rice beers saying, "though it is not tasty drink with us, there again they will drink along with them". The brothers also praise their sisters that today our sisters make them special in such a way after many years, they praise each other and shed tears due to their love and remembrance of the past. Meat prepared by the host would not be brought home due to the traditional belief they give to their sisters who married to other villages. After finishing their luncheon, an old man will shout, 'let us ready to go again' and they all will shout with their voice sounding 'aho- aho- aho'. On the way to the village the wife sisters will come and receive them with good foods (*khala*).

Return (Coming Back to the Village)

All the participants of the peace settlement after reaching their village they would be shouting with their voice as 'aho- aho' some of them will be jumping due to happiness and blank-fire their guns into the sky, the sound would be like thunderstorms and bursting maize in the roasting pot. At that time, some courageous men will jump and shook their heads with the spear and shield pronouncing that "I am like an ox, if any one who stand against me will do like this!" All the villagers, children and womenfolk will be watching them pushing each other and tears will come down due to their deep love. After this, everyone will go home and the next day will called cleansing genna in the village and will complete the process of peace settlement.

The Host Village on the Next Day of the Settlement

After the guests left the village there will be a cleansing genna (phehremani), village elders will drink the remaining rice beer and will calculate the presentation, the amount who gave most and how much with that money will do in which purpose. After the settlement, the villagers will talk about which guests own what items, shot put, High jump, Long jump, etc. Whose guest is handsome, who is good to others and will discuss on the way to paddy fields or wherever they go.

To Remember/Gist

Friendship during the peace settlement will not break till the end of life but also will make friendship with their sons and grandsons.

No Restriction to Each Other

For the people of Mao there are many gennas and rituals; as for example, not to enter inside the house due to "first day of seedling or first day of digging paddy fields", etc. But for the guests after friendship settlement, there would not be restriction if any friendship coming as guests, host friends welcomed the guests and to kill a chicken for them, if there is no chicken at home, they would ask from the neighbours or anywhere around the village. They two villages will go for the funeral without fail if any one of them died, they will come by for mourning the dead body and the living friend will give presentation shawls. Making friendship has given many benefits at the time of worries, sadness or happiness both the villages can get help from each other as far as possible. Friendship settlement will not break till the end of life and is passed down to their generations.

Conclusion

Peace settlement, which has been in practice in Mao society even from the bygone preliterate days, is very relevant and important in the present society. After modification some of the terms are adjustable and applicable in the present society. In the state of Manipur, restrictions and differences between Meiteis and Pangals, Meitei-Naga, Naga-Kuki are prominent, that is, few decades back Meitei community restricted the tribals to come into their kitchens. Peace settlement can change and do away with this restriction if there is friendship. Such Settlement between the hosts and the guests will help in bridging the gap and bring closer the relationship amongst the different communities in Manipur. If peace settlement is conducted between the two villages or between the two communities they will be friends forever which cannot break as per the settlement terms and conditions if it is obliged in letter and spirit. If parents died their grand-children also will make friends through their parents. If any of their friends died, they will come for condolence without fail. If a friend who is a party to such settlement visited his friend in another village, the host friend will not keep any restrictions from entering the house, the host must welcome warmly and be treated properly like killing chicken for the guest, if chickens are not available at home he will ask from his neighbours. If any land dispute or problems arises, they will defend together against the enemies. If this peace settlement can be brought about between the different communities, it will be helpful in bringing peace and harmony and they will be closer to each other communities or neighbouring villages.

Index